OXFORD STUDIES IN AFRICAN AFFAIRS

IMPERIALISM AND NATIONALISM IN THE SUDAN

IMPERIALISM AND NATIONALISM IN THE SUDAN

A STUDY IN
CONSTITUTIONAL AND POLITICAL
DEVELOPMENT
1899–1956

BY

MUDDATHIR 'ABD AL-RAḤĪM
Head, Department of Political Science
University of Khartoum

OXFORD
AT THE CLARENDON PRESS
1969

Oxford University Press, Ely House, London W. 1
GLASGOW NEW YORK TORONTO MELBOURNE WELLINGTON
CAPE TOWN SALISBURY IBADAN NAIROBI LUSAKA ADDIS ABABA
BOMBAY CALCUTTA MADRAS KARACHI LAHORE DACCA
KUALA LUMPUR SINGAPORE HONG KONG TOKYO

PRINTED IN GREAT BRITAIN

TO

MY PARENTS

AND

COUNTRYMEN

'The Soudan is a useless possession, ever was so, and ever will be so. . . .'

GENERAL C. GORDON, 1884

'We reach now the Sudan itself, one of the most fabulous countries of the world. . . . Politically, Sudan is, I think, the most exciting country we saw in all Africa with the possible exception of Nigeria.'

JOHN GUNTHER, 1955

PREFACE

THE Sudan is the largest country in Africa and was the first to achieve independence after the Second World War. Geographically, socially, and culturally it is a microcosm of Africa. Its colonial history, its present problems, and its future prospects and potentialities are in many respects typical of those of other African or Afro-Asian countries. A study of the Sudan's constitutional and political development therefore should throw some light on the nature and methods of colonial governments in general, and on the interaction between these and the liberating nationalism which has, during the last two or three decades especially, swept through the 'third world', and, finally, on the processes whereby an increasing number of Afro-Asian countries have recently acquired the status of sovereign statehood.

But the Sudan has in many respects been distinguished by certain characteristic features which set it apart from other countries and make it of special interest and appeal. Among these was the peculiar constitutional arrangement in accordance with which the Sudan was governed throughout its more recent history as a dependency from 1899 to 1956. The Anglo-Egyptian Agreement—more commonly, but incorrectly, known as the 'Condominium Agreement'—was signed, in January 1899, by representatives of the Egyptian and British Governments with a view to organizing the future administration of the Sudan which had just been conquered by their joint forces. The conquest was conducted in the name of the Khedive of Egypt who—as a vassal of the Ottoman Sultan in whom sovereignty over the Sudan had, in theory, resided—was recognized as the ruler of both Egypt and the Sudan until 1885 when, as a result of the Mahdist Revolt in the Sudan and British policy in Egypt, the remaining Ottoman-Egyptian forces were withdrawn. Although the question of sovereignty was not mentioned in the Agreement, the British Government subsequently claimed that the Agreement had established an Anglo-Egyptian 'Condominium' in the Sudan—which implied that Egypt and Britain had become jointly the sovereign authority of the conquered territory. But Egypt, which was itself under British occupation, declined to accept this interpretation of what was, in her view, an agreement for the administration of an Egyptian province over which the Khedive, and subsequently the King of Egypt, was sovereign. And when they were again able to speak for themselves, the Sudanese—who had not been consulted about the Agreement—rejected both interpretations and, instead, wanted sovereignty over the Sudan to be restored to the Sudanese. Although they were agreed on the ultimate objective of independence however, some sections of Sudanese opinion preferred to seek the realization of this aim by means of co-operation with Britain while others preferred co-operation with Egypt. The resulting pattern of political relations was further complicated, on the one hand, by the existence of other differences in the Sudan—the most important being the regional differences between the Northern and Southern parts of the country and between the urban and nomadic, or semi-nomadic, sections of the population—and, on the other hand, by policies which, deliberately introduced and, for several years, vigorously implemented by the British Government of the Sudan, had the effect of increasing these differences and making them more acute.

The interactions between these forces are examined in the following pages as they affected and were affected by the constitutional development of the country from 1899, when the regime was established, to 1956 when the Sudan regained its independence. Anglo-Egyptian relations and other developments in the international field are discussed whenever relevant, but throughout the study emphasis is put on the internal evolution of the Sudan. The physical and human environment in which these developments took place are outlined in the introductory chapter. In Part I an attempt is made to analyse the forces which gave rise to the Anglo-Egyptian regime. The terms of the Agreement are examined and the nature of the regime which was thereby established is then discussed and its development until 1936 described. Chapter IV is devoted to an analysis of Sudanese nationalism and the growth of the main political groupings in the country. In chapter V the first attempt of the Sudan Government to associate the Sudanese with the central government is discussed and the experiment of the Legislative Assembly is reviewed in chapter VI. In chapter VII an outline of the development of local government, as distinct from the Native Administration of an earlier period, is given. Finally the steps leading to the termination of the Anglo-Egyptian regime and the transfer of power to the Sudanese are discussed. The constitutional and political problems and developments of the Sudan after 1955 will be examined in a later study of government and politics in the independent Sudan. M. A-R.

London, 19 July 1967

ACKNOWLEDGEMENTS

THE main sources of this study have been unpublished documents in the Sudan Government Central Archives and the Ministry of Interior, Khartoum; the Public Record Office, London; the School of Oriental Studies, Durham; and the Library of New College, Oxford. I wish to record my appreciation and sincere thanks to the custodians and staff of these institutions for giving me access to the documents and for valuable help while consulting them. I am particularly grateful to Dr. Muḥammad Ibrahīm Aḥmad, the Director of the Central Archives; to Sayyids Mirghani al-Amīn, Ḥusain Muḥammad Aḥmad Sharfi, and Ja'afar Muḥammad 'Ali Bakhīt of the Ministry of Interior; and to Mr. Richard Hill of the School of Oriental Studies, Durham—all of whom were most helpful to me in the years from 1959 to 1962, the period during which I collected the bulk of the material on which the present study is based.

I also wish to thank the many Sudanese politicians and administrators who so generously gave of their time to discuss various aspects of the subject. I am especially grateful to Sayyid Sir 'Ali al-Mirghani, the late Sayyid al-Ṣiddīq al-Mahdi and Sayyids Isma'īl al-Azhari, 'Abdalla Khalīl, Muḥammad Aḥmad Maḥjoub, Mirghani Ḥamza, Ibrahīm Aḥmad, Aḥmad Khair, and Da'ud 'Abd al-Laṭīf.

The original version of this study was a thesis submitted for the degree of Ph.D. at the University of Manchester in April 1964. In this connection it is a most pleasant duty to thank Professor W. J. M. Mackenzie—then Head of the Department of Government, Manchester University—who insisted that, as a colleague, I should in effect be my own supervisor while preparing the thesis and thus gave me a heightened sense of responsibility which informed my work throughout and has thereby made it less defective than it might have been otherwise. Professor Mackenzie's comments and searching questions, like those of Professor P. M. Holt and Professor H. J. Hanham, have been of the greatest help to me in preparing this version. I have also received generous help and encouragement from Dame Margery Perham, Professor Kenneth Robinson, Professor Makki Shibaika, and Dr. Norman Daniel. Needless to say I alone am responsible for this work and all the faults it may contain.

I owe a special debt of gratitude to two who have greatly stimulated my interest in this field of study. The first is my late uncle, Aḥmad Afandi Qindīl, in whose house and under whose stimulating guidance and that of his distinguished circle of friends I, as a boy some twenty years ago, was first awakened to the fascinating world of history, government, and politics. Secondly, I am grateful to the late Professor Sa'ad al-Dīn Fawzi for having guided my first steps in the systematic study of the social sciences and for subsequently having given me generous encouragement in developing my interest in politics.

I am also indebted to the University of Khartoum, the University of Manchester, the Rockefeller Foundation, and the British Council for having made it possible for me to make a number of visits to the Sudan, Egypt, and Britain in connection with my research; to the British Museum, the Arts Library of Manchester University, and the Central Library of the City of Manchester for allowing me to use their facilities for extended periods of time over the last seven years, and to the authors and publishers of works from which quotations have been reproduced in this study.

To my students at the Universities of Khartoum and Manchester (especially the post-graduate students in the latter institution during my time there from 1960 to 1965), I am grateful for the stimulus of their interest and questioning, without which many points made in this study would have been left unelucidated or less clearly stated.

I am also grateful to Sayyids Khalīfa 'Abbās and al-Nour 'Ali Sulaiyman of the Ministry of Foreign Affairs, Sayyids 'Ali Ḥasan 'Abdalla and 'Abd al-Salām al-Khiḍr of the Ministry of Local Government, Sayyids al-Ṭayyib 'Abdalla and 'Abdalla 'Umar of the Ministry of Interior, Sayyid Muḥammad Maḥjoub Mālik of the Central Archives, and the staff of the offices of the Attorney-General for facilitating my work; to Sayyid Bashīr Ramli for helping me with the transliteration of Arabic characters; to Sayyid 'Uthman Satti of the Geography Department, University of Khartoum, for drawing the map; and to Sayyid 'Abd al-Raḥīm Muḥammad 'Abd al-Raḥmān of the Department of Political Science for undertaking, at short notice, a considerable amount of last-minute typing and retyping with remarkable efficiency and forbearance.

The material on which the discussion of 'Southern Policy' in Chapters III and VI is based was used—together with other documents which I had the honour of preparing for the Round Table

Conference on the Southern Sudan which was held in Khartoum in March 1965—on several occasions in the past, including the United Nations General Assembly session of 1965, and subsequently formed the substance of an article 'The Development of British Policy in the Southern Sudan', which was published in *Middle Eastern Studies* in April 1966. Some of the material which appears in Chapter IV was likewise used in an article on 'Early Sudanese Nationalism' which appeared in *Sudan Notes and Records*—also in 1966. I am grateful to the editors of the two journals for permitting me to use these articles in this study.

Last, but not least, I would like to record my most grateful thanks to my wife for having saved me from many errors in English and for her consistent and selfless support throughout.

CONTENTS

PREFACE vii

ACKNOWLEDGEMENTS ix

NOTE ON TRANSLITERATION xvii

INTRODUCTION: The Sudan and the Sudanese 1

PART ONE

THE ANGLO-EGYPTIAN AGREEMENT AND ADMINISTRATION TO 1936

I. THE POLITICAL CONTEXT OF THE ANGLO-EGYPTIAN AGREEMENT OF 1899 13

1. The Ottoman-Egyptian roots of the Anglo-Egyptian regime 14
2. Britain's involvement in Egypt and the Sudan 18
3. Imperial diplomacy and the birth of the new regime 23

II. THE TERMS OF THE AGREEMENT 29

1. Some basic considerations 29
2. Analysis of the Agreement 32

III. THE DEVELOPMENT OF ADMINISTRATION TO 1936 39

1. The foundations of the new administrative system 39
2. The Governor-General's Council 46
3. Provincial administration 49
4. The impact of the Egyptian Revolution: relations with Egypt 51
5. The impact of the Egyptian Revolution: trial and error in adjustment 64
6. The politics of reaction: Indirect Rule 65
7. The politics of reaction: 'Southern Policy' 70
8. Winds of change 83

PART TWO

THE ROAD TO INDEPENDENCE

IV. THE RISE OF SUDANESE NATIONALISM 89
1. Resistance: Mahdist and non-Mahdist styles 89
2. The impact of the First World War 94
3. The Revolt of 1924 102
4. Challenge and response: the aftermath of the Revolt 108
5. The Graduates' Congress: its rise, development, and demise 117

V. THE ADVISORY COUNCIL 135
1. From paternalism to partnership 135
2. The structure and functions of the Council 137
3. The Council and the nationalists 140
4. The gathering storm: politics after the war 152
5. The search for new policies 157

VI. THE LEGISLATIVE ASSEMBLY 159
1. The Sudan Administration Conference 159
2. The abandonment of 'Southern Policy' 166
3. The making of the new constitution 172
4. Towards self-government: the conflict of parties and policies 179
5. Towards self-government: The Constitution Commission and the abrogation of the Agreement 190
6. The Self-Government Statute: drafts, debates, and diplomacy 197

VII. THE STATE OF LOCAL GOVERNMENT 201
1. Objections to Native Administration 201
2. The coming of Local Government 205

VIII. THE TRANSFER OF POWER 213
1. The Agreements of 1952 and 1953 213
2. The first national elections 216
3. Sudanization and self-determination 219

APPENDICES 228

SELECT BIBLIOGRAPHY AND A NOTE ON PRIMARY SOURCES 261

A NOTE ON ANGLO-EGYPTIAN WRITINGS ON THE CONSTITUTIONAL AND POLITICAL DEVELOPMENT OF THE SUDAN 265

INDEX 269

NOTE ON TRANSLITERATION

In the transliteration of Arabic characters I have, in general, followed the recommendations approved by the majority of participants at the International Society of Orientalists' Conference of 1961. In transliterating names of persons, however, I have followed Sudanese practice in pronunciation rather than the classical forms of literary Arabic. I have thus written of Shaikhs and Khair instead of 'Shaykhs' and 'Khayr'. And while I have taken liberties with the rendering of the names of smaller towns and places to make them fit this pattern, I have followed general practice in writing the names of bigger and better-known places. I have thus written of Barbar and Khartoum instead of 'Berber' and 'al-Kharṭoum'.

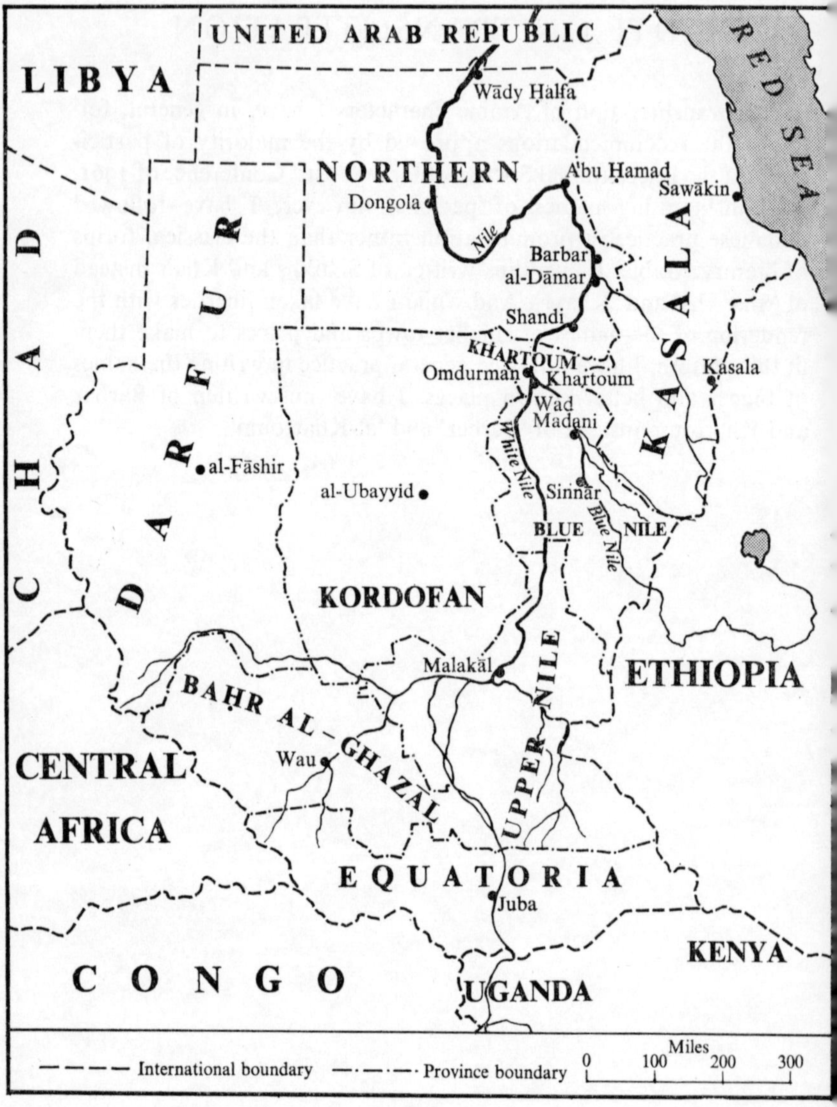
UNITED ARAB REPUBLIC
LIBYA
RED SEA
Wādy Ḥalfa
NORTHERN
Abu Hamad
Sawākin
Dongola
Nile
Barbar
al-Dāmar
Shandi
KHARTOUM
Omdurman
Khartoum
Kasala
Wad Madani
KASALA
CHAD
DARFUR
al-Fāshir
al-Ubayyid
White Nile
Sinnār
Blue Nile
BLUE NILE
KORDOFAN
Malakāl
ETHIOPIA
BAḤR AL-GHAZĀL
UPPER NILE
CENTRAL AFRICA
Wau
EQUATORIA
Juba
KENYA
CONGO
UGANDA
International boundary
Province boundary
Miles
0
100
200
300

INTRODUCTION

THE SUDAN AND THE SUDANESE

THE word 'Sudan' is Arabic. It derives from the expression 'Bilād al-Sūdān'—i.e. the Land of the Blacks—which was used by medieval Arabs as a generic name for the regions lying to the south of the Sahara, from the Red Sea and the Indian Ocean to the Atlantic.[1] In this sense the term is still used by Western scholars—especially orientalists and anthropologists—but very rarely by contemporary Arab writers.

In its more restricted and modern sense, however, 'the Sudan' means the Republic of the Sudan, formerly the Anglo-Egyptian Sudan. But this has sometimes been questioned. For instance when the French colonial territories in West Africa became independent in 1960 'the Soudan' naturally assumed the name of 'the Soudanese Republic'. The resulting confusion between this and the Republic of the Sudan induced some people in Khartoum to suggest (and the idea was, for a while, seriously discussed in the local press) that the country should revert to the older name of 'Sinnār', or even the pre-Islamic 'Nubia', in the same way as the Gold Coast for example had reverted to Ghana and Abyssinia to Ethiopia.[2] However, the debate was soon brought to an end when the Soudanese Republic adopted the name of Mali.

[1] Ibn Khaldoun uses the term in this sense, but also states that 'the Sudanese' inhabit the vast belt of land extending from West Africa to the southern parts of the Yemen, Ḥejāz, Persia, India, and South-East Asia in general (*Tarīkh*, vol. vi, p. 198, Cairo, n.d.). This is almost identical with 'Ethiop' (meaning burnt-face) and 'Ethopia' (his homeland) as used by Homer and Herodotus.

[2] The area which roughly corresponds to the modern Sudan was known to the ancient Semites, including the writers of the Bible, as the Land of 'Cush', while to the Greco-Romans it was known as 'Ethopia'. By the third century A.D. however the Ancient Egyptian term 'Nubia'—meaning the land of gold—seems to supplant Cush and Ethopia. From the sixteenth century onwards the expression 'Fūnj' gains currency, especially with reference to the areas now comprising the central Sudan, but 'Nubia' lingers on until the nineteenth century, when 'the Sudan' becomes prominent. At present Cush survives only amongst certain tribes in Kordofan in Western Sudan; 'Nubia' and 'Nuba' are used with reference to Ḥalfa and Dongola districts in the Northern Province, and the Nuba Mountains in the mid West respectively, while 'Ethiopia' has, of course, been

A similar uncertainty attached, not unnaturally, to the definition of the territory which properly constituted the Sudan. The present boundaries were substantially settled with the coming of the Anglo-Egyptian regime in 1898 and its subsequent establishment in the country.[1] During the Mahdist period (1885–98) the boundaries of the state varied with the variation in the power of the government and its ability to elicit obedience from the people over whom it claimed to exercise authority.[2] This was firmly established throughout the central Sudan, from Ḥalfa in the north to Rajjāf in the south and from Sawākin in the Red Sea to Darfur in the west, but tended to diminish or even to be completely ineffective on the outer fringes of the country—particularly where no permanent garrisons were stationed, e.g. in the South, and on the Abyssinian borders, where (to use Gibbon's phrase regarding medieval Islam and Christendom in general) an intermittent armed debate was conducted between the two countries.

During the latter part of the Ottoman-Egyptian administration of Muḥammad 'Ali Pasha (1821–85), the Sudan formed part of a huge empire which extended from the Mediterranean to the Great Lakes of Central Africa and included considerable portions of what are now Ethiopia and Somalia.[3] As in the days of the Mahdiyya, however, there were no definite frontiers in the modern European sense of the word,[4] and boundaries simply ebbed and flowed with the rise and fall of the effective power of the state. Before the coming of 'the Turks',[5] however (which is generally accepted as marking the beginning of the modern era in Sudan history), the country did not even exist as a single administrative unit. The South was a little-

officially adopted by Abyssinia. Cf. J. Arkell, *A History of the Sudan to 1821* (London, 1955), pp. 171 ff.

[1] Darfur was not brought under the authority of the Anglo-Egyptian regime until 1916; and in 1910 the northern part of the Lado Enclave, which had been leased by Britain to King Leopold of Belgium in 1894, was restored to the Sudan.

[2] See P. M. Holt, *The Mahdist State in the Sudan* (Oxford, 1958), chapters vii to ix.

[3] 'Abd al-Raḥmān al-Rāfi'i, *Miṣr wa-l Sūdān* (Cairo, 1948), pp. 82–3.

[4] R. Hill, *Egypt in the Sudan* (London, 1959), p. 153.

[5] It is generally known, as Richard Hill has pointed out, that the 'Turks' who governed the Sudan were, in fact, a wide cross-section of the various nationalities (Turks, Greeks, Circassians, Albanians, etc.) which were welded into the Ottoman Empire. To the less sophisticated Sudanese, therefore, the word 'Turk' came to signify the alien ruling classes of their country, so that even the British of the Anglo-Egyptian regime were often referred to as 'Turks' and their regime as the 'Second Tūrkiyya'.

known part of 'Darkest Africa',[1] occasionally raided for booty and slaves, and the North was divided into a number of competing tribal domains roughly organized under three medieval sultanates which were centred on Sinnār, Ḥalfayat al-Mūlouk, and al-Fāshir.

As it exists today the Sudan is an immensely vast country—the largest in Africa. Stretching from latitude 22° north to latitude 4° near the Equator and from the Red Sea to Chad in Equatorial West Africa, it covers about one million (967,500) square miles, or over two and a half million kilometres—an area as vast as that of the United Kingdom, Sweden, Norway, Denmark, Belgium, France, Italy, Spain and Portugal; or more than ten times that of Britain. It shares boundaries with Egypt and Libya to the north, Ethiopia to the east, Kenya, Uganda, and the Congo to the south, and the Republic of Chad and the Central African Republic to the west.

Climatically the Sudan lies wholly within the tropics; and apart from the narrow plain on the Red Sea, where certain maritime characteristics are introduced, it is entirely land-locked and has a predominantly continental climate.[2] With the exception of the 'Sudd' region in the south, where there are extensive swamps, and a few areas on the Red Sea and in the west and mid west, where some hills are to be found with local climatic effects, this large territory consists almost entirely of one vast plain.[2] It may conveniently be divided into three fairly distinct zones. The northern zone, from latitude 22° to about 18° north, consists of desert land and forms part of the Sahara. With temperatures as high as 38 °C on an average, and northerly winds blowing from the Sahara throughout the year, this is one of the hottest and driest parts of the world.[3] The central belt, from about latitude 18° to about 12° north, contains the richest agricultural and grazing lands in the country, including the 'Jazīra' (meaning 'Peninsula') between the White and the Blue Niles, which was traditionally considered to have been the granary of the Sudan and now grows its most important export product and earner of foreign currencies—namely, cotton. Here, the climate is somewhat milder than it is in the northern zone, but it can be almost as hot on

[1] Arkell states that 'what is known as the southern Sudan today, has no history before A.D. 1821', op. cit., p. 2.

[2] J. D. Tothill, *Agriculture in the Sudan* (London, 1948), pp. 63–4.

[3] W. C. W. Rath, 'The Climate of the Sudan: A factor in the Social and Economic Development of the Country', *Proceedings of the 1953 Annual Conference of the Philosophical Society of the Sudan* (Khartoum, 1955), p. 105.

occasions; and the amount of rainfall gradually increases from a few millimetres in the north to well over 1,250 millimetres (or 50″) in the south, thus causing a gradual drop in temperature and a corresponding rise in humidity from the fringe of the desert to the Equator. Consequently, the vegetation changes from thorny desert scrub in the north, to richer grasslands in the centre and thickly forested jungle in the extreme south of the country.

Traversing these three zones and, in a sense, uniting them with one another as well as with the neighbouring countries to the south, the east, and the north, is the River Nile and its tributaries. The most important of these is the Blue Nile which rises from Lake Tana in the Ethiopian Plateau and, when in full flood, moves rapidly into the Sudan bringing with it the bulk of the water and the silt[1] which gives life to the valley as far as Alexandria and Rosetta. At Khartoum it is joined by the more steady, if rather sluggish White Nile, which flows from the Great Lakes of East and Central Africa. On its way it is fed by numerous tributaries, the most important of which are Baḥr al-'Arab from the west and the River Sobāt from the east. From the point where it meets the latter, a few miles south of Malakal, the White Nile slowly makes its way to Khartoum spreading, at points, to over two or three miles in breadth. Beyond Khartoum, where it is joined by the Blue Nile, there are no important tributaries except the River Atbara which rises in northern Ethiopia and meets the main Nile about 200 miles north of Khartoum. From that point to the Mediterranean, a distance of about 1,700 miles, there are no tributaries; and with less and less rainfall, both animal and human life become increasingly dependent on the Nile.

In these circumstances, it is hardly surprising that the population of the Sudan is a mosaic of different races and colours with a roughly corresponding variety of languages and traditions.

The total population of the country was estimated on 17 January 1956 (the date on which the first population census was held) at 10,262,536.[2] Of these, over half a million (about 3 per cent) were foreigners—mainly West Africans, Egyptians, and Greeks. The remainder represented no less than 572 Sudanese (mainly Southern) tribes, with 'many more sub-tribes'[3] on record. At the time of the

[1] H. E. Hurst, *The Nile* (London, 1952), pp. 1, 8, and 234.

[2] The Republic of the Sudan, Ministry for Social Welfare: *First Population Census of the Sudan: Twenty-one Facts about the Sudanese* (1958), p. 13.

[3] Ibid., p. 23.

census approximately 39 per cent of the total population claimed membership of Arab tribes,[1] 30 per cent were Southerners—mainly Nilotics and Nilo-Hamites, and 13 per cent Westerners, i.e. West Africans claiming Sudanese status. The rest were members of the Nuba tribes of the mid West, the Beja of the Red Sea Hills (the 'Fuzzi Wuzzies' of Rudyard Kipling), and the Nubians, or Berberines, of Northern Sudan and Upper Egypt.

Although Arab tribes predominate in the provinces of Khartoum, Blue Nile, Kordofan, and Northern Province, the Beja in Kasala, Westerners in Darfur, and the Nilo-Hamites in Equatoria, it is obvious that considerable racial mixing has taken place, particularly in the central parts of the country. A clear indication of this is the wide range of colours and features among the Sudanese Arabs (over half of the total population) who are, on the whole, much darker than other Arabic-speaking peoples north of the Sahara and across the sea in Arabia. As the above-mentioned census report points out however, the two Southern provinces of Baḥr al-Ghazāl and the Upper Nile are almost exclusively[2] populated by Nilotics, thus showing a much higher degree of insularity than is usual throughout the country as a whole.

Culturally, however, the country is far more homogeneous than it is racially. For although slightly more than one-third of the total population claim Arab descent, over half speak Arabic as their mother tongue,[3] while most of the rest, including the Southern Sudanese, use Arabic, or a pidgin form of it as a 'lingua franca'.

This is easy to explain. In the first place, the majority of the Sudanese are Muslims, and historically speaking the spread of Islam went hand in hand with that of the language of the Qurʿān. Secondly, the fact that Arabic is the national language and that it is the language used in business, education, journalism, broadcasting, and in government offices—where it is now officially supposed to be supplanting English—at once explains and propagates its adoption throughout the country. In so far as the Southern provinces in particular are concerned, this has been facilitated by the reversal, since 1947, of the

[1] The census reports, using a racial definition of the term 'Arab', state that approximately 39 per cent of the Sudanese are Arabs, the rest being considered non-Arabs. But if the generally accepted definition of Arab is applied, i.e. one whose mother tongue is Arabic, 51 per cent of the Sudanese must, according to census figures, be Arabs—and not 39 per cent as the reports state.

[2] *First Population Census of the Sudan*, p. 25.

[3] Ibid., p. 26.

(British) government's 'Southern Policy', which was, among other things, aimed at counteracting the spread of Islam and the Arabic language 'by every practical means' and installing Christianity and the English language instead.[1] Finally, as the above mentioned report states, the unifying force of Arabic is likely to grow with improved means of transport and greater intermixing of the population.[2] For the time being, however, more than 40 per cent of the Sudanese, mostly concentrated in the three Southern provinces but also, though to a much lesser extent, existing in the Red Sea Hills, the Dongola and Ḥalfa districts of the Northern Sudan, and certain parts of the Western Sudan, speak languages other than Arabic at home and use Arabic only as a lingua franca.

Both the extent and the limits of Arabization in the Sudan can be explained in terms of the historical evolution of the country which, in turn, has been largely determined by the geographical considerations which have been indicated above. It is generally agreed that relations between the eastern and western coasts of the Red Sea have existed ever since rafts and boats were first built by man. But the Arabization of the Northern Sudan, as indeed of the whole of North Africa, did not come about until, and by reason of, the rise of Islam in the seventh century A.D. and its subsequent spread. The twin processes of Islamization and Arabization were primarily brought about through the agency of Muslim Arab immigrants who—coming from Arabia across the Red Sea, from Egypt and, at a later stage, from the Maghrib—gradually infiltrated the Christian kingdoms of Nubia and, being free from racial prejudice, readily mixed with the indigenous population and freely intermarried with them.[3] By the end of the fourteenth century they had effected a social and cultural revolution which resulted in the total transformation of Nubia and the establishment, in 1504, of the Islamic Kingdom of the Fūnj, which lasted until 1821. With the added advantage of political control over the central Sudan they were then able to penetrate all those parts which, being geographically similar to the Arabian peninsula,

[1] Civil Secretary to Governors of the three Southern provinces, 25 Jan. 1930 (CS/I.C.I./Khartoum, Government Archives, Khartoum). 'Southern Policy' is discussed in Chapters III and VI below.

[2] *First Population Census of the Sudan*, p. 27.

[3] Needless to say, Islam and Arab culture continue to be closely related and are, in fact, inseparable in the minds and social institutions of the Sudanese—as is the case with the modern Arabs in general whether they are Muslim or Christian, in Africa or in Asia.

they found agreeable to themselves. And the further they penetrated the greater became their power and momentum through the twin mediums of racial assimilation on the one hand and Islamization—which owed a great deal to the religious fraternities (or Ṭariqās)[1]—on the other. But they were barred from entering the South by swamps, flies, and tropical humidity, none of which were suitable for camel-breeding nor attractive to desert people. Some of them therefore turned eastwards, entered Abyssinia, and settled there, while others moved westwards into the great plains of Kordofan and Darfur and, moving further west, reached as far as Lake Chad and Bornu in Central West Africa.[2]

In so far as the modern Sudan is concerned the outstanding result of these happenings is that while the Northern Sudan has thereby become almost completely Islamized and to a large, though lesser extent, also Arabized, the South remained virtually untouched by these influences until the nineteenth century. In spite of their common nationality and African identity,[3] therefore, the North and the South of the Sudan—like the northern and southern regions of the chain of African states that runs from the Red Sea to the Atlantic (often referred to as 'Sudanic' states)—have, on many occasions, tended to show signs of estrangement and difference rather than harmony and unity. This tendency has, in the past, been stimulated by two main factors: the traffic in slaves, which followed the conquest of the Sudan by Muḥammad 'Ali Pasha,[4] and the above-mentioned

[1] It is important to note that these fraternities do not in any sense constitute 'sects' such as the Catholics and Protestants in the history of Christianity, but are simply religious associations which are usually formed around the ideas and the personality of a teacher or saint who may encourage communal worship on mystical lines within the bounds of Islam. Membership being open to all, Ṭariqās have cut across tribal boundaries and thus played, and still play, an important part in Sudanese life and politics.

[2] Arkell, p. 199.

[3] The often-used cliché that the Northern Sudanese are Muslim and Arab while the Southerners are African and pagan or Christian—though it may be useful in giving a quick idea of the nature of the Sudan—is misleading in that it assumes the existence of a clear cut racial or cultural boundary between the two regions, suggests a definition of Africanism and Arabism in racial terms, and therefore wrongly implies (among other things) that the Northern Sudanese are not truly African.

[4] As Richard Gray has pointed out, the slave trade was conducted not only by Europeans of different nationalities, Egyptians, and Northern Sudanese, but also by the Southern Sudanese tribes between themselves. One of the most famous Southern slave-dealers was Mopoi, an Azande chief, who dealt in 'thousands upon thousands' of slaves, which he obtained either from 'the slave tribes' that

'Southern Policy', which was vigorously pursued by the British administration of the Sudan until 1947. The latter aimed at the separation of the Southern provinces from the rest of the country with a view to 'lumping' them with neighbouring 'possessions' in order to build an East African Federation under British control. To-day, the slave trade is, of course, a long dead issue; but this has not prevented its use by propagandists hostile to the unity of the Sudan. British policy, on the other hand, has saddled the independent Sudan with its most intractable problem by creating a form of local patriotism in the South which, though it is not universally accepted there, has sought to speak in the name of the whole region and, in its more extreme brands, has—reportedly with the assistance of Israel and other foreign countries[1]—stood for the establishment, by means of violence, of a separate Southern state. Other factors—including mistakes which have been committed by successive governments of the independent Sudan, especially the military regime of General 'Abboud (1958–64)—have added to the difficulty of an already complicated problem. It is not surprising therefore that both the enlightened public and the various governments which came to office since the Revolution of October 1964 (which resulted in the restoration of civilian government in the Sudan) have devoted much of their thought and energy to the settlement of this problem, by peaceful and democratic means. Fortunately, these efforts have so far met with considerable, though as yet incomplete, success. It is generally realized however that without the successful resolution of this problem the search for a permanent constitution, which began soon after the achievement of independence, over ten years ago, would be futile and meaningless, and that the chances of the two regions holding together would, to that extent, be reduced. If the neutralization of the separatist 'Southern Policy' of the British administration was an important and basic issue in the Sudan's struggle for independence, therefore, the establishment of a more perfect union between its two

he had subjected or 'by raids organized against the surrounding nations' (R. Gray, *A History of the Southern Sudan*, London, 1961, pp. 68 ff.).

[1] *The Economist*, 23 Nov. 1963, and the *Sunday Telegraph*, 10 Nov. 1963. Referring to the same subject during a speech which he gave in the Uganda Parliament on 3 Mar. 1965, Mr. F. K. Onama, the Minister of Internal Affairs in Uganda, stated that there was 'positive action from certain nations to frustrate, not only the genuine desire of the Government of the Republic of the Sudan, but also to frustrate Uganda, in its attempts to bring the two factions in the Republic of the Sudan together. . . . This is an example of the encouragement of external agents to disrupt the peace of Africa.'

regions has already shown itself as the main preoccupation of the Sudanese in their post-independence history and may prove to be of still greater importance in the future. Needless to say the fulfilment of this objective is not merely of administrative or constitutional significance for the Sudanese. It is central to their vision of themselves as a creative link between the worlds of Africa and the Middle East. And—considering especially the growing importance, on a world-wide scale, of developing better and more humane relations between the different races of mankind—it is also of key importance to the role which the Sudanese aspire to play in the world at large.

PART ONE

THE ANGLO-EGYPTIAN AGREEMENT AND ADMINISTRATION TO 1936

CHAPTER I

The Political Context of the Anglo-Egyptian Agreement of 1899

THE geographic position of the Sudan between the worlds of the Mediterranean and the Middle East on the one hand and Central Africa on the other, coupled with the fact that the Nile and its tributaries run through Sudanese territory for hundreds of miles before it reaches Egypt, has always played an important part in determining the character and the politics of the country from biblical times to the present day. In almost all cases of contact between the Sudan and the outside world Egypt has been the most important link and, especially since the rise of Islam, by far the greatest single influence. Thus the Pharaohs, the Persians, the Greeks, the Romans, the Arabs, the Turks, and the British; all those who governed or conquered Egypt in the past have in turn found it either necessary or expedient to attempt (with varying degrees of success) to extend their influence, if not their power, beyond the traditional boundaries of Egypt, between the first and the second cataracts, into the lands which now constitute the Republic of the Sudan. Conversely, the inhabitants of these lands, or at any rate those of them who lived in the northern parts of the country, have always had to choose between three alternative policies. They could either submit to the domination of their lands and themselves by Egypt or whatever power happened to be supreme therein at the time; or devote their energies and resources to the cause of complete independence with—normally—friendly relations with their neighbours; or else they could attempt to conquer Egypt and establish their own authority in it. Each one of these possibilities was actually realized at one time or another. At no time, however, could either of the two countries ignore the other or minimize its importance for its own being—a fact that, in the hands of modern Egyptian nationalists, became one of the main arguments for the Unity of the Nile Valley, for many years the *raison d'être* of Egyptian foreign policy.

1. *The Ottoman-Egyptian roots of the Anglo-Egyptian regime*

In order to have an adequate appreciation of the constitutional development of the Sudan during the period under consideration—as, indeed, of the modern history of the country in general—it is necessary to refer back to the conquest of the Sudan by the Ottoman-Egyptian forces of Muḥammad 'Ali Pasha in 1821.

There is no evidence that the Viceroy had obtained permission from the Sublime Porte for conquering the Sudan; nor did he discuss his motives for undertaking this enterprise.[1] His subsequent policies however—particularly in connection with building a modern and efficient army and navy and establishing an Egyptian-Arab empire independent from that of the Sultan in Constantinople[2]—leave little doubt that he had two main objectives. The first of these was the illusory one of finding gold and other precious minerals in the country. The other was expressed in a dispatch to the Defterdar, one of his generals in the Sudan, in which the Pasha stated: 'You are aware that the end of all our efforts and this expense is to procure negroes. Please show zeal in carrying out our wishes in this capital matter.'[3] It being impermissible for Muslims to enslave Muslims, the raids for slaves had to be directed to the pagan hinterlands of the White Nile and the Nuba Mountains from which about ten thousand slaves were annually exported to Egypt.[4] A great camp was set up in Aswan to receive the captives. There they were vaccinated, clothed, and instructed in the fundamentals of Islam. A certain proportion was absorbed in domestic slavery; but, in accordance with his instructions, all able-bodied males were recruited into the Viceroy's French-trained army. In this capacity many of them distinguished themselves during the campaigns in Syria, Arabia, and—during Sa'īd's reign—in Mexico, where they fought on the side of the Pasha's friend, Napoleon III.[5]

Muḥammad 'Ali's successes, however, especially when they threatened to undermine the authority of the Porte and replace it by a new, vigorous, and perhaps unmanageable Muslim state astride the routes to India, were unacceptable to Britain, whose policy was then aimed at the maintenance of Turkish command over

[1] Hill, pp. 7–8.
[2] George Antonius, *The Arab Awakening* (London, 1961 edition), pp. 23–7.
[3] Quoted in Hill, p. 13.
[4] Gray, pp. 5–6.
[5] Hill, pp. 24–8 and 104.

the straits and an independent but inactive administration in Egypt.[1] Largely as a result of British intervention, therefore, Muḥammad 'Ali was forced to withdraw from Syria and relinquish his plans for the creation of an Afro-Asian Arab state.[2] As compensation he was given the hereditary Pashalik of Egypt. And the Firman of 13 February 1841, which conferred this position on the Viceroy, also recognized him as the governor of 'the provinces of Nubia, Darfur, Kordofan, Sinnar, and all their dependencies outside the boundaries of Egypt, but without the right of heredity'.[3] The inclusion of Darfur in this list was an anomaly, for Darfur had not yet been conquered; and when this happened it was not Egyptian forces which accomplished it, but the private army of the Sudanese adventurer al-Zubair Pasha wad Raḥama who had defied the Viceroy, defeated his representative in Baḥr al Ghazāl, and established himself as a rival power in the Southern Sudan. In June 1876, Zubair Pasha went to Cairo in order to settle differences with the Khedive[4] Ismā'īl Pasha. When discussions were over, however, Zubair found that he had become a respected captive of his host. A rebellion broke out in Darfur under the leadership of Zubair's son, Sulaymān, but was crushed by an Italian mercenary, Romolo Gessi, who had fought under Garibaldi before enlisting in the Khedive's service.[5]

Other mercenaries and expatriates, including the British Sir Samuel Baker and General Charles Gordon, were also employed by Ismā'īl in order to execute his enlightened policy with regard to the abolition of the slave-trade and to secure the whole of the Nile Basin for him. With the aid of such men and the modern techniques and equipment of warfare Ismā'īl succeeded in extending the boundaries of his empire as far as the Great Lakes of Central Africa.[6] Realizing the increased importance of the Red Sea after the opening of the Suez Canal in 1869, the Khedive directed his attention to the Horn of Africa

[1] Chatham House Study Group, *British Interests in the Mediterranean and Middle East* (London, 1958), p. 2.

[2] G. Lenczowski, *The Middle East in World Affairs* (Cornell, 1960), pp. 16–17. Also Antonius, pp. 23–7.

[3] Imperial Firman in *al-Sūdān min 13 Fabrayir 1841 ilā 12 Fabrayir 1953*, a documentary record published by the Presidency of the Council of Ministers (Cairo, 1953), p. 1.

[4] The Firman of 8 Jan. 1867 raised the Viceroy of Egypt to the rank of Grand Vizier with the title 'Khedive' and empowered him to conclude commercial and other treaties of a non-political nature (Egypt, no. 1 (1879), C. 2395, p. 43).

[5] Gray, pp. 120–5.

[6] al-Rafi'i, p. 83.

where, by 1877, the Somali coast as far as Ras Hofun was recognized as Egyptian territory under the suzerainty of the Sultan.[1] Further north on the Red Sea coast, the ports of Sawākin and Musawwa'—which had previously been administered by the Ottoman Wali of the Ḥejāz—were handed over to Egypt by the Firman of 27 May 1866. The same Firman amended the earlier decree of 1841 by extending the hereditary principle to the Sudan, so that 'henceforth the Government of Egypt, with the territories which are annexed to it, and its dependencies, and with the Kaimakamates of Suakin and Massawah, shall be transmitted to the eldest of their male children, and, in the same manner, to the eldest sons of their successors'.[2]

Within this vast, but loosely organized empire, the Sudan had by virtue of its proximity to Egypt, an important place. Being viewed as a province of Egypt it was, at first, put under the control of area military commanders who answered to a Mudīr (Governor), himself an army officer, whose headquarters were in Khartoum, a small hamlet which, from 1833, became the capital of the Sudan. In 1835, however, the Mudīr of the Sudan was elevated to the position of Hākimdār (Governor-General) in whose person civil and military power over the Sudan was vested. At the same time, the provincial military commanders, hitherto known as Māmūrs (roughly, 'executives') were designated Mudīrs.[3] The provinces were themselves divided into smaller units which tended to follow the traditional tribal and territorial boundaries of the Fūnj period.

The personnel of the new regime was a mixture of Circassian, Turkish, European, and Armenian officers of the Ottoman Egyptian Army who were helped, at the lower levels of the administration, by Sudanese Shaikhs and tribal leaders. Being Muslims and men who knew the country well however, these were not excluded from high office in what was, after all, a multi-racial Muslim administration. Thus, a number of Sudanese were, in due course, appointed provincial governors, or made Pashas.[4]

But the administration was subjected to continuous and, usually,

[1] Hill, pp. 141–2.

[2] Egypt, no. 4 (1879): *Firmans Granted by the Sultans to the Viceroys of Egypt, 1841–73*, with correspondence relating thereto (C. 2395 (1879), p. 4).

[3] Hill, pp. 22–3.

[4] The first Sudanese to be made provincial governors were Aḥmad Bey Abu-Sin, the Shaikh of the Shukriyya tribe and Muḥammad Bey Rāsikh, from Barbar. The former was appointed Governor of Khartoum province, the latter became the Governor of Barbar and, afterwards, Governor of Barbar and Dongola together.

arbitrary interference from Cairo; there was no regular system of pay; and politically undesirable persons were, as a rule, exiled to the Sudan, where they were given military and administrative posts. Under these conditions inefficiency and arbitrariness, especially in the levying and collection of taxes, gradually assumed phenomenal proportions and the seeds of discontent were thereby sown. The difficulties of the empire were increased by the policy of rapid but poorly organized expansion, which was followed by Muḥammad 'Ali's successors, especially the Khedive Ismā'īl. Harassed by European intervention on the one hand and being unable to solve its internal financial and administrative problems on the other, the Ottoman-Egyptian 'empire' began to crumble under its own weight. Gordon, who was invited by Ismā'īl to serve on a commission of inquiry on the financial situation in Egypt in 1878, was quick to understand the situation. In an interesting letter to Baker, he recorded his impressions in the following terms:

> My visit to Cairo opened my eyes to (Ismā'īl's) great weakness. He has no one to guide him in any way, his ministers are only his servants. He is a wonderful man but the weight is too much for him and there must come a collapse . . . not one of the places Zeyla, Tajurah, Berbera, or Harar anything like pay their expenses, neither does Darfur. The most sensible thing would be to evacuate all of them. This is sad after the expenditure of so much money and so many lives. Darfur must have cost, at least the death of 30,000 . . . Under a foreign master at Cairo and with a subvention of 80,000 pounds, and 20 officers, I could manage this country, but I think I would vacate a lot of it; query what will be the ultimate use of the Equator province?[1]

Baker's and Gordon's own violent and yet ineffective methods in abolishing the slave-trade in accordance with Ismā'īl's wishes alienated large sections of the population, caused considerable social and economic dislocation, and to that extent weakened the government's control over the country.[2] To make matters worse, the Khedive, to whom the administration naturally looked for financial support, was himself fighting a losing battle against his European creditors. And, in desperation, he ordered the Governor-General to appropriate the revenues of Dongola and Barbar and raise an additional £150,000 per annum for the Egyptian treasury. The Governor-General found this an impossible task, and he was recalled to Cairo to explain his failure to conform with the Khedive's directions.[3] In 1879 the Khedive

[1] Quoted in Gray, p. 137. [2] Holt, pp. 24–8. [3] Hill, p. 143.

himself was deposed by the Sultan who, seeing that the deposition of Ismā'īl would be the inevitable result of pressure by European Powers, preferred that the act should emanate from him, rather than suffer yet another open intervention in the affairs of the empire by Britain and France.[1]

Meanwhile, discontent was mounting in the Sudan. But when the Sudanese religious leader Muḥammad Aḥmad 'Abdalla claimed that he was the Mahdi (i.e. the Divinely Guided One) in March 1881 and called upon the people to rally with him against the Turks and for the reformation of Islam, Ra'ūf Pasha, the then newly appointed Governor-General, did not take the matter seriously. In a desperate attempt to economize, in accordance with Cairo's instructions, he decided moreover, to disband several military formations—thereby simultaneously weakening his own position as Governor and boosting the ranks of the discontented.[2]

The Mahdi, on the other hand, showed remarkable skill in manœuvre and organization; and under his able leadership the apparently minor rebellion was rapidly transformed into a 'jihād' and a nation-wide revolution. The consequences, both for Egypt and the Sudan, were great.

2. *Britain's involvement in Egypt and the Sudan*

Ismā'īl's mismanagement of Egypt's finances not only cost him his position as Viceroy, and aggravated matters in the empire, it also paved the way to the occupation of Egypt by Britain in 1882—a year after the outbreak of the Mahdist revolution in the Sudan. The occasion which gave rise to the occupation was the revolt, led by 'Urābi Pasha, against the intervention in Egyptian affairs of European powers—principally Britain and France—which followed the establishment of the Dual Control over Egypt's revenues and expenditure with a view to protecting the interests of her creditor-states and their subjects. The revolt was crushed in September, and Britain assumed control of the country. At first, this was presumed to be temporary,[3]

[1] The Earl of Cromer, *Modern Egypt* (London, 1911 edition), p. 108.

[2] Hill, p. 149.

[3] In Dec. 1883 Baring considered that the British occupation of Egypt was likely to last 'from five to ten years' (P.R.O. FO/78/3562, no. 642). In January 1884 he wrote to Granville: 'I hope you will fully understand that what I am chiefly aiming at is eventual withdrawal, and although the policy will now take longer than we originally hoped, I see no reason why it should not eventually

but in fact it continued until 1922, when Egypt was granted formal independence as a monarchy under Fuʿād I, Ismāʿīl's sixth son.

Once in Egypt, the British Government could not avoid taking interest in whatever was happening in the Sudan. For, as the British Agent and Consul-General in Egypt, Sir Evelyn Baring (later Lord Cromer), then said, it was impossible, at that time, wholly to disconnect the Sudan from the rest of the Egyptian question[1]—whether on financial or strategic grounds.

Conceived in the light of what was then viewed as a temporary occupation of Egypt, however, British interest in the Sudan took the form of a policy of 'wait and see', which saw no point in direct intervention in the country and, at the same time, refused to accept any responsibility for the operations in the Sudan which were undertaken by the Egyptian Government and its agents. The British Foreign Secretary, Lord Granville, was at pains to explain his Government's position in this respect and repeated the essence of it in more than one of his dispatches to the British representative in Cairo. When General Hicks—who had left for the Sudan at the head of the largest Egyptian army ever to march against the Mahdi—persisted in communicating with the British Agent in Egypt with regard to the financial difficulties of the expedition, Granville hastened to remind the latter that the British Government accepted no responsibility whatsoever in regard to the conduct of affairs in the Sudan, adding that General Hicks should know that although they were glad to receive information, Her Majesty's Government did not want to be associated with the actions of the Egyptian Government in that quarter.[2] By the end of October 1883 Baring's instructions were still '. . . not to interfere in Soudan matters . . . we will not take any responsibility . . . and . . . we will under no circumstances send troops'[3] to the Sudan.

A series of happenings, however, soon followed which completely transformed British policy both in Egypt and in the Sudan.

The first of these was the news, confirmed in Cairo on 22 November,[4] that General Hicks's army had not merely been defeated by the

be carried out if you keep the Tories out of office' (P.R.O. FO/633, vol. viii, no. 20).

[1] Baring to Granville, P.R.O. 30/29/160 (29 Oct. 1883).

[2] Granville to Malet, 8 Aug. 1883, P.R.O. FO/78/3551.

[3] Baring to Granville, 29 Oct. 1883, P.R.O. 30/29/161.

[4] Mekki Shibeika, *British Policy in the Sudan 1882–1902* (London, 1952), p. 113.

Mahdists, but almost completely annihilated at Shaikān, near al Ūbayyid in Kordofan. From then on it became quite clear that the fall of Khartoum to the Mahdi was a matter of time and that the very existence of the Egyptian regime in the Sudan had been brought into serious doubt. In a private letter to Lord Granville, Baring said that both local opinion at Khartoum and all the best military opinion in Cairo were agreed on this point.[1] As for his own views on the situation, Baring said[2] that he was in complete agreement with Colonel Stewart who had reported from the Sudan in the following terms: 'I am firmly convinced that the Egyptians are quite unfit in every way to undertake such a task as the government of so vast a country with a view to its welfare, and that both for their own sake and that of the people they try to rule, it would be advisable to abandon large portions of it. The fact of their general incompetence to rule is so generally acknowledged that it is unnecessary to discuss the question.'[3]

Baring then proceeded to explain the significance of the new situation. He pointed out that apart from the heavy blow which the abandonment of the Sudan would inflict upon the authority of the Khedive and his Government, which had already been badly shaken by the 'Urabi Revolt, the presence on the Egyptian borders of a population flushed with religious enthusiasm and military success would endanger Egypt itself and might quite conceivably spark off a pro-Mahdist rising in its southern provinces. 'It may be', Baring continued, 'that, as circumstances develop, Her Majesty's Government will be obliged to reconsider some portions of their Egyptian policy . . . I had hoped that within a year or so it would have been possible to withdraw the British garrison from Egypt. I must now reluctantly admit that a more prolonged occupation will, in all probability, become an almost unavoidable necessity.'[4]

The only way of averting this prospect was to reverse the whole process—by checking the Mahdi, turning his victories into defeat, and re-establishing Egypt's authority in the Sudan, at least as far as Khartoum. This, the Egyptian Government of Sharīf Pasha was determined to do, or try to do, at almost any price,[5] as the only

[1] Baring to Granville, 22 Nov. 1883, P.R.O. 30/29/161.

[2] Baring to Granville, 3 Dec. 1883, P.R.O. FO/78/3560.

[3] Quoted in Baring to Granville of 3 Dec. above. The whole document was published under the title *Report on the Sudan* by J. D. H. Stewart, Cmd. 3670 (1883).

[4] Baring to Granville, 3 Dec. 1883, P.R.O. FO/78/3560.

[5] Baring to Granville, Midnight, 10 Dec. 1883, P.R.O. 30/29/161.

course compatible with their dignity and the independence of their country.[1] Convinced of their own inability to undertake such a task, however, the Egyptian Government proposed to seek the assistance of either the British or the Turkish Governments. The reaction of the British Government to Sharīf's request for British or Indian troops was that, in general, they could do nothing which would throw upon them the responsibility of operations in the Sudan[2] and, in particular, that they had no intention of employing either British or Indian troops in the country.[3]

With regard to Sharīf's proposal to call in the Sultan instead, Granville informed Baring that: 'Her Majesty's Government have no objection to offer to the employment of Turkish troops provided they are paid by the Turkish Government and that such employment be restricted exclusively to the Soudan, with their base at Suakin.'[3]

These conditions, as Cromer was to say some twenty years later, were practically prohibitive.[4] As if to remove any possible doubt as to their real meaning however, the dispatch continued that 'Except for securing the safe retreat of garrisons still holding position in the Soudan Her Majesty's Government cannot agree to increasing the burden on the Egyptian revenues by expenditure for operations which even if successful, and this is not probable, would be of doubtful advantage to Egypt. Her Majesty's Government recommend the Minister of the Khedieve to come to an early decision to abandon all territory south of Assouan, or at least Wady Halfa. They will be prepared to assist in maintaining order in Egypt proper and in defending it as well as the ports on the Red Sea.'[5]

Sharīf refused to accept the policy of abandonment thus recommended. In doing this, 'He', Baring wrote to Granville, 'was much moved by the danger which he sees to the future independence of Egypt. He argues, and with truth, that the policy of abandonment will almost certainly entail an increase in the British garrison . . . It is impossible to deny that whatever solution be adopted the future independence of Egypt is in danger.'[6] For Sharīf, however, this last

[1] Baring to Granville, 16 Dec. 1883, P.R.O. 30/29/161.
[2] Granville to Baring, 25 Nov. 1883, P.R.O. FO/78/3550.
[3] Granville to Baring, 13 Dec. 1883, P.R.O. FO/78/3550.
[4] Cromer, *Modern Egypt*, p. 295.
[5] Granville to Baring, 13 Dec. 1883, P.R.O. FO/78/3550.
[6] Baring to Granville, 16 Dec. 1883, P.R.O. 30/29/161. Baring added: 'I fancy that Cherif and others think that the policy of abandonment is merely a snare, and is recommended in order to render our presence permanently necessary in

point was by no means self-evident. On the contrary, he argued, Egypt's independence could best be safeguarded if a policy—based on borrowing 10,000 men from a foreign power—of re-establishing the Khedive's authority in the Sudan was adopted instead of that of abandonment. Besides, Sharīf pointed out, the Khedive was forbidden by the Firman of 7 August 1879 to cede any territory entrusted to him by the Sultan.[1] The recommendation of Her Majesty's Government, therefore, was both unwise and unconstitutional.

In the trial of strength which followed, the Khedive threw his weight behind Sharīf. Baring was thereby led to the conclusion that under no amount of persuasion or argument would the existing ministry consent to the policy of abandonment, and that the only way in which this policy could be carried out was for him to inform the Khedive that the British Government insisted on that course.[2] He later added, in a private telegram to Granville, that in his opinion it was impossible to get out of so serious a situation without some serious interference on his part. 'When once I speak it is very desirable that the Ministerial crisis should be short, sharp and decisive.'[3] The Foreign Secretary approved the suggestion and instructed him to inform the Egyptian Government that it was essential in matters affecting the administration and safety of Egypt, that the advice of Her Majesty's Government should be followed, and that ministers and advisers must carry out this advice or forfeit their office.[4]

Four days later, Baring was able to tell Granville: 'I have got the Khedieve entirely on my side . . . send me something pleasant which I can show him. He will do everything he is told.'[5] Nūbār Pasha, who succeeded Sharīf after the latter's resignation, would also do everything he was told[6] and he wanted to have one or more English ministers in his cabinet.[7] Under Nūbār the question of abandonment

Egypt. I would not give any pledges . . . because the force of circumstances may compel us to eat our words.'

[1] Sharīf's Memorandum to Sir Evelyn Baring, *al-Sūdān 1841–1953*, p. 214. Also, Baring to Granville, 22 Dec. 1883, P.R.O. FO/78/3560.

[2] Baring to Granville, 22 Dec. 1883, P.R.O. FO/78/3560.

[3] Baring to Granville, 4 Jan. 1884, P.R.O. 30/29/162.

[4] Granville to Baring, 4 Jan. 1884, *al-Sūdān 1841–1953*, p. 3; also Cromer, *Modern Egypt*, p. 296.

[5] Baring to Granville, 8 Jan. 1884, P.R.O. 30/29/162.

[6] Baring, writing privately to Lord Rosebery, said that: 'Nubar's strength, politically speaking, is that of a woman. It consists in his weakness. If he is told officially that he must yield on a point to which he attaches great importance, he will not resist any further, knowing that resistance is useless, but he will resign' (Cromer to Rosebery, 16 May 1886, P.R.O. FO/633/7, no. 58).

[7] Baring to Granville, 14 Jan. 1884, P.R.O. 30/29/162.

was no longer a matter of policy but of administration. The task was entrusted to General Charles Gordon who proceeded to the Sudan and began making arrangements for the evacuation of Egyptian and European troops and civilians. By that time, however, the Mahdist Revolution had grown too strong for even this limited task to be fully accomplished. Khartoum fell to al-Mahdi on 26 January 1885 and Gordon himself was killed. His death caused a great outcry in Britain and left a deep impression on the minds of its people, but no change of policy was effected, and for the next decade Britain was content to stay in Egypt and watch events in the Sudan.

3. *Imperial diplomacy and the birth of the new regime*

Baring, who was by then already recognized as the *de facto* ruler of Egypt, decided on this line of policy and, until 1896 defended it and succeeded in persuading successive British Governments to accept it, on the strength of three basic arguments. The first of these was that as long as British forces, or Egyptian forces under British officers, were available the Mahdist regime in the Sudan could not present a serious threat to Egypt, since all attempts to invade the country were certain to be checked[1]—as indeed they were in 1889, when General Grenfell defeated the Khalīfa's[2] army under Amir 'Abd al-Raḥmān al-Nujumi, at Argīn and Toshki—thereby negating a cardinal point in the Mahdi's programme of conquering Egypt and reviving the Muslim world. Secondly, that as long as Egypt's security was thus safeguarded, no attempt should be made to reconquer the Sudan unless and until Egypt's military and financial resources admitted of such a step being taken with prudence.[3] Otherwise, Baring insisted, an unnecessary strain would be imposed on the Egyptian Treasury which would hinder the country's recovery and reduce its ability to reconquer the Sudan when the right time came. In the light of this argument it was decided, in 1895, to give priority to the construction of the Aswān Dam over premature attempts at reconquering the Sudan, it being suggested at the time that the increase of revenue derived from the resultant agricultural expansion would provide funds to make possible the reconquest.[4] Finally, and in so far as

[1] Baring to Rosebery, 26 Jan. 1886, P.R.O. FO/633/7, no. 65.

[2] al-Mahdi died soon after the fall of Khartoum and was succeeded by the Khalīfa (Caliph) 'Abdullahi al-Ta'āiyshi.

[3] Baring to Rosebery, 12 Apr. 1895, P.R.O. FO/633/7, no. 205.

[4] Cromer, pp. 522–3.

Egypt's welfare depended on the Nile, Baring argued that there was in fact no need to worry as long as the Mahdists, and not a European Power, were in control of the Sudan, since they, unlike France for instance, possessed neither the resources nor the engineering skill to do any real harm to Egypt.[1]

By 1896 none of these arguments had been undermined. On 12 March of the same year, however, the British Government suddenly —and somewhat prematurely as both Cromer and Salisbury had feared[2]—decided to embark on the reconquest of the Sudan. The immediate cause of this sudden reversal of policy was the humiliating and unexpected defeat of the Italians (whose presence in the Horn of Africa was then favoured by Britain) by the Abyssinians, at Adua on 1 March 1896. It was rumoured at the time that the Abyssinians were seeking an alliance with the Khalīfa, who was also preparing to attack the Italians at Kasala, in eastern Sudan. The Italian ambassador in London appealed to the British Government to intervene, and it was decided therefore, that Dongola should be occupied.[3] In a private letter to Cromer the day after, Salisbury explained that the decision was 'inspired by a desire to help the Italians at Kasala and to prevent the Dervishes from winning a conspicuous success which might have far-reaching effects'.[4]

More important, the scramble for Africa which marked the 1880s had already begun and the Nile Valley was 'in the diplomatic market', France and Belgium being the main bidders apart from Britain.[5]

Almost exactly a year before the cabinet's decision, Cromer had warned the British Government of the consequences of maintaining a purely passive attitude towards the Sudan while the French were already pushing their way from Central Africa towards the Nile. He argued that Britain had to choose between two courses against both of which great objections could be urged. She could either yield to the French and tolerate the consequences; or she could, at the risk of going to war with France, seek to establish her own authority throughout the Nile Valley. Cromer preferred the second course, and

[1] Baring to Rosebery, 12 Apr. 1895, P.R.O. FO/633/7, no. 205.

[2] Ibid. Also Salisbury to Cromer, 13 Mar. 1896, P.R.O. FO/633/7, no. 171. Cromer later recorded that if about 1896 he had been asked how long a time would probably elapse before the Egyptian Government could assume an offensive policy in the Sudan, his answer would have been 'about 25 years' (*Modern Egypt*, p. 522).

[3] Salisbury to Cromer, 12 Mar. 1896, P.R.O. FO/78/4893.

[4] Salisbury to Cromer, 13 Mar. 1896, P.R.O. FO/633/7, no. 171.

[5] Salisbury to Cromer, 1 Apr. 1896, P.R.O. FO/633/7, no. 173.

with a view to reducing the possibility of war which was inherent in such an undertaking, and in order to disarm the French—diplomatically speaking—in the event of war, he suggested that Britain should place herself on the grounds of strict international right by conducting the reconquest of the Sudan in the name of Egypt, under English guidance: 'The country belonged to Egypt by right of conquest; the right was ratified by the Sultan, and is now acknowledged by France. The Egyptians were obliged to retire temporarily. Let us assume that they are now able and willing to re-enter into possession. Why should they not be allowed to do so? This argument appears to me to turn the flank of the French.'[1]

Cromer's suggestions became official policy, and his views with regard to the diplomatic position Britain should take were also accepted. The Egyptians, however, were reluctant to 're-enter into possession' under these circumstances; and the Sultan, presumably on the instigation of the Russians and the French,[2] was not prepared to give his blessings without further question.

In Egypt the reigning Khedive, 'Abbās II, who, unlike his father, was a confirmed Anglophobe and nursed a general dislike of Europeans and European intervention in Egypt,[3] strongly disapproved of the Dongola Campaign and spoke of it as conceived mainly in Italian interests.[4] The nationalists condemned it even more vigorously for not being dictated by the interests of Egypt.[5] And when it was decided that the campaign should not stop at Dongola for two or three years as had been originally hoped,[6] but that it should be extended into a full attack on the Khalīfa, the Khedive could not help but feel that any advantage gained in the Sudan constituted an

[1] Cromer to Rosebery, 12 Apr. 1895, P.R.O. FO/633/7, no. 205. In a private letter to Lord Kimberly dated 29 Mar. 1895, he also said the following: 'Surely it is impossible for all time to have the Soudan in its present condition; and if the Egyptians do not take it the French or the Italians will some day walk in. I greatly doubt the possibility of keeping them out by arrangements on paper. It is surely undesirable in our interest that this should happen. I had always hoped that the question might be left to stand for some years. What I now fear is that the activity of the French will force on a premature consideration of the issue. Remember that, though the French might object to English reconquest, as to which I conceive there can be no serious question, they could make no objection to reconquest by Egypt' (P.R.O. FO/633/7, no. 236).

[2] Salisbury to Cromer, 24 Apr. 1896, P.R.O. FO/633/7, no. 174.

[3] Cromer to Salisbury, 25 Apr. 1898, P.R.O. FO/78/4956.

[4] Cromer to Salisbury, 14 Mar. 1896, P.R.O. FO/78/4893.

[5] Cromer to Salisbury, 18 Mar. 1896, P.R.O. FO/78/4893.

[6] Cromer to Salisbury, 30 Oct. 1896, P.R.O. FO/633/7 and Salisbury to Cromer, 24 Apr. 1896, P.R.O. FO/633/7.

English rather than Egyptian success. The nationalists regarded Kitchener's victories as disasters to Islam and even hoped that the Egyptian army, under Kitchener, would be defeated and that the Mahdists would occupy Cairo.[1]

But, despite his feelings, the Khedive knew that neither in Egypt nor in the Sudan could he take any important step contrary to the wishes of the British Government or without their consent.[2] The hostility of the small but influential group of nationalists who looked to the Khedive for guidance could also be discounted as long as the mass of the people were kept in a condition of comparative material prosperity.[2]

The Sultan's protestations were equally ineffectual. For instance, on 27 March 1896 the Grand Vizier telegraphed the Khedive to remind him that the military force of Egypt was a part of the Imperial Army and that the use of these troops—especially when directed against Muslims, as was the case with the Mahdists, depended absolutely and entirely on the will and permission of His Imperial Majesty. Such permission had neither been sought nor granted in the case of the Dongola Campaign, and the whole enterprise was not in the interest of Egypt. It was, therefore, 'absolutely impossible that this expedition should be sanctioned by the Imperial Government'.[3] The Khedive's reply, framed after due consultation with Cromer, denied any infringement of the Imperial Firmans, and stated that the Sultan had not been informed of the expedition merely because it resembled those which had previously been sent to the Sudan—even before the appearance of the Mahdists, who were heretics and molested the people of Islam. In any case, the dispatch continued, 'the military undertaking against Dongola was not one originally conceived by the Egyptian Government. It was the result of agreement with the views and proposals of the English Government which is now in military occupation of Egypt'.[4] Two days later His Imperial Majesty conveyed his cordial greetings to the Khedive and informed him that his reply had caused great satisfaction and pleasure.[5]

Although such episodes—with varying degrees of protest and forbearance—were repeated at different stages of the war, they were of little consequence to British policy in the Nile Valley. The British

[1] Cromer to Salisbury, 25 Apr. 1898, P.R.O. FO/78/4956.
[2] Cromer's Memorandum to the Cabinet, 15 June 1898, P.R.O. FO/78/4956.
[3] Cromer to Salisbury, 31 Mar. 1896, P.R.O. FO/78/4761.
[4] Ibid., Inclosure II.
[5] Ibid., Inclosure III.

Government looked upon them as a nuisance rather than a real challenge,[1] and was by and large able to ignore them until the time came when 'the shadowy claims of Turkish suzerainty were practically . . . swept away by a stroke of the pen'.[2]

French opposition, however, was bound to be stronger and far more real than that of either Egypt or Turkey. Partly in order to forestall this opposition, but also with a view to gratifying the Egyptians in whose name and with whose material support the reconquest was being undertaken, and in order to give a clear indication to the French that the control of the Nile was more an English than an Egyptian question[3]—Kitchener was instructed, when once Khartoum had fallen to him, to hoist the British and Egyptian flags side by side.[4]

The last battle between Kitchener and the Khalīfa was fought at Karari, a few miles north of Omdurman, on 2 September 1898. Kitchener's forces entered the Mahdi's capital on the 2nd, and on the 4th the British and Egyptian flags were hoisted with due ceremony on the wall of the palace at Khartoum.[5] Soon afterwards Kitchener proceeded south on the White Nile, and on the 19th reached Fashoda, a point about one thousand miles from Khartoum, where he found a French force of about 130 men under a Captain Marchand flying the French flag.[6] He judiciously hoisted the Egyptian flag, but not the British, and protested in the strongest terms against the occupation of Fashoda by the French and the hoisting of their flag 'in the domains of His Highness the Khedieve', and informed Marchand that this was regarded as a direct violation of the rights of Egypt and Great Britain.[7]

Marchand said that he had no objection to the Egyptian flag being hoisted;[7] but he also stated that he had orders from the French Government to occupy Baḥr al-Ghazāl as far as Fashoda and could not retire without further orders.[8] An acute diplomatic crisis was thereby precipitated which led Britain and France to the brink of war. During the controversy which followed the principal arguments of the French were that the country bordering the White Nile, though

[1] Salisbury to Cromer, 3 June 1898, P.R.O. FO/78/5050.
[2] Cromer, p. 550.
[3] Cromer to Salisbury, 15 June 1898, P.R.O. FO/78/4956.
[4] Salisbury to Cromer, 2 Aug. 1898, P.R.O. FO/78/5050.
[5] Sirdar to Cromer, 4 Sept. 1898, P.R.O. FO/5050.
[6] Salisbury to the Queen, 25 Sept. 1898, P.R.O. FO/78/5051.
[7] Kitchener to Cromer, 21 Sept. 1898, P.R.O. FO/78/5051.
[8] Salisbury to the Queen, 28 Sept. 1898, P.R.O. FO/78/5051.

formerly under the Government of Egypt, had become '*res nullius*' by its abandonment on the part of the Egyptian Government, and that the French had a right to a position on the Nile as much as the Germans or the Belgians, and that they had retained that right to occupy the banks of the Nile whenever they thought fit.[1] In reply, the British Government argued that the Egyptian title to the banks of the Nile had certainly been rendered dormant by the military successes of the Mahdi, but that the amount of right which had been alienated from Egypt, had been entirely transferred to the conqueror. How much title remained to Egypt, and how much was transferred to the Mahdi and the Khalīfa had been settled on the field of battle. But the controversy did not authorize a third party to claim the disputed land as derelict.[1]

The problem was finally resolved by dividing Central Africa into French and British spheres of influence in accordance with the terms of a declaration, signed on 21 March 1899,[2] which left the Sudan for Egypt to govern—'under English guidance'.[3]

[1] The Marquess of Salisbury to Sir E. Monson, 6 Oct. 1898, Egypt, no. 3 (1898), C. 9055.

[2] *Declaration Relating to the British and French Spheres of Influence in Central Africa*, C. 9134 (Egypt, no. 2, 1899).

[3] Cromer to Rosebery, 12 Apr. 1895, P.R.O. FO/633/7.

CHAPTER II

The Terms of the Agreement

1. *Some basic considerations*

IN his letter to Cromer, in which the decision of the British Government that the British and Egyptian flags were to be hoisted at Khartoum side by side, Lord Salisbury stated that

> This decision will have no reference to the manner in which the occupied countries are to be administered in the future. It is not necessary at present to define their political status with any great precision. These matters can be considered at a later period. You will, however, explain to the Khedieve and to his ministers that the procedure I have indicated is intended to emphasise the fact that Her Majesty's Government consider that they have a predominant voice in all matters connected with the Sudan, and that they expect that any advice which they may think fit to tender to the Egyptian Government in respect to Soudan affairs, will be followed.[1]

In the light of these instructions, Cromer, for a while, considered the possibility of allowing matters to drift, settling each point on its own merits as it came up for solution.[2] However, he soon came to the conclusion that this course—though, in his opinion, it was quite feasible for the governance of the Sudanese themselves—was not really adequate for regulating the country's relations with the outside world, particularly in connection with those Europeans who wished to reside, to invest capital, to trade, and to acquire real property in the Sudan.[2] Unless a distinctly separate regime was established in the Sudan which rendered it immune to such abuses, Europeans, Cromer found, would assume that they had the same status and privileges to which they were accustomed in Egypt and which, under the system of the Capitulation,[3] had enabled European

[1] Salisbury to Cromer, 2 Aug. 1898, P.R.O. FO/78/5050. The Khedive's Government were informed accordingly—on 4 Sept., i.e. two days after the battle of Omdurman (Rodd to M. le Ministre, 4 Sept. 1898, P.R.O. FO/78/5050).

[2] Cromer to Salisbury, 10 Nov. 1898, P.R.O. FO/78/4957.

[3] Under this system the rulers of the Ottoman Empire, including the Khedive of Egypt, customarily granted 'letters of privilege' to Europeans who wished to

smugglers to carry on their illicit trade under the eye of the law, and had been 'turned to such base uses that they have protected the keeper of the gambling-hell, the vendor of adulterated drink, the receiver of stolen goods, and the careless apothecary who supplies his customer with poison in place of some healing drug'.[1] And with the Capitulations it was certain that 'all the cumbersome paraphernalia of internationalism'[2] which had made Egypt a judicial and legislative Babel,[3] would also be introduced—thus rendering the government of the Sudan unnecessarily difficult, particularly from the point of view of the British administrator who, instead of having a predominant voice in all matters connected with the Sudan,[4] would find himself competing with the agents and representatives of 'Powers, some or other of whom might at some future time become the enemy of England'.[5]

In order to avert these prospects, therefore, and so that Britain's position in the country should be finally and unequivocally established, it was necessary that a constitutional charter be drawn up for the Sudan.

Considering the various possibilities which lay before him in drafting such an instrument, Cromer decided against the direct annexation of the Sudan by Britain, because this would have meant throwing a new financial burden on an unwilling British Parliament,[6]

reside or conduct business in the Empire. With the decline of the Ottomans, from the seventeenth century onwards, these privileges gradually came to be regarded, at any rate by the Europeans who enjoyed them, as 'rights' and not privileges. In the absence of any effective checks on the manner in which they were exercised, these 'rights' were habitually abused and exploited by the adventurers who held them in order to further their illegal as well as their legal interests. The situation was particularly hopeless in Egypt where Europeans could not be tried under the laws of the land, and Egyptian courts had no jurisdiction over them. Instead cases involving Europeans were tried by Consular Tribunals of which there were no less than seventeen. Before these Tribunals however, 'Europeans were systematically acquitted of crimes and offences which there was no difficulty in proving, while it was difficult for natives to come by their rights when the aggressors were aliens' (Sir A. Ward and C. P. Gooch, *Cambridge History of British Foreign Policy* (Cambridge, 1923), iii. 164).

[1] Cromer, *Modern Egypt*, pp. 795 and 796.

[2] Ibid., p. 548.

[3] Ibid., p. 799.

[4] Salisbury's words in his letter to Cromer of 2 Aug. quoted above.

[5] Cromer, p. 548.

[6] Cromer, p. 548. Salisbury often urged Cromer not to forget the extreme difficulty they always had in persuading the House of Commons to incur any heavy expenses in connection with Egypt. 'The pressure of taxation here is very heavy. Motions in the direction of economy will unite many who ordinarily

and also because annexation would have unnecessarily reawakened French, Turkish, and Egyptian hostility.[1] At the same time, however, he was, of course, not prepared to recognize the Sudan as a portion of Egypt or the Ottoman Empire.[1] Under these circumstances, therefore, Cromer decided to create a 'hybrid form of government'[2] which enabled Britain to become the *de facto* ruler of the country, without having to shoulder the cost of its administration, and which, at the same time, gave the Egyptians the satisfaction of seeing themselves as the co-governors of the Sudan—thereby inducing them to accept more willingly than might otherwise have been possible, the responsibility for paying the bulk of the cost of the country's administration, as they had done in financing its reconquest.[3] Besides, this hybrid arrangement had the further convenience of enabling Cromer to state, in his published works, that annexation by Britain was excluded on the grounds of equality, as well as policy, since—in view of the fact that the whole campaign had been carried out in the name of the Khedive—'it would have been very unjust to ignore Egyptian claims in deciding on the future political status of the Sudan'.[4]

vote apart, and the decision of the House on such points cannot be confidently foretold.' Salisbury to Cromer, 11 Feb. 1887, P.R.O. FO/633/7.

[1] Cromer's words were: 'I understand that, for many obvious political reasons, we do not wish to annex' (Memorandum of 10 Nov. 1898, P.R.O. FO/78/4957).

[2] Cromer, p. 549. Almost fifteen years before the conclusion of the Agreement, Cromer—in a very long and interesting private letter to Granville—discussed the various alternative policies which Britain could pursue with regard to the Sudan, after Gordon's death. Dismissing the three courses of establishing a quasi-independent ruler in the Sudan, inducing the Sultan to intervene, and arranging for the Italians to take over the government of the country, he proceeded to examine 'the fourth solution which . . . involves the establishment in some form or another of English Rule in the Sudan. I say "in one form or another" because the execution of this policy admits of several modifications in detail. Thus we may either annex the country outright, or we may establish an Englishman as a quasi-independent Ruler, or as a Governor-General under the Khedieve —with the accompaniment, which I should consider necessary, of an English force, or, at all events, of a force officered by Englishmen to keep him in his place, or perhaps a Company might be formed somewhat on the model of the old East India Company. But all these plans virtually rest on the same foundation. Under all of them England would virtually take in hand the Government of the Soudan' (Cromer to Granville, 3 Apr. 1885, P.R.O. G. & D. 30/29/165).

[3] The total cost of the campaigns of 1896–8 was £2,354,000 of which rather less than £800,000 was paid by the British, and the balance of about £1,554,000 by the Egyptian Treasury. Cromer, p. 541. As will be seen in the next chapter, Egypt also paid the bulk of the cost of administration for many years after the reconquest.

[4] Cromer, p. 548.

The result of Cromer's considerations was the 'Agreement between Her Britannic Majesty's Government and the Government of His Highness the Khedieve of Egypt relative to the future Administration of the Sudan', which was signed in Cairo, on 19 Jan. 1899.

2. *Analysis of the Agreement*

The Anglo-Egyptian Agreement for the Administration of the Sudan, more commonly known as the Condominium Agreement (which wrongly implies the establishment in the Sudan of a regime wherein sovereignty was jointly held by the two governments concerned) in fact altogether ignored the question of sovereignty as such. Nor was any reference made in it to the Ottoman Sultan in whom, theoretically speaking, sovereignty over the Sudan was still vested. Instead the Agreement was concluded with the Government of the Khedive who, from the legal point of view, was merely a vassal of the Sultan and was as such specifically forbidden by the Imperial Firmans to conclude Treaties with any foreign power other than commercial and customs conventions.[1]

As a matter of fact, however, the Ottoman Empire had long been nothing but 'the sick man of Europe'; Egypt was a British 'sphere of influence'; and Cromer (who was nicknamed 'The Lord' by his subordinates speaking behind his back)[2] was naturally convinced that British authority should be firmly established in the Sudan and that 'the Egyptians should not have conferred on them a "bastard freedom" to repeat the misgovernment of the past'.[3]

These facts and convictions were given formal expression in the preamble as well as in the main body of the Agreement. In the former part allusion was made 'incidentally and inferentially'[4] to the rights of the Khedive in the Sudan—before the Mahdist revolution; but no mention was made of such rights after the reconquest. The fact that the campaign had been conducted in the name of the Khedive was similarly ignored; and the reconquest was described as the result of the joint military and financial efforts of the British and

[1] *al-Sūdān 1841–1953*, pp. 2–4.

[2] A typical reference to Cromer by his juniors occurs in a private letter written by Cecil of the British Agency in Cairo in which he tells Wingate that he was afraid 'The Lord may blow up' about the way some of the Agency's work was being done (the Wingate Papers, School of Oriental Studies, Durham University, Ref. 277/E3).

[3] Cromer, p. 548.

[4] Cromer's Memorandum to Salisbury, 10 Nov. 1898 (P.R.O. FO/78/4957).

Egyptian Governments without any indication as to the proportions in which the total costs of the campaigns had been divided between the two Governments.

By contrast the claims which accrued to Britain by virtue of her role in the reconquest were explicitly stated in the preamble, and the desire to give effect to these claims was presented as one of the objectives of the Agreement. The further statement was therefore added that Her Britannic Majesty's Government was entitled 'by right of conquest' to share in the present and future working and development of the (Sudan's) system of administration and legislation.[1]

Article III provided that this should be headed, as in the days of the Turco-Egyptian regime, by a single officer termed 'The Governor-General of the Sudan' in whom was to be vested the supreme military and civil command in the country. He was to be an Egyptian official, appointed and dismissed only by Khedivial Decree. He could not, however, be appointed except on the recommendation of the British Government, nor could he be removed without their consent. This, obviously, meant that although the Governor-General of the Sudan was nominally and formally an Egyptian official, he was in fact, a British agent. The Agreement was silent as to his nationality; but in the light of what has already been said, it is hardly surprising that all those who held the office of Governor-General under the Anglo-Egyptian Administration were, without exception, British.

Consistent with the provisions of Article III, which vested the supreme military and civil command of the Sudan in him, Article IV empowered the Governor-General to make, alter, or abrogate, by proclamation, all laws, orders, and regulations with the full force of law, for the good government of the Sudan, and for regulating the holding, disposal, and devolution of property within its boundaries. The only limitation imposed on him in this connection was that he

[1] In the original draft of his Memorandum of 10 Nov. 1898, Cromer argued: 'that the reconquest has been effected by English troops and Egyptian troops officered and trained by Englishmen; that the Soudan consequently belongs by right of conquest to England'. Sir Malcolm McIlwraith, the Judicial Adviser of the Egyptian Government, who helped Cromer with the drafting of both the Memorandum and the Agreement, commented, 'I think that this is rather strong', and added that if a Power helped another to reconquer dominions which that Other had for some time lost, the helping Power was entitled—in International Law and convention—to become a preponderating influence in the future of the country; but it could not rightly claim that the country in question belongs to her. He suggested that it would be quite sufficient for their purpose that the British Government claims that the reconquest confers on them a predominant right in the determination of the future of the Sudan (P.R.O. FO/141/333).

was required to notify such proclamations as he may from time to time make or issue, to Her Britannic Majesty's Government—through the British Agent and Consul-General in Cairo—and to the President of the Council of Ministers of His Highness the Khedive.

In his concern for finding a way whereby the Governor-General could be held under the effective control of his peers, Cromer had originally intended to make the issue of proclamations by the Governor-General conditional upon the prior consent of the British and Egyptian Governments, except where they had specifically agreed to exempt proclamations from this obligation—in which case the proclamations in question were to be notified to them within a given period of time after the date of issue.[1] Cromer, however, considered that it would be a great mistake to centralize the administration in the hands of any authority, British or Egyptian, in Cairo.[2] He also felt that the Governor-General should appear absolutely supreme in the eyes of the population of the Sudan.[2] For these reasons, and since it was clearly in the interest of efficiency that the Governor-General who was, after all, the trusted representative of the two governments, should, as far as possible, be given a free hand in governing the country—the condition of prior consent on proclamations was dropped[3] from the final text of the Agreement. He was, therefore, only required to notify the two governments after proclamations had been made.

In the light of these same considerations, and in order to ensure the Governor-General's complete freedom from the shackles of international (including Egyptian) interference, Article V stipulated that no Egyptian law, decree, ministerial *arrêté*, or other enactment could, in future, apply to the Sudan or any part thereof, except where the Governor-General's approval had been specifically granted, by proclamation. Similarly, Article VIII provided that the jurisdiction of the Mixed Tribunals (in which civil cases involving Egyptians and Europeans were tried in Egypt) should not extend nor be recognized for any purpose whatsoever, in any part of the Sudan, except in the town of Sawākin, which continued to have a special status until July 1899.

[1] Cromer's draft of the Agreement, P.R.O. FO/141/333. See Appendix I.
[2] Cromer to Salisbury, 10 Nov. 1898, P.R.O. FO/78/4957.
[3] As will be seen in the next chapter, this was largely due to the insistence of Kitchener and Salisbury that the Governor-General should be allowed to govern without too much control from the Agent and Consul-General (pp. 51–7 below).

The implications of these two articles for Europeans were explicitly stated in Article VI of the Agreement. This explained that in the definition by proclamation of the conditions under which Europeans were to be at liberty to trade with or reside in the Sudan, or to hold property within its limits, 'no special privilege shall be accorded to the subjects of any one or more Power'. Cromer felt that this, like other features of the Agreement, was almost certain to be challenged on the grounds that the Sudan was part of the Ottoman Empire and could not legitimately be treated in a different way from, for instance, Egypt.[1] He was, nevertheless determined to exclude the loathsome effects of internationalism and legislation by diplomacy (which he considered to have been the most cumbersome form of legislation in the world)[2] from the country. As if to make doubly sure that this objective would be fulfilled Cromer inserted another Article, number X, which made it impossible for Consuls, Vice Consuls, or Consular Agents to be accredited in respect of, or to reside in, the Sudan without the previous consent of the British Government. Europeans who might find this unpalatable, he argued, could be conciliated by proclaiming the commercial policy of the 'open door' in the Sudan,[3] and by ensuring that they—however Anglophobic their governments may be—would be treated with perfect justice under the British flag.[4] To those who could not or would not be satisfied with the benefits of Free Trade and British Justice, and more especially to those who considered it essential that their marriages or burials should be attested by the Consular representatives of their respective countries, Cromer had one simple reply: namely, that they should not go to the Sudan, but 'remain in the territory lying north of the 22nd parallel of latitude'.[5]

This, it was stated in Article I, was to constitute the northern boundary of the country. Other boundaries to the east, west, or south were not fixed, for the time being at any rate, with anything approaching the exactitude, not to say the arbitrariness, with which the Sudanese–Egyptian border was thus determined. However, according to this Article the 'Sudan' was carefully defined so as to include three fairly recognizable categories of territory—all lying to the south of the 22nd parallel.

[1] Cromer to Salisbury, 10 Nov. 1898, P.R.O. FO/78/4957.
[2] Cromer, *Modern Egypt*, p. 708.
[3] Cromer to Salisbury, 10 Nov. 1898, P.R.O. FO/78/4957.
[4] Cromer, *Modern Egypt*, p. 552.
[5] Ibid., p. 551.

The first of these categories comprised territory which had never been evacuated by Egyptian troops since 1882, the second year of the Mahdist revolution. This formula was adopted in order to include Wadi Ḥalfa and Sawākin,[1] both of which had traditionally belonged to the Sudan and, as was stated in the preamble to the Agreement, could best be administered in conjunction with the reconquered provinces to which they were respectively adjacent. Unlike Ḥalfa, however, the ancient port of Sawākin continued, until July 1899, to be administered as part of Egypt and not the Sudan. During the intervening six months therefore, the jurisdiction of the Mixed Tribunals was recognized in Sawākin, and the Egyptian flag alone was hoisted in it. This anomalous position was temporarily tolerated by Cromer because of the emotional attachment which Egyptians felt towards this ancient outpost of their bygone empire, and his consequent fear that any sudden change might raise a great and obviously unwanted outcry in Egypt.[1] A few months later, however, it appears that Cromer was convinced that he had been somewhat over-cautious about this issue, and a 'Supplementary Agreement' was signed on 19 July 1899, which brought Sawākin in line with the rest of the country.

The second category referred to territories 'which having before the late rebellion in the Sudan been administered by the Government of His Highness the Khedieve were temporarily lost to Egypt and have been reconquered by Her Majesty's Government and the Egyptian Government, acting in concert'. In other words, it was not the intention of the signatories that the Anglo-Egyptian Sudan should be identical with the Ottoman-Egyptian empire as it existed in 1881. The new administration was to be limited to those parts of the said empire which, having rebelled against the authority of the Khedive, had now been reconquered by the combined efforts of Egypt and Britain. Otherwise, as Cromer explained to Salisbury, considerable areas in the Equator as well as the Somali coast would have been included in the Anglo-Egyptian Sudan, which was inconsistent with Britain's imperial interests in East and Central Africa.[1]

Cromer's views in this connection were explicitly stated in his commentary on the third category of lands which were to form part of the new Sudan. These were described as territories 'which may hereafter be reconquered by the two Governments acting in concert'.

[1] Cromer to Salisbury, 10 Nov. 1898, P.R.O. FO/78/4957.

Pointing out the significance of these words Cromer said that, apart from indicating the possible extension of the Sudan southwards or westwards they were intended 'to exclude extensions from Uganda northwards, made by the English Government acting alone'.[1]

Throughout the Sudan so defined the British and Egyptian flags were to be used, according to Article II, on land and water (except in the town of Sawākin in which locality the Egyptian flag alone was hoisted until July 1899)—thus generalizing what had hitherto been the practice only in Khartoum.

The remaining four Articles of the Agreement were more administrative than political in character. Thus Article VII exempted goods from Egyptian territory from import duties. By virtue of Article IX the whole country (with the exception of Sawākin) was put under martial law. This was considered expedient in view of the fact that the country was still far from settled. Article XI prohibited the exportation and importation of slaves, but said nothing as to the more difficult question of how to deal with domestic slavery. And the concluding Article, number XII, declared that special attention would be paid to the enforcement of The Brussels' Act of 2 July 1890 regarding the sale and manufacture of firearms and spirituous liquors.

As may be expected this Agreement had a mixed reception. Diplomatists of a conservative turn of mind, Cromer tells us, were shocked 'at the creation of a political status hitherto unknown to the law of Europe'.[2] The Sultan too produced some ineffectual murmurs of protest.[2] In Egypt, as will be seen in the following chapters, the nationalists viewed the Agreement as a betrayal to their country, and a few years later, Cromer himself described it as 'the child of opportunism', adding that 'should it eventually die and make way for some robust, because more real, political creation, its authors need not bewail it'.[3]

Being fully aware of its various weaknesses—particularly the fact that it was, to put it mildly, of dubious legality and that it could therefore be easily maintained only as long as Britain was in control

[1] Cromer to Salisbury, 10 Nov. 1898, P.R.O. FO/78/4957.

[2] Cromer, *Modern Egypt*, p. 551. It seems that Cromer was unaware that, as a result of the Congress of Vienna, the district of Moresnet had been put under the joint control of Prussia and the Netherlands in 1819 and that, half a century later, the province of Schleswig-Holstein was subjected to a similar arrangement between Prussia and Austria.

[3] Ibid., p. 552.

of both Egypt and the Sudan, the British Government, as will be seen in Chapter III, did seriously consider, after the outbreak of the Egyptian Revolution of 1919, the possibility of replacing the Agreement by a more 'robust, because more real, political creation' as Cromer had suggested. This, however, was prevented by the very facts of the Revolution and the subsequent independence of Egypt which, from Britain's point of view, seemed to make the change necessary or, at least, highly desirable. As a result British and Egyptian Governments were forced to engage in lengthy and complicated legal debates on the real meaning and purpose of the Agreement and whether it had created an Anglo-Egyptian condominium in the Sudan as Britain argued or only an Anglo-Egyptian administration, leaving the question of sovereignty in the hands of the Egyptian crown as the Egyptians claimed. And the longer they debated the issue, the more obvious became the weakness of the Agreement and the fact that it was, both legally and politically, unsatisfactory—from both Egypt's and Britain's points of view.

Be that as it may, the Agreement lasted for over half a century, during which it provided the constitutional framework within which all legal and practical action in the Sudan took place. It is to this that we now turn.

CHAPTER III

The Development of Administration to 1936

1. *The Foundations of the new Administrative System*

ONCE the main force of the Mahdiyya had been broken, on 2 September 1898,[1] Kitchener[2] and his lieutenants—working under the general direction of Cromer—turned their attention to the establishment of the new Sudan administration.

Following Turkish and Mahdist precedents, the country was divided into a number of provinces which were in turn sub-divided into districts; and these were further split into smaller units, each answerable to the division above, through districts and provinces, to the general headquarters in Khartoum.[3]

Fiscal legislation was also 'based on the unquestionably sound principle that, in the assessment and collection of the taxes, no innovation, based on Western ideas, should be introduced unless its introduction were altogether unavoidable'.[4] Explaining his position in this connection, Cromer stated that

> The main fault of Oriental fiscal administration has generally been, not so much that the principles on which the taxation is based are unsound, as that the method of applying them has been very defective. On going through the list of the taxes which were collected under the Khalīfa's rule, it was found that, although the manner in which they had been levied was cruel and extortionate to the last degree, they were based on principles which are generally recognized in all Moslem countries. No radical change of system

[1] The Khalīfa 'Abdullahi himself escaped death at Karari and, with a small group of followers, tried to resume the fight from Western Sudan, but he was killed in November 1899.

[2] Kitchener was appointed first Governor-General of the new Sudan on the same day on which the Agreement was signed, 19 Jan. 1899.

[3] Khartoum, first established as the Sudan's capital by the Turkish regime of Muḥammad 'Ali, was not used for this purpose by the Mahdist regime. Omdurman, on the western bank of the Nile, was the seat of the Mahdist government. Today it is regarded by the Sudanese as their 'national capital'—Khartoum being the official centre of the country.

[4] *Annual Report* for 1899, Egypt, no. 1 (1900), Cd. 95, p. 46.

was, therefore, necessary. Broadly speaking, all that was required was that the rates of taxation should in each case be fixed by law; that the taxes should be moderate in amount;[1] and that every care should be taken that no demands were made on the taxpayers save those which the law allowed.[2]

Accordingly, only land, herds, and date palms were taxed at the beginning, and the general principle was laid down that local custom should be observed in the methods of levying taxes and recovering them in case of default.[3]

In personal matters, such as marriage, divorce, and inheritance, the traditional Islamic Sharī'a law was allowed to operate. But the penal and criminal codes, which were introduced in 1899, were both modelled on the British Imperial system as developed in India and the Zanzibar and East African Protectorates.[4] The administration of the Sharī'a courts was, naturally, left to Sudanese and Egyptian Muslim civilians, but that of the civil and criminal law—as indeed of all other branches of government—was, at first, dominated by British officers of the Egyptian Army.[5]

At the head of the administration was the British Governor-General who, in this capacity, was the supreme military and civil commander of the Sudan. Until 1925, he was also the 'Sirdār', or Commander-in-Chief, of the Egyptian Army. His chief lieutenants, most of whom were British officers on secondment from the Egyptian Army,[6] were assisted by Egyptian officers and these, in turn, used Sudanese subordinates from the armed forces.[7]

But civilians were, of course, indispensable—especially in rural areas where no government could reasonably hope to function with-

[1] In his *Annual Report* for 1901, Cromer stated: 'A somewhat long experience of the East has led me to attach more importance to low taxation than to reforms, however necessary these may, from the European point of view, appear' (p. 76).

[2] *Annual Report* for 1899, p. 47.

[3] Ibid., pp. 46–7 and 49–50.

[4] Ibid., p. 52.

[5] The *Annual Report* for 1899 states that 'the Magistrates are all military officers'. Six years later, Cromer reported that 'broadly speaking military officers are employed to a considerable extent in the administration of criminal and to a lesser extent in the administration of civil law. Civilian judges are being gradually introduced and now deal with all the more important civil cases', *Annual Report* for 1905, Egypt, no. 1 (1906), Cd. 2817, p. 144.

[6] A notable exception was Rudolf von Slatin (or Salāṭīn Pasha, as he is still remembered in the Sudan), an Austrian officer who had seen service in the Sudan with General Gordon, and afterwards suffered long captivity under the Khalīfa. He was appointed Inspector-General—a specially created post which he held from 1901 until the outbreak of the First World War.

[7] The Egyptian Army was composed of Sudanese as well as Egyptian (and British) soldiers and officers.

out the co-operation of the tribal shaikhs. Besides, a cadre of competent artisans and clerks was needed to fill minor posts in the administration both in Khartoum and in the provincial administrative centres. Since the class of tribal shaikhs could not provide the required type of artisan and junior official, and the importation of these in sufficient numbers would have proved too expensive, the so-called Gordon College[1] was established[2] in order to meet this need.[3]

The higher ranks of the administration (both in Khartoum and in the provinces), however, were dominated by army officers, and the country was, until 1926, governed under martial law.[4] In its earlier stages, therefore, the system of government could best be described as an 'autocracy on military lines for civil purposes'.[5]

Cromer, who believed that the military career 'besides much that is worthy of admiration, has the tendency to excite some of the worst passions in the human breast',[6] did not always find dealing

[1] Writing on the Gordon College in his *Annual Report* for 1898, Cromer felt it necessary 'to explain that the use of the word "college" in connection with this institution is possibly somewhat misleading inasmuch as it conveys the idea that a more ambitious programme will be adopted than, for the time being at all events, will be the case. Lord Kitchener tells me that for the present "The College will be a school, teaching much on the lines of the Assouan and Wadi Halfa schools". These are what are known in Egypt as Higher Primary Schools. The age of admission is seven years and upwards. The course of study lasts for four years' (Egypt, no. 3 (1899), C. 9231, pp. 6–7).

[2] The fact that the construction of the 'college' was largely financed out of funds raised in Britain in response to Kitchener's appeal, in the name of General Gordon, led some enthusiasts to the conclusion 'that "not a single penny of Moslem money is in it". . . . [This] is erroneous. The College cost £23,000 to construct. Of this sum, the Soudan Government provided £12,000. The annual expenditure is £5,400. Of this, £3,400 is from the Endowment Fund. The balance of £2,000 is provided by the Sudan Government out of the proceeds of general taxation paid almost exclusively by Moslems' (Cromer to MacInnes, 15 May 1905, P.R.O. FO/633/8, p. 408).

[3] In 1901, 'the educational needs' of the country were officially defined as follows:

(i) The creation of a native artisan class.
(ii) A diffusion among the masses of the people of education sufficient to enable them to understand the merest elements of the machinery of government.
(iii) The creation of a small native administrative class who will ultimately fill many minor posts (*Annual Report* for 1900, Egypt, no. 1 (1901), Cd. 441, p. 76).

[4] MacMichael, *The Sudan* (London, 1952), p. 67.

[5] MacMichael, *The Anglo-Egyptian Sudan* (London, 1932), p. 108.

[6] Cromer to Salisbury, 8 Mar. 1900, P.R.O. FO/633/8, no. 322. In a letter to Lansdowne, he said: '. . . I have found the universities, rather than the army, the

with soldier-administrators very congenial. In a private letter to Lord Lansdowne he said it always made him shudder when soldiers began to discuss semi-political questions. 'They always seem to me to treat the population and Government of various countries as if they were so many inanimate pawns on a chess-board in the office of the Intelligence Department. This is not exactly the case.'[1] Sometimes, as he told Salisbury, this was an unending source of amusement. 'The other day', for instance, 'I told him [Kitchener] that land speculators were sending money to the Greeks in the Sudan in order to make purchases, and that some little care was necessary, as there were at present no legal means for acquiring a valid title. He replied that he abounded in my view, and would I like him to expel every Greek from the Country who bought or sold anything without his consent?'[2] But, more often than not, the effects of such drastic and peremptory methods were alarming. In 1899, for example, a state of near famine was brought about, largely because of the Sirdār's not allowing sufficient people scope for private trade;[3] and in the following year, Kitchener's 'very stern discipline' caused so much discontent[4] among the XIVth Sudanese battalion at Omdurman that a mutiny broke out which was only put down with difficulty.[5] Besides, the English officers, with few exceptions, were ignorant of the Arabic language and were, consequently, far too much in the hands of their Egyptian subordinates.[6] 'The only remedy', Cromer concluded, 'is gradually to train up a number of young English civilians who will be prepared to stay in the country and acquire a thorough knowledge of the language.'[7] The same conclusion was reached by Kitchener's successor, General Reginald Wingate, viewing the situation from a different angle. He wrote in his first Annual Report:

There is one serious drawback to this system: the military officers being borne on the active list of the British Army[8] are liable to recall for various reasons, or they may tire of their arduous work and desire to return to

best recruiting ground' (Cromer to Lansdowne, 14 Nov. 1900, P.R.O. FO/633/6, no. 329).

[1] Cromer to Lansdowne, 28 Nov. 1902, P.R.O. FO/633/8, no. 338.

[2] Cromer to Salisbury, 10 Feb. 1899, P.R.O. FO/633/8, no. 309.

[3] Cromer to Salisbury, 22 Apr. 1899, P.R.O. FO/633/8, no. 312.

[4] Cromer to Salisbury, 17 Mar. 1899, P.R.O. FO/633/8, no. 311 and 27 Apr. 1900, P.R.O. FO/633/6, no. 324.

[5] R. Wingate, *Wingate of the Sudan* (London, 1955), pp. 131–3.

[6] Cromer to Salisbury, 8 June 1900, P.R.O. FO/633/8, no. 325.

[7] Ibid.

[8] They served with the Egyptian Army on secondments from the British.

their own service and the more congenial surroundings of stations at home or abroad. In short, the British officers cannot be counted on as a permanency and, in consequence, provision must be made gradually to introduce into the machinery of civil government a more permanent element in the shape of young and carefully-selected civilians, who will enter the Soudan with the intention of making their careers in the country.[1]

Accordingly a small number of 'very carefully-selected young English civilians' were appointed as an experiment in 1901[2] and a few more were recruited each year beginning from 1902, when the Boer War deprived the Sudan Government of still more of its soldier-administrators—including Kitchener. Recruits were usually selected from among young graduates, not for their academic brilliance, but on the principle of *mens sana in corpore sano*. In the early days they were sent back to the universities in order to study Arabic for a year before proceeding to the Sudan where, after a few months, they were required to pass another examination in Arabic and, two years later, a third—in law.[3] Later, when the number of Arabic-speaking administrators had increased, the teaching of Arabic was provided in the Sudan.

As may be expected, however, the replacement of officers by civilians, especially at the top level of the administration, was a slow process. Thus it was not until 1909 that the first civilian Province Governor was appointed, and in 1912 there were only two (out of twelve) civilian Governors.[4] It is important to note, however, that the slow pace of replacing military officers by civilians was not entirely unintentional; for in the early days even Cromer felt that the use of the military in the administration was necessary owing to the fact that the country had just been conquered and the process of 'pacification' was still far from complete. In particular, it was felt that Mahdism, even after the death of the Khalīfa, was still a force to be reckoned with—especially as almost every year, during the first two decades, a new rebel claiming to be a Mahdi or a Nabi 'Īsa (Prophet Jesus)[5] tried to rally people against the regime. The

[1] *Annual Report* for 1900, Egypt, no. 1 (1901), Cd. 441, p. 86.

[2] *Annual Report* for 1901, Egypt, no. 1 (1902), Cd. 1012, p. 58.

[3] MacMichael, *The Sudan*, p. 105.

[4] Based on the table appended to MacMichael's *The Anglo-Egyptian Sudan*.

[5] The word 'Mahdi' means 'the Divinely Guided One'. Traditionally it is believed that a Mahdi appears once every century, who strives to revive Islam and restore its classical greatness, and that the appearance of the last Mahdi will be followed by the return of the Messiah, who, completing the work of the Mahdi would 'fill the earth with justice as it had been filled with iniquity'.

Southern provinces, still a part of 'Darkest Africa', were not completely subdued until 1928. Until then, hardly a year had passed since the conquest without the need for a punitive expedition against one or other of the Southern tribes and, even in 1928, it was felt that occasional bombardment from the air might still be necessary in order to elicit obedience from the 'turbulent, warlike and inaccessible people'.[1] And in Western Sudan, Sultan 'Ali Dinār continued to govern Darfur—an area as large as France—until the First World War when, through the Sanousi of Libya, he got in touch with the Young Turks and joined the Axis with a view to attacking the British administration in the Sudan. But he was killed in 1916 and Darfur was thereby brought within the bounds of the Sudan. Under such conditions, therefore, it was clear that an efficient administration which was reinforced by military personnel and run on military lines was the best means of safeguarding the interests of the Anglo-Egyptian regime in the Sudan.

Gradually, however, it became clear that the authority of the regime had been firmly established, and that the emphasis in the administration could safely be shifted from 'pacification' to reconstruction. This, coupled with the outbreak of the war, which further reduced the number of officers in the administration, enhanced the already growing tendency to replace military men with civilians and to separate the military from the administrative branches of the government. Thus, the number of civilian Governors rose from two in 1912 to five in 1914 and to fourteen in 1933.[2]

In order to maintain the high standards of efficiency of the earlier days and guard against possible deterioration in changed circumstances, Cromer had, from the beginning, insisted that only 'the right class of Englishman'[3] should be appointed. In November 1900 he wrote, in a private letter to Lord Lansdowne: 'The principle on which I have always acted here is that, if I cannot afford to pay for the sort of man I want, I would rather go without anyone. English waifs and strays . . . are a great deal worse than useless: also I may mention that I have found the Universities, rather than the Army, the best recruiting ground.'[4] This is a recurring theme in his private and official correspondence.

[1] *Annual Report* for 1928, Sudan, no. 2 (1929), Cmd. 3403, p. 13.
[2] MacMichael: the appendix to *The Anglo-Egyptian Sudan.*
[3] Cromer to Murray, 4 Mar. 1909, P.R.O. FO/633/12, pp. 175–6.
[4] Cromer to Lansdowne, 14 Nov. 1900, P.R.O. FO/633/6, no. 329.

I have pointed out over and over again to the F.O. the danger of appointing third-rate Englishmen with very low salaries. . . . If there is one point more than another on which I have been convinced during my Oriental experience, it is the very great objection to endeavouring to rule subject races through the agency of low-class Europeans . . . (for) once you lower the character of the European, you run a risk of cruel and unsympathetic treatment of the subject race, and also a risk of corruption of one sort or another creeping into the service. I was so strongly impressed with this in connection with the Sudan that although the financial situation was always pretty severe, I invariably refused to employ young Englishmen unless they were well paid. I tried to get the pick of the military services and of the Universities, and I think I may say that to a certain extent I succeeded. . . .'[1]

Another factor which contributed to the formation of a successful civil service in the Sudan was the generosity of the terms of employment and their suitability to the conditions of the country. Retirement was possible after twenty years[2] and service in the hot and humid areas south of the 12th parallel was counted as double service.[3] A particularly attractive feature of the system was that, unlike the Indian Civil Service, which virtually compelled recruits to stay in India until they were retired, the Sudan Government made leave in Europe compulsory for three months every year[4]—thus giving her British employees the opportunity of refreshing themselves and maintaining contacts with the outside world. Expressing his satisfaction with these arrangements, Wingate wrote to Cromer in 1905:

. . . there is no doubt that the African climate—especially in its lower latitudes—has a most marked effect on the nervous system and however sound a man's normal judgment may be, he is never really normal in the hot weather here. You were never more correct than when you insisted on British officers and officials taking leave annually. If we can keep it up and prevent ourselves from being submerged in the rush of work it will be our surest guarantee of success.[5]

Under these conditions, the Sudan Political Service, as it came to be known, grew steadily and the administration was gradually transformed from a military to a civilian machine with a high reputation for both efficiency and congenial organization. But it continued to

[1] Cromer to Murray, 4 Mar. 1909, P.R.O. FO/633, vol. 12, pp. 175–6.
[2] Wingate, p. 135.
[3] Percy Martin, *The Sudan in Evolution* (London, 1921), p. 55.
[4] Wingate, p. 135.
[5] Wingate to Cromer, 24 Apr. 1905 (the Wingate Papers, Durham).

have a military flavour which survives to this day in the khaki uniform and coloured stripes of the civilian administrators of the independent Sudan.

2. *The Governor-General's Council*

A second important consequence of the shift of emphasis from pacification to construction, from the state of emergency of the earlier days to something approaching normality, was the transformation of the position of the Governor-General from that of a virtual dictator to a position comparable, in some restricted respects, to that of a Prime Minister in the modern British cabinet system. For, with the growth of the administration, technical questions assumed an ever-increasing importance; the rush of work to which Wingate refers as early as 1905 (in his above-quoted letter) gathered momentum, and the machinery of government began to evolve along professional lines.[1] It, therefore, gradually became the practice of the Governor-General, encouraged, it may be assumed, by his increasing civilian subordinates, frequently to assemble his main lieutenants—both military and civilian—for informal consultation before decisions were finally made. By 1910, this practice had become so well established that it was decided it should be formalized and made more regular.[2] In the words of Cromer's successor, Sir Eldon Gorst:

> . . . it was thought that the time had arrived when it was desirable to go a step further and create a duly constituted Council to be associated with the Governor General in the discharging of his executive and legislative powers. The view was taken that such a body would conduct its deliberations with a greater sense of responsibility than could be expected under the informal

[1] MacMichael, *The Anglo-Egyptian Sudan*, p. 109.

[2] The first time the idea of a Governor-General's Council occurs is in an interesting letter dated 7 June 1908, which Major P. R. Phipps, the then Civil Secretary, wrote to Wingate: 'We have done as much of the piles of work awaiting the conferences of L.S., F.S., and C.S. [i.e. Legal, Financial, and Civil Secretaries respectively], as has been humanly possible. Unfortunately we have not cleared up everything . . . These present arrangements cannot go on: there is no elasticity and no reserve of any kind. I have had a talk with Bonham [the Legal Secretary]. His work is hopelessly behind and he knows he is dreadfully slow. I only kept my head above water by absolute slavery, and it is more by luck than by good management we have as few mistakes in our work. But it cannot go on—the service must suffer: there is no time to consider questions: it is a case of taking up your pen, writing quickly and chancing doing the right thing. We must have a sort of Governor-General-in-Council arrangement and every odd, unusual or unlegislated question must come before it' (the Wingate Papers, Durham).

conditions which had hitherto prevailed, and would prove a valuable safeguard against precipitate action on the part of the executive, or the adoption of insufficiently considered measures. . . .

'Both Sir R. Wingate and I', the Consul-General concluded, 'anticipate that the new system will tend to promote administrative stability and continuity of policy in Soudan affairs, and will prove a very useful part of the machinery of government.'[1]

'The new system', which was in some respects inspired by the example of the Executive Council of the Governor-General of India,[1] was formally approved by the British and Egyptian Governments early in January 1910, and the first meeting of the Council was held in Khartoum on 27 January.[2] The Ordinance in accordance with which it was established[3] provided that the Governor-General was to preside over the meetings of the Council. The Inspector-General, the Legal Secretary, the Financial Secretary, and the Civil Secretary were *ex officio* members of the Council. In addition, the Governor-General was to appoint not less than two and not more than four members as he saw fit. Each one of these additional members was to hold office for three years and was eligible for reappointment. Decisions were to be taken according to majority opinion, but the Governor-General, like his counterpart in India, was empowered to overrule majority decisions. In such cases, however, he was obliged to record his reasons and refer the matter to the British and Egyptian Governments. Any member who wished to dissent from the decision of the majority was likewise entitled to have the reasons for his dissent recorded in the minutes. Amongst the matters which were to be brought before the Council and formally decided by the Governor-General-in-Council were ordinances, laws, and regulations to be made by proclamation of the Governor-General by virtue of the provisions of Article IV of the Anglo-Egyptian Agreement; the annual budget and supplementary credits, whether out of reserve or out of current revenue; and administrative and legislative matters which the Directors of Departments or the Governor-General himself considered of sufficient importance to be submitted to Council.[4]

[1] *Annual Report* for 1909, Egypt, no. 1 (1910), Cd. 5121, p. 62.

[2] Minutes of the Proceedings of the Governor-General's Council, 1910 (Archives, Khartoum).

[3] The Governor-General's Council Ordinance, 1910, *Sudan Gazette*, no. 174, Khartoum, 15 Apr. 1910. See Appendix V.

[4] Gorst to Governor-General, Sudan, 12 Jan. 1910, in the Minutes of the first meeting of the Governor-General's Council, 1910 (Archives, Khartoum).

But questions of defence, military matters, and matters concerning appointments and promotions could be considered by the Council only in an advisory capacity and on the invitation of the Governor-General who could disregard Council opinion without giving reasons.[1] In these matters, as in matters of major policy and questions affecting foreign subjects or involving serious changes in the taxation and revenue system, the Governor-General was to act—except in cases of emergency—in consultation with Her Majesty's Agent and Consul-General in Cairo.[2] The Consul-General, moreover, was to be informed of ordinary routine administration in sufficient detail to enable him to keep in touch with developments in the Sudan, and the minutes and proceedings of the meetings of the Governor-General's Council in particular were to be regularly communicated to him. In general, no action involving major policy was to be taken by either the Governor-General acting alone, or by the Governor-General-in-Council before consulting the Consul-General in Cairo, in order that he might represent, and if necessary, ascertain the views of the British and Egyptian governments.[2]

Thus constituted, the Governor-General's Council continued—with certain amendments—to be the central organ of the Sudan Government until 1948 when it was decided, on 15 June, that it should be replaced by an Executive Council to which Sudanese members were to be appointed for the first time.[3] Of the amendments which had been introduced in the meantime was that of 1919 when, following the retirement of Slatin Pasha and the consequent suppression of the office of Inspector-General,[4] it was decided that only the Civil, the Financial, and the Legal Secretaries were to be *ex officio* members, while the number of additional members was to be raised from four to five.[5] Another amendment, introduced in 1926, made the Kaid el Amm (al-Qāʿid al-'Aām), i.e. the Commander-

[1] Dispatch from H.M. Agent and Consul-General in Cairo to Governor-General, Sudan, 12 Jan. 1910 (Archives).

[2] Dispatch from H.M. Agent and Consul-General in Cairo to Governor-General, Sudan, 13 Jan. 1910 (Archives).

[3] Minutes of the 572nd Meeting of the Governor-General's Council, 15 June 1948 (Archives).

[4] Sir Rudolf von Slatin Pasha held this (especially created) post from 1901 till 1914. Being an Austrian, however, the outbreak of the war necessarily severed his relation with the Sudan where, with his unique acquaintance with the country and the people, he was, for over a decade, 'the Government's principal adviser on all questions that concerned native affairs' (*Governor-General's Report*, 1914–1919, Egypt, no. 1 (1920), Cmd. 957, p. 93).

[5] *Sudan Government Gazette*, no. 342, 16 Feb. 1919.

in-Chief of the newly-constituted Sudan Defence Force, an *ex officio* member of the Council.[1]

3. *Provincial administration*

Before discussing further developments in the organization of central government, however, we must turn to provincial administration and the impact on it—indeed on the entire structure and politics of the Sudan Government—of the political developments in Egypt which followed the First World War.

As has already been pointed out, after the conquest the Sudan was divided into a number of provinces (Mudīriyyas) each of which was put under the direct rule of a British military Governor. The Governor was assisted, at the district (Markaz) level, by Inspectors who were also British officers of the army and, at lower levels, by Egyptian 'Māmūrs' and Sudanese Shaikhs and Chieftains.

The number of provinces varied from six in 1898[2] to fourteen in the period after the First World War,[3] but was eventually reduced to nine, some of which were larger than France in area.

The increase in the number of provinces in the early days was, in some cases, the result of territorial expansion such as followed the conquest of Darfur in 1916 or the reversion, from the Belgian Congo, of the Lado enclave (an area of about 17,000 square miles) after the death of King Leopold, in 1910. But the existence of comparatively small provinces, such as those of (old) Kordofan and Nuba Mountains which were amalgamated in 1928, owing largely to improved communications,[4] also contributed to the large number of provinces during the first two decades of the regime.

The amalgamations, and hence the reduction of the number of provinces was not, of course, always or solely the consequence of improved communications and means of transport. The creation of, for example, an enlarged Kordofan Province incorporating the former province of the Nuba Mountains, just mentioned, was also based on important political considerations relating to the introduction, a few years previously, of the principles of Native Administration which aimed, amongst other things, at the revival and

[1] *Sudan Government Gazette*, no. 473, 31 May 1926.

[2] These were: Dongola, Barbar, Kasala, Fashoda, Kordofan, and Khartoum.

[3] MacMichael, the appendix to *The Anglo-Egyptian Sudan*.

[4] *Annual Report* on Sudan for 1928, Sudan, no. 2 (1929), Cmd. 3403, p. 14.

consolidation of the tribal system. For the same reason, the Red Sea Province, in the Eastern Sudan, was abolished and an enlarged Kasala Province, incorporating the core of the Beja tribes was established instead. Financial and economic considerations also played an important part in this respect. In 1934, for example, the provinces of Ḥalfa, Dongola, and Barbar were made into a single Northern Province whose capital was al-Dāmar. The motive force behind this move, which followed the Great Depression, was a general drive 'to check the growth of administrative expenditure, to ensure the most economical use of existing staffs and to provide the requirements of further developments in the cheapest possible way'.[1] It was in that year that the enlarged Kasala Province was created and the total number of provinces was reduced from fourteen to eleven.[2]

More important than the question of numbers and areas was the manner in which the provinces were administered. In this connection, two (in a sense opposite) principles were recognized right from the beginning. The first of these was the principle of provincial decentralization *vis-à-vis* the headquarters in Khartoum. Both in the interest of efficiency and because of the vast area of the country and the poor system of transport, especially in the Western and Southern parts of the country, each Governor was given a free hand, within the general framework of existing laws, in the administration of his province. Apart from the obvious requirements of regular reporting on the conduct of affairs with a view to keeping the Governor-General, whose representative he was, well informed, and keeping himself within the bounds of the law, a Governor could look upon his province as, in effect, an *imperium in imperio*.

The internal administration of provinces, however, was based on the opposite principle and, generally speaking, the lower the level of provincial administration, the greater was the degree of control from above. Thus, while Senior Inspectors (or District Commissioners, as they were later designated) could, in some cases, behave as if they were Governors in their own right,[3] their subordinates, the Māmūrs, were subjected to closer control from above and they, in turn, kept a close watch over the Shaikhs and the Chiefs.

But tribal organization and tribal chiefs, though they had a definite

[1] *Annual Report* on Sudan for 1934, Sudan, no. 1 (1935), Cmd. 5019, p. 8.
[2] Ibid., p. 10.
[3] Martin, p. 48.

and useful position in the system were not, during the first two decades, looked upon as key agents of government and their place in what might be called the administrative philosophy of the day was comparatively small.[1] The guiding principle of the prevailing philosophy was Direct Rule. This was personified in the District Commissioner, who, as judge, administrator, chief surveyor, inspector of education, chief of police, and military ruler all in one, was the symbol of the paternalism of the new regime and was rightly described as a jack of all trades.

This situation, however, was radically transformed during the twenties, and especially after the publication in 1922, of Lugard's *The Dual Mandate in British Tropical Africa*, a book which made a creed of 'Native Administration' or 'Indirect Rule', not only in the Sudan but throughout the British Empire.

In order to see this transformation in its proper perspective, however, and to appreciate the forces which governed the timing of the introduction of its different stages in particular, it is necessary to review the country's relations with Egypt and the impact on the Sudan of the Egyptian Revolution of 1919.

4. *The impact of the Egyptian Revolution: relations with Egypt*

As the architect of the Agreement of 1899 Cromer had very definite views on the relationship of Egypt and the Sudan which he strongly held and advocated until his retirement in 1907. Briefly, he held that the Sudan was a province[2] of Egypt. But, since it was such a vast province, and in order to keep the French and what he impatiently called the paraphernalia of internationalism out, the Sudan had to be governed not from Cairo or London, but from Khartoum, by a Governor-General who was to be the final arbiter in all matters of detail and local importance. In matters of policy and major importance, however, the Sudan administration was to follow the guidance of the Agent and Consul-General in Cairo, acting on

[1] 'Umdas and Shaikhs received no pay for their services until after the close of the second decade of the Anglo-Egyptian regime (ibid., p. 53).

[2] Cromer used the word 'province' with reference to the Sudan in much of his writings, including one of his last letters as Consul-General (Cromer to Sir Edward Gray, 19 Apr. 1907, P.R.O. FO/633/13).

The preamble of the Agreement also refers to the Sudan as the 'reconquered provinces'.

behalf of the British Government. Indeed, Cromer considered that, from this point of view, Egypt and the Sudan constituted a single country and was 'horrified' at any suggestion that they were not. 'I will not listen to anything which tends in this direction. . . . The only reason why the British flag is flying, why the Soudan has a Governor General and special laws, is to avoid the capitulations and the rest of the international paraphernalia. . . .'[1] He had no patience with those officials who tended to look upon Egypt and the Sudan as different countries with separate governments. Thus, in a private letter to Wingate in 1904, he wrote:

> . . . Mr. Sterry's memorandum was to my mind strongly confirmatory evidence that many of the Soudan officials entertain a wholly erroneous idea of the status of the Soudan Government. Mr. Sterry, who is a trained lawyer and 40 years of age, speaks throughout as though the Soudan was an independent Government. It is nothing of the sort. The sooner this idea is got out of the head of all your officials the better.[2]

There were two main reasons why Cromer held to this view and was so emphatic in advocating it.

The first of these was his deep-seated mistrust of and lack of faith in the soldier-administrators who were his agents in the Sudan.[3] 'There must be some sort of general control over the soldiers', he wrote in a private letter to Salisbury, 'or else they will land us in all sorts of trouble.'[4] It was in the light of this conviction that Cromer, in Article IV of his original draft of the Anglo-Egyptian Agreement, proposed that 'Proclamations of the Governor General shall be issued only with the prior consent of H.H. the Khedieve, acting under the advice of his Council of Ministers, and of H.B.M.'s Government, through H.B.M.'s Agent and Consul General in Cairo',[5] and that 'the whole of the Soudan revenue shall be at the disposal of the Egyptian Government'.[6]

Kitchener, however, objected to these provisions and suggested instead that the relevant section of Article IV should read: 'All such proclamations or ordinances of the Governor General shall after promulgation be forthwith notified to the President of the Council of Ministers of H.H. the Khedieve and to H.B.M.'s Agent and Consul-

[1] Cromer to Wingate, 25 Jan. 1904, P.R.O. FO/623/8, p. 390.
[2] Cromer to Wingate, 3 May 1904, P.R.O. FO/633/8, p. 396.
[3] See above, pp. 41–2.
[4] Cromer to Salisbury, Dec. 1898, P.R.O. FO/633/8, no. 306.
[5] P.R.O. FO/141/333.
[6] Ibid., Article VI.

General in Cairo. . . .'[1] With regard to the proposed Article VI of the draft Agreement Kitchener wrote:

I do not see what the object of this declaration is unless it means that the finances of the Soudan are to be administered entirely by the Finance Ministry in Cairo. Such a centralization appears to me to be very undesirable. Almost everything in the administration of a country must have a financial aspect and it follows that, if this statement is read to mean that the revenue of the Soudan is an integral part of the revenue of Egypt it would possibly entail interfering from Cairo in every detail of law and administration in the Soudan. If this is not intended, I do not see the object of the statement as it may eventually turn out to be a very inconvenient declaration to have made. . . .[1]

He then proceeded to propose an alternative but somewhat complicated formula aimed at putting the administration of the finances of the Sudan under the direction of the Governor-General assisted by a Financial Secretary to the Sudan who was to be appointed by Khedivial decree in a similar manner to the Governor-General. The central supervision of these finances was to be vested in the Ministry of Finance in Cairo, the Egyptian Government being solely responsible for all civil and ordinary military expenditure in the Sudan while the British Government undertook the whole cost of any British troops who may be stationed in the Sudan. In case of the dispatch of special or additional British expeditions to the Sudan, the question of the division of cost was to be the subject of special arrangement between the two Governments.[2]

With the two men holding such different views, Salisbury had to intervene. Having discussed the draft agreement with Kitchener, he told Cromer, in a private letter, that he felt Kitchener was probably right on two main points:

. . . they are that the Governor General of the Soudan is to govern and is to spend the money he has. In both cases he is, of course, to obey orders received from you, and his proceedings may be revised and altered by you, but that he shall not by a formal document be forbidden to pass an Ordinance or to spend 100 £ without a preliminary approval. . . . Your Constitution should be such that it has a fair chance of working when neither you nor the Sirdar will be there to control it. . . .[3]

[1] Memorandum from Kitchener, appended to Cromer's letter to Salisbury, 10 Nov. 1898, P.R.O. FO/78/4957.

[2] Ibid. The latter part of the suggestion—from 'the Egyptian Government being solely responsible . . .' to the end—is in conformity with Cromer's original draft.

[3] Salisbury to Cromer, 9 Dec. 1898, P.R.O. FO/633/8.

Accordingly, the condition that proclamations and ordinances were to be approved by the Consul-General in Cairo before they were promulgated was dropped from the final text of the Agreement. Instead, it was only required that proclamations be forthwith notified to Her Britannic Majesty's Agent and Consul-General in Cairo and to the President of the Council of Ministers of His Highness the Khedive.

Financial matters, it was also agreed, were not to form part of the Agreement, but were to be settled by administrative means independent of its provisions.

This brings us to the second reason why Cromer felt that Egypt and the Sudan should, in all matters of policy, be considered to constitute a single country: namely that until 1913, as it happened, the Egyptian Treasury met the deficit in the Sudan budget while Egypt practically got nothing in return except its nominal share in the government of the Sudan.

The Egyptian nationalists who, as has already been indicated, did not approve of the new regime in the Sudan were far from satisfied with this arrangement.

In trying to justify this policy to them, and to the world in general, Cromer argued that, since the Sudan was an Egyptian possession, it was only fair that the cost of its administration should be borne by the Egyptian Treasury. Seeing that this argument by itself was not sufficient to reconcile the nationalists some of whom were 'not likely to be convinced by anything I can say'[1] Cromer put forward the further point[2] that it was in Egypt's interest that the Sudan had been conquered and was gradually being developed.

Had it not been for the reconquest, he argued, Egypt would have had to pay for the maintenance of a large and permanent force in order to guard her southern frontier against Mahdist invasion. Not only was this unnecessary now that the Sudan had been conquered, but Egypt's all-important water supply had also been safeguarded. And apart from the material benefits accruing to Egypt from the

[1] *Annual Report* for 1904, Egypt, no. 1 (1905), Cd. 2409, p. 119.

[2] It is important to note in this connection that Cromer's Annual Reports on Egypt and the Sudan were 'translated into Arabic, that they were widely circulated in Egypt, and that, in respect at all events to some points in which the Egyptians take an interest, they', as Cromer saw it, 'constitute practically the only opportunity which is afforded to them in the course of the year of acquiring full or accurate information' (*Annual Report* for 1900, Egypt, no. 1 (1901), Cd. 441, p. 1).

reconquest and development of the Sudan, Cromer insisted that 'in view of the present prosperous state of Egypt, it would be morally quite indefensible to leave the large Moslem population of the Sudan in their present condition without making every effort to assist them'.[1] Accordingly, the Egyptian Treasury which, of course, was itself under British control, met the deficit in the Sudan budget until 1913 when,

TABLE 1

The Revenue and Expenditure of the Sudan Government for the years 1899–1913 and 1936, 1946, and 1956/7

	Revenue £E	*Expenditure* £E
1899	126,569	230,238
1900	156,888	331,918
1901	242,309	407,335
1902	270,226	516,945
1903	462,605	616,361
1904	579,013	628,931
1905	665,411	681,881
1906	817,921	827,961
1907	975,973	1,012,357
1908	979,343	1,163,657
1909	1,104,599	1,153,519
1910	1,171,007	1,214,676
1911	1,311,218	1,350,854
1912	1,428,605	1,490,668
1913	1,654,149	1,614,007
1936	4,462,309	4,204,917
1946	8,288,985	8,207,802
1956/7	45,869,401	32,698,657

for the first time, there was a surplus (of £40,000)—revenue being £1,654,000 and expenditure £1,614,000. In addition, Egypt also provided the capital, interest free, necessary for public works—her total contribution, until 1913, being £5,354,000.[2] In the meantime 'England's only commitment was one battalion and a battery of artillery stationed at Khartoum'.[3] Apart from that, 'England spent

[1] *Annual Report* for 1904, Egypt, no. 1 (1905), Cd. 2409, p. 120.

[2] Martin, p. 112.

[3] Wingate, p. 129. In this connection it is interesting to note that 'the Defence Committee in London consider that the British force in Egypt and the Sudan is "from an Imperial point of view" of no value "strategically". Hence they expect Egypt to pay the whole cost—amounting at present to £40,000 a year!' (Cromer to Wingate, May 1904, quoted in Wingate, p. 139).

not a penny on the administration or rehabilitation of the Sudan'[1] until 1913 when the British Treasury, pressed by Lancashire men,[2] guaranteed a £3-million loan with a view to developing the Sudan as a cotton-growing country.

In this situation, Cromer felt that any suggestion that the Sudan was independent from Egypt would undermine his already-precarious arguments in justification of spending Egyptian money in the Sudan. To quote him once more: '. . . the only justification for paying large sums from the Egyptian Treasury to the Soudan Government is that the Soudan is *not* independent of Egypt. It is already difficult enough to reconcile people here to this expenditure. If ideas of independence get abroad the ground is obviously cut from under my feet.'[3] And again,

I really cannot say to the Egyptians, albeit I am somewhat accustomed to anomalies—'You have to pay a large Soudan deficit; all your surplus revenues, which you want to employ in Egypt, are to go to make Soudan Railways; I know you think that those railways will do you harm; but I know better than you: you *ought* to want them; you are to have practically nothing to do with the administration; nevertheless if you want cattle (from the Sudan) you are to pay (custom duties) for having them.'[4]

The position is not only unjust and impolitic, but almost ridiculous.

In politics as in music those who pay the piper have a right to call the tune.

Pray get all these ideas of independence out the heads of your officials. The result of putting them forward is to make people here think—and with some reason—that there is need of more stringent control.

It could not be officially conceded then that the Sudan was independent of Egypt. And, consistent with this, the British Agent and Consul-General in Cairo was to supervise and control the policy-making and administration of the government in the Sudan. As if to ward off the accusation of undue centralization Cromer was always careful to point out in this connection that he only wanted 'to control

[1] Wingate, p. 130. One of Wingate's favourite anecdotes was that of his meeting with Mr. Arnold Foster, a member of Mr. Balfour's Government, who asked him what were the figures of England's expenditure in the Sudan. Wingate's reply was 'By the Condominium Agreement, the British and Egyptian flags must always be flown together, but for several years past I have had the greatest difficulty in getting the Admiralty to supply the bunting for the British flag. I hope you can help me. That is the only British commitment that I can think of.'

[2] Arthur Gaitskill: *Gezira—a Story of Development in the Sudan* (London, 1959), pp. 53–8 and 65–6.

[3] Cromer to Wingate, 3 May 1904, P.R.O. FO/633/8.

[4] Cromer to Wingate, 25 Jan. 1904, P.R.O. FO/633/8.

the big questions but leave all the detail and execution to be managed locally'.[1] And by the word 'big' he meant all such measures as involved any serious interference with the water supply of the Nile or any large concessions to Europeans or others.[1] Lord Salisbury and the British Government approved this arrangement and accordingly directed the Governor-General of the Sudan 'to obey whatever instructions he may from time to time receive from the British Agent and Consul-General in Cairo, and . . . to keep the latter fully informed of all important current events connected with the affairs of the Soudan.'[2] The main object of the Agreement, Cromer commented, was to enable an adequate control to be exercised by the British and Egyptian Governments over all important matters connected with the Sudan, whilst at the same time conferring sufficient powers on the Governor-General to settle all matters of local detail on the spot, without reference to Cairo. Cromer never tired of repeating these points whenever occasion demanded and allowed, and his last recommendation before going on final leave in 1907, was that firm control of the Sudan administration by the Consul-General should at no time be allowed to lapse, adding that 'no government in the world has been so little controlled as that of the Sudan'.[3] He had confined himself to an annual review of reports and some financial control, and the Parliament at Westminster only occasionally concerned itself with the affairs of the Sudan, and the country was 'without any free press, without European newspaper correspondents, and without any semblance of free institutions. The time will inevitably come', he proceeded to warn, 'when greater attention will be directed to the affairs of that country, and in that case, Wingate will have to choose between the very light control exercised from here, or a much more stringent control exercised from a London office. If he is wise, he will not resist the former in order that he may not incur the very serious evils of the latter.'[3]

Under Cromer's successor, Sir Eldon Gorst, relations between the Consul-General and the Government of the Sudan continued much as before. And when the Governor-General's Council was created in 1910, the principle of supervision and general control from Cairo was confirmed. The only alteration was that, instead of the Consul-General

[1] Cromer to Kitchener, 19 Jan. 1899, P.R.O. FO/633/8.
[2] Cromer to Salisbury, 19 Jan. 1899, P.R.O. FO/78/5022.
[3] Cromer to Gray, 19 Apr. 1907, P.R.O. FO/633/13.

exercising his powers by means of 'close unofficial relations'[1] between himself and the Governor-General as had been the practice until that time, the matters on which the Consul-General expected to be consulted were laid down (by Gorst) in general terms 'for the information and guidance of the members of the Council'[1] and in order to round off the tidying process which was occasioned by the creation of the Council.

Three years later, Egypt's subventions to the Sudan Government were discontinued, but this did not lead to any radical departure from existing policies. Egypt and the Sudan continued to be regarded as closely connected units of the same dominion. This attitude was confirmed in 1914 when, following the declaration of war on Britain and her allies by Turkey, in whom sovereignty over Egypt theoretically still resided, Egypt was, for the first time, formally declared a British protectorate—thus bringing theory in line with long-established practice. Possible French opposition to such a step had, of course, been eliminated since 1904 by the *entente cordiale* which gave France a free hand in the Mahgrib while Britain's hegemony in Egypt was recognized by France and, owing to the coming of the war, was indeed replaced by open, though perhaps grudging, approval.

By 1914, therefore, Britain's position in the Nile Valley was apparently stronger than it had ever been.

But the coming of the war, the Egyptians' resentment of the formal declaration of their country as a British protectorate, the apparent success of the Arab Revolt of 1916, and President Wilson's fourteen points and doctrine of self-determination greatly stimulated the already-growing sentiment of nationalism in Egypt. The outcome was the Egyptian Revolt of March/April 1919. This, and the increased danger to British interests of the spreading of the spirit of nationalism into the Sudan—where the majority of the population were, by virtue of their common language, religion, and recent experience, generally inclined to sympathize with the Egyptians—induced the British Government to revise, indeed to reverse its former policy—with regard to the relationship of Egypt and the Sudan—whose chief author and advocate had been Lord Cromer.

The reasons for this radical change were clearly set out in a letter which Sir Reginald Wingate, who by then had been transferred from

[1] Gorst to Wingate, 13 Jan. 1910, in the Minutes of the Proceedings of the Governor-General's Council (first meeting), 27 Jan. 1910 (Archives, Khartoum).

the Governor-Generalship of the Sudan to the British Residency in Cairo, sent to Lord Hardinge in December 1918, i.e. three months before the outbreak of the Revolt. The letter, which was originally private but was afterwards made an official document,[1] set the tone of future development of British policy in the Sudan, and its arguments and conclusions were, in one form or another, echoed in subsequent statements of policy including Lord Milner's Report of 1920. In the letter, Wingate emphasized 'in the strongest possible manner, the importance—from a British Empire point of view— of keeping the Egyptian and Sudan questions totally apart'. He continued:

As long as we hold the Sudan we hold the key to Egypt because we control the source of its water supply. Therefore, whatever the eventual political fate of Egypt may be, I beg that the Sudan may be entirely excluded from its orbit. As it stands, the Sudan is of the greatest importance to us strategically—besides being a future asset to the Empire of no mean value. But as an *apanage* of Egypt (under a form of independence or even quasi-independence) it would be a positive danger to us—for it would at once become a hotbed of Egyptian and foreign intrigue and would draw into its sphere of disturbance the adjoining possessions of Central Africa, Abyssinia, Eritrea, etc. I cannot too strongly emphasize this danger, nor can I too emphatically urge on H.M.G. the importance of maintaining the *status quo* of the Sudan. I would even suggest that should a favourable opportunity occur, its severance from Egypt could be rendered still more complete by obtaining the assent of the Powers at the Peace Conference to its definite acquisition by Great Britain. . . .[1]

Wingate was strongly supported in his main argument by local (British) opinion, including that of his successor in the Governor-Generalship, Sir Lee Stack.[2] Being more directly concerned with the practical aspects of the question, however, Stack felt it was necessary to caution Wingate against making too much haste in the implementation of the policy of separating the Sudan from Egypt. 'In the first place' he pointed out

there is not yet a large enough number of educated persons in the country to take the place of the Egyptians now holding posts in the administration. The Egyptians are to useful too be dispensed with hastily. . . . In the second place, the military needs of the country will have to be supplied without

[1] The Milner Papers, New College, Oxford: Appendix 'F' to the Note by Sir R. Wingate for the use of the Special Mission. The date of the letter is 27 Dec. 1918.

[2] Private letter from Stack to Wingate, 17 Jan. 1919, ibid. Stack was appointed Governor-General on 14 Mar. 1919; until then he had been Acting Governor-General.

the use of Egyptian troops. . . . In the third place, there is the question of finance which is the most difficult of all. The revenues of the Sudan are adequate to the present civil needs of the country but we could not yet pay for a sufficient military force without help from outside. It would be unwise, even if it were possible, to put on the Sudan the burden of taxation that the maintenance of an adequate military force would involve.[1]

Unless assistance could be obtained from the Empire, therefore, no immediate action was to be taken to separate the Sudan from Egypt either militarily or financially, nor was it advisable, at that stage, to separate the offices of Sirdār and Governor-General.[2] But given a fair transitional period during which the Sudan Government could readjust to the new circumstances of the post-war period, arrangements could be made to increase the financial power of the administration and to replace the Egyptian personnel with adequate numbers of Sudanese trained in the work of the governmental bureaucracy and shaikhs and chiefs employed at the lower levels of the judiciary with powers to try minor civil and criminal cases.[3]

Time, however, was against the Governor-General; for a month later the Egyptian Revolution broke out, taking him and the Sudan Government completely by surprise.[4] He was thus forced to give up his cautious attitude and urge instead that a definite pronouncement be made, when the status of Egypt was settled, which finally removed the Sudan from the jurisdiction of the proposed Egyptian Parliament. Otherwise, he pointed out, there would be a sensible loss of British prestige in the Sudan, the position of the Governor-General would be undermined, and the way would thus be prepared for either Pan-Islamism or nationalistic fraternization with the Egyptians.[5]

Thus, by December 1919, when the Special Mission under the chairmanship of Lord Milner arrived in Egypt, agreement had already been reached by those who were on the spot that, whatever the Commission's recommendations with regard to Egypt, the Sudan question was to be treated as entirely different. As for the manner in which this policy might be implemented, it was confidentially reported to Lord Milner that:

[1] Stack to Wingate, 23 Feb. 1919, note on growth of Nationalism. The Milner Papers, New College, Oxford.

[2] Stack to Wingate, 26 Jan. 1919, ibid.

[3] Stack to Wingate, 23 Feb. 1919, ibid.

[4] On 7 Apr. Stack wrote to Wingate: 'The outbreak descended on us here like a bolt from the blue, and before we knew where we were, communication with Egypt, both telegraphic and railway was cut', ibid.

[5] Stack to Wingate, 8 May 1919, ibid.

From a Sudan [Government] point of view, the ideal solution would be an immediate clear cut from Egypt. The Turkish Peace Treaty would declare that all Turkish rights in Egypt and the Sudan (the Nile Basin) were ceded to Great Britain. Lord Milner's Report would recommend such measure of internal self government for Egypt as might be considered right, but would point out the absurdity of claims made by Egypt to Egyptian Nationalism for the Sudan, stating at the same time how the Sudan differs in race, tradition and sympathy from Egypt, and showing that Egypt's only legitimate interests in the Sudan are the safe-guarding of her water supply and the protection of her frontiers from external aggression. For these, H.M. Government would assume full responsibility, and, at the same time, take full charge of the Sudan which would develop on lines of Sudanese Nationalism under British guidance, training and cultivating her institutions and watching over the interests of her people.

Our intentions would be carefully explained to the tribal and religious chiefs throughout the country, and there is no doubt that they would be with us to a man. In fact, the only danger is that their enthusiasm, when the moment comes, might prove uncomfortable for unpopular Egyptian officials.

Steps could then be taken to put into immediate execution the portions of the annexed programme which deals with the Army, and as the last Egyptian soldier left the country, the Egyptian flag would be hauled down.

Alternatively, if no mention of the Sudan is made by Lord Milner in his report, and H.M.G. are unable to make a declaration in regard to the Sudan, the programme of freeing the Sudan from all Egyptian influences can be gradually followed out until the time is ripe for an understanding with Egypt on the matter.[1]

In the light of this it is not surprising that the published Report[2] of the Mission (two of whose members had paid a visit of several weeks to the Sudan)[3] described the Sudan as 'a country entirely distinct from Egypt in its character and constitution'[4] and that it was, therefore, excluded from the Commission's recommendations to the British Government.

It is interesting to note the reasons which, according to the (published) Report, made it 'wholly impossible to contemplate, in the case of the Sudan, a settlement on the lines proposed for Egypt' and the manner in which they were expressed. The Report granted that

[1] Keon-Boyd to the High Commissioner, 14 Mar. 1920, enclosed in Allenby's letter to Lord Milner, 24 Mar. 1920 (File E, Milner Papers).

[2] Egypt, no. 1 (1921), Cmd. 1131. A confidential version of the Report containing—in brackets—the genuine reasons for its recommendations, was sent to Lord Curzon, the Foreign Secretary, who then presented it to the Cabinet. The original draft of this version forms part of the Milner Papers in Oxford.

[3] MacMichael: *The Anglo-Egyptian Sudan*, p. 140. [4] Cmd. 1131, p. 32.

the Arabs of the Sudan speak dialects of the same language as the people of Egypt and are united to them by the bond of religion. Islam, moreover, is spreading even among the non-Arab races of the Sudan. These influences mitigate in various degrees, but they have not overcome the antagonism of the two countries which rankling memories of Egyptian misgovernment in the past have done much to intensify.

The political bonds which have at intervals in the past united Egypt with the Sudan have always been fragile. Egyptian conquerors have at various times overrun parts and even the whole of the Sudan. But it has never been really subdued by, or in any sense amalgamated with Egypt. The Egyptian conquest of the Sudan in the last century was especially disastrous to both countries, and ended in the complete overthrow of Egyptian authority in the early eighties by the Mahdist rebellion. For more than ten years no vestige of Egyptian authority was left in the Sudan except in a small district surrounding Suakin. As a consequence of this breakdown, Great Britain was obliged to undertake several costly expeditions for the rescue of the Egyptian garrisons and the defence of Egypt, which was in danger of being overrun by the Mahdist hordes.[1]

The contrast between this line of argument and the earlier one used against the French and the Powers—especially over Fashoda and in justification of the conquest (or the reconquest as it was then called) of the Sudan and of the Agreement—is too obvious to require comment. The Egyptians, as it was correctly predicted, found it absolutely noxious and unpalatable. In deference to their susceptibilities,[2] therefore, the Mission insisted that Egypt had

an indefeasible right to an ample and assured supply of water for the land at present under cultivation, and to a fair share of any increased supply which engineering skill may be able to supply. A formal declaration on the part of Great Britain that she recognizes this right and is resolved under all circumstances to uphold it would go far to allay the uneasiness which prevails in Egypt on this subject.

The crux of the matter as presented by the Mission was how to 'secure the independent development of the Sudan while safeguarding the vital interests of Egypt in the waters of the Nile'.

In the eyes of the Egyptian nationalists, however, Egypt's vital interests went beyond the simple matter of safeguarding a fair share

[1] Cmd. 1131, p. 33.

[2] In the confidential version of his Report, Milner recommended that 'in pursuing this policy we must take account of the sensitiveness of the Egyptians, of their self-importance and love of forms and phrases, and seek to give to the future status of Egypt the greatest appearance of independence compatible with the maintenance of the absolutely indispensable minimum of British control' (Milner to Curzon, 17 May 1920, Milner Papers).

of the waters of the Nile, and were seriously compromised by the existence of a British-controlled Sudan over which Egyptian sovereignty was not recognized. Therefore, they continued to be discontented and, understandably, considered the recommendations of the Mission (which they had effectively boycotted from the beginning) as humiliating as they were prejudicial to the interests of their country. Under these circumstances, negotiations between the British and Egyptian Governments continually failed until February 1922, when Britain unilaterally declared the termination of the Protectorate and the independence of Egypt subject to certain reservations, one of which was the future of the Sudan—the others being the defence of Egypt, the security of imperial communications and the protection of foreign interests in Egypt. The settlement of these issues became the subject of a long series of conferences and negotiations during which successive Egyptian Governments steadfastly held to their traditional view of the Agreement: namely, that this, as was indicated in its title, had sought to establish an Anglo-Egyptian administration in the Sudan, the legal question of sovereignty over the country having been left out because, they maintained, sovereignty was recognized—by the British Government as well as others—to vest in the Egyptian crown. The Sudan was therefore an Egyptian territory and as Egypt was now an independent country the British had no legal right to stay in the Sudan. The British Government having lost control over the (admittedly) independent Egypt could no longer justify their position in the Sudan in terms of the legal arguments which had been forged by Cromer. Indeed, these, as was amply demonstrated by the Egyptians, could be used to undermine the British position. Having decided against the direct annexation of the country as had, once again, been suggested at the time of the Egyptian Revolution, British Governments, for their part, had no alternative but to stick equally steadfastly to what was to become, from now onwards, their traditional view of the Agreement: namely that it had established in the Sudan, not merely an Anglo-Egyptian administration, but also an Anglo-Egyptian 'Condominium', whereby the British, like the Egyptians, shared in legal sovereignty over the country and were therefore legally entitled to stay in it.

Whatever the merits or weaknesses of these arguments (and they were frequently carried to such degrees of refinement that they could only be described as juridical theology) Britain, as the power in command of the greater force, was able to implement its new policies—not only in the Sudan but also in the formally independent Egypt—just as it had done before.

5. *The impact of the Egyptian Revolution: trial and error in adjustment*

In the Sudan, the policy of replacing the Egyptian personnel of the administration by Sudanese was, within the limits of available funds, energetically pursued from 1919 onwards. A special course was introduced in that year for the training of Sudanese sub-Māmūrs and the number of recruits was increased to about ten per annum.[1] Within five years there were 102 Sudanese sub-Māmūrs as against 35 Egyptians and one Syrian.[1] The training of Sudanese medical assistants was started in 1922 and two years later the Kitchener School of Medicine (generously endowed by 'Abd al-Laṭīf Bey al-Baghdādi, an Iraqi philanthropist who had settled in the Sudan) was opened. The military college increased its intake of Sudanese cadets. Artisans, engineers, agriculturists, and telegraphists were also trained in greater numbers. In the three towns of Khartoum, Khartoum North, and Omdurman a consultative municipal council was constituted in 1921 with a number of Sudanese sitting as nominated members.[2] A similar municipal council was also constituted in Port Sudan one third of whose members were Sudanese. In other provincial towns, Sudanese notables were appointed as third-class magistrates as from 1920 onwards.[3]

In 1922, the financial problem of the Sudan, acutely felt since 1913, when Egyptian subventions were stopped, was tackled by proceeding with the development of the Gash Delta and the Jazīra Scheme. In his Annual Report of that year, the Governor-General correctly described the provision (on loan guaranteed by the British Government) of funds for this purpose as a step which 'may well prove to be the turning point in the economic history of the country'.[4]

With increased financial resources (owing to rising cotton production and high prices in the following years) it might have been expected that the administrative history of the Sudan would also be

[1] MacMichael, *The Anglo-Egyptian Sudan*, p. 174.
[2] *Annual Report* on the Sudan in 1921, Sudan, no. 1 (1923), Cmd. 1837, p. 174.
[3] *Annual Report* for 1922, Sudan, no. 2 (1923), Cmd. 1950, p. 6.
[4] Ibid., p. 4.

transformed by the acceleration of the rate at which Sudanese personnel were trained for service in the different branches of the government bureaucracy. But this did not take place, and the policy which had recently been initiated for the training and education of Sudanese suffered a severe setback from 1924 onwards.

6. *The politics of reaction: Indirect Rule*

The termination of the limited and short-lived experiment in 'Sudanization' which has been indicated above was precipitated by the nationalist rising which—dramatized by the militancy of a Sudanese battalion which fought to the last man—took place in 1924 as an expression of solidarity with Egyptian nationalism. The suddenness and intensity of the rebellion coupled with the fact, revealed in the course of subsequent investigations, that it was largely inspired by Egypt, where Sir Lee Stack, the Sirdār and Governor-General, had in the meantime been murdered,[1] left a deep impression on the Government. The Government in the words of Sir James Currie, a former Director of Education in the Sudan, 'took fright',[2] and proceeded to react with unprecedented violence. In the circumstances relations between the Government and the small class of educated Sudanese, who were now seen as the collective enemy of the British, deteriorated rapidly and a period of intense bitterness began which lasted well into the thirties and was much aggravated by the Depression and the consequent retrenchment of salaries. The development and consequences of these events will be examined in the following pages, especially Chapter IV. At this juncture, it is sufficient to note that when Currie visited the Sudan in 1926, he found that 'enthusiasm [among English officials] for education had largely evaporated, and "Indirect Rule" was the prevalent administrative slogan'.[3] Noting the part which had been played by the Turkish

[1] Following this, all the purely Egyptian units of the Egyptian Army in the Sudan were evacuated from the country, their place being taken by a Sudan Defence Force which, formed from the Sudanese units of the Egyptian Army, took an oath of allegiance to the Governor-General instead of the Khedive of Egypt, as had been the practice hitherto. At the same time the Sirdārship of the Egyptian Army was separated from the Governor-Generalship of the Sudan and the Governor-General was henceforth made directly accountable to the Foreign Office in London.

[2] Sir James Currie: 'The Educational Experiment in the Anglo-Egyptian Sudan, 1900–1933' in the *Journal of the African Society*, xxxiv (1935), p. 49.

[3] Ibid., p. 48.

and Mahdist regimes in unifying the country and breaking the barriers of tribalism in the Sudan, Sir James continued: '. . . in spite of the loyalty of the educated Sudanese to the Government that had given them opportunity, the spectacle could be beheld of young administrators diligently searching for lost tribes and vanished chiefs, and trying to resurrect a social system that had passed away for ever'.[1]

Indirect Rule, though it did not become a creed until after 1924, had been accepted as a policy since 1920, when the Milner Mission, in response to the Governor-General's suggestions,[2] recommended that the administration of the Sudan 'should be left, as far as possible, in the hands of the native authorities, wherever they exist, under British supervision. A centralized bureaucracy', continued the Report, 'is wholly unsuitable for the Sudan. Decentralization and the employment, wherever possible, of native agencies for the simple administrative needs of the country, in its present stage of development, would make both for economy and efficiency'.[3] It was in the light of this that 'The Powers of Nomad Sheikhs Ordinance, 1922' was introduced. The preamble of the Ordinance reads as follows: 'Whereas it has from time immemorial been customary for sheikhs of nomad tribes to exercise powers of punishment upon their tribesmen and of deciding disputes among them, and whereas it is expedient that the exercise of these powers should be regularized . . .', etc.[4] Three observations can be made. In the first place, the Ordinance was concerned with the powers of Shaikhs of nomad tribes; sedentary or partly sedentary and partly nomadic tribes (not to mention the de-tribalized peoples of the larger villages and towns) were not included in its provisions. Secondly, the powers of Shaikhs of nomadic tribes herein described are purely judicial in character. No administrative functions, such as the assessment of taxes or road maintenance, for example, were mentioned. Thirdly, the Ordinance did not set out to expand the judicial powers of these Shaikhs, but merely to regularize them. Thus punishable offences were enumerated in a Schedule and divided into 'major' and 'minor' offences the nature of which was to be settled, in case of doubt, by the Governor of the Province. Major offences could only be dealt with by a Shaikh sitting as a President of a Majlis, or Council, of tribal elders while minor

[1] *Journal of the African Society*, xxxiv (1935), p. 49. [2] Above, p. 60.
[3] Report of the Special Mission, p. 34.
[4] *Sudan Government Gazette*, no. 396, 15 June 1922.

offences could be handled, if so directed by the Governor of the Province, by a Shaikh sitting alone. The maximum fine which could be imposed under the Ordinance was fixed at £25 or its equivalent in kind, but, in case of theft or damage to property, a Shaikh was empowered, in addition to the fine imposed, to issue orders for restitution or reparation to the extent of the loss or damage sustained, normally not exceeding the value of £50. In all cases, local custom was, as far as was possible, to be followed and the Ordinance also provided that small offences not mentioned in the Schedule should be punished in accordance with customary law.

By 1923, three hundred Shaikhs of nomadic and semi-nomadic tribes were, in the words of the Annual Report, enjoying powers which, under the Ordinance of 1922, had the full support of Government authority.[1] At the same time, the possibility of creating village courts among the sedentary population of the Northern Sudan was considered[2] but nothing was done until after the rising of 1924. In fact Native Administration, until 1924, was primarily thought of as complementary to the policy of training educated Sudanese for service in the hierarchy of the central government. Stack definitely thought of these two forms of 'Sudanization' as complementary to one another[3] and, following his example, the Milner Mission, despite all they had to say about the unsuitability of centralized bureaucracy for the Sudan, did not sufficiently distinguish between them.[4] The paramount consideration in both cases was the replacement of Egyptians by Sudanese.

After 1924, however, Native Administration (meaning government through the Shaikhs and Chiefs of tribes) was looked upon as an alternative to the employment of educated Sudanese in the government bureaucracy and, as such, it was vigorously pursued especially from 1926 onwards. In his Annual Report of that year, the Governor-General confirmed his agreement with the objectives defined in the Milner Report with regard to centralization, adding that whereas Native Administration was an instrument of devolution, the selection of Sudanese executive officials for the public service was one of

[1] *Annual Report* for 1923, Sudan, no. 2 (1924), Cmd. 2281, p. 6.

[2] Ibid., p. 7.

[3] Above, p. 60.

[4] 'At the present time', the Report stated, 'the officials of local origin are still largely outnumbered by those introduced from Egypt, with whom service in the Sudan is by no means popular. This difficulty will be overcome as education progresses and a greater number of Sudanese themselves become capable of filling official posts' (Cmd. 1131, p. 34).

costly bureaucracy, the elaboration of which was impossible to contemplate with equanimity. Under the impulse of new ideas and with the rise of a new generation, however, tribal organization, tribal sanctions, and old traditions tended 'to crumble away unless they are fortified betimes'. The time factor was, therefore, important if Native Administration was to be successfully established. And although some progress had already been made

it is essential that experiments of wider scope should be made while the ideal is rendered comparatively easy of realization on account of the survival of the older personalities. . . . By the judicious and progressive application of devolutionary measures in districts where conditions are suitable, and by ensuring that the native agencies which are to be responsible for administering these measures are remunerated on a scale sufficient to give them their requisite measure of status and dignity, it should be possible not only to strengthen the fabric of the native organisation but, while maintaining our supervisory staff at proper strength, gradually to reduce the number of sub-mamurs, clerks, accountants and similar bureaucratic adjuncts in the outdistricts.

The most obvious line of advance towards the realisation of the object in view has been generally agreed to be that of strengthening the authority wielded by the native chiefs over their people as judges in criminal and civil cases, for the power and status required by the chief as a judge, whether sitting alone or as president of a tribunal of elders, must naturally tend to enhance his authority as the administrative and executive head of his tribe or district.[1]

Accordingly, the training courses for sub-Māmūrs were ended in 1927 and an Ordinance[2] was passed which considerably enhanced the status and power of tribalism and the tribal Shaikhs. The preamble of the Ordinance which, unlike that of 1922, was not confined to nomads but applied to the Shaikhs of all tribes, stated that its object was to extend and regularize the powers of Shaikhs and not, as was the case with its forerunner, merely to regularize them. Whereas the Governor of the Province was the source of power in 1922, it was the Governor-General himself who granted powers to the Shaikhs under the Ordinance of 1927 and the Shaikhs, together with the elders qualified to sit as members of their courts, were specified by name in the warrant. The older Ordinance allowed Shaikhs of nomad tribes to exercise power in punishing certain scheduled

[1] *Annual Report* for 1926, Sudan, no. 2 (1927), Cmd. 2991, pp. 5–6.

[2] The Powers of Sheikhs Ordinance, 1927, in the *Sudan Government Gazette*, no. 494 of 15 Aug. 1927.

offences (such as theft, hurt, or mischief) among their own tribesmen who were under their authority. The 1927 Ordinance, by contrast, empowered Shaikhs to try any case except certain offences (such as homicide, and offences against the State or relating to the Military Forces) in which those subject to their tribal or local jurisdiction were involved. Under the Ordinance of 1922, the maximum penalty was a fine of £25 unless theft or damage to property were involved, when restitution or reparation to the extent of the loss or damage sustained, not normally exceeding £50, could be ordered. The maximum penalty under the 1927 Ordinance, on the other hand, was a fine of £100 and two years' imprisonment.[1] And, for the first time, Shaikhs and Chiefs were paid, out of public funds, for their services in order 'to give them their requisite measure of status and dignity'.[2]

Under these circumstances, it is not surprising that a distinct tendency was observed in 1927 for the smaller tribal units, willingly or with some reluctance, to coalesce or attach themselves to larger tribes in the neighbourhood.[3] Equally natural was the fact that this tendency was officially regarded as 'eminently healthy and one to be encouraged'.[3] With this object in view, a further ordinance was passed in 1928 especially to reinforce and extend the powers of 'inter-tribal or inter-regional councils for the settlement of inter-tribal or inter-regional disputes'.[4]

In addition to expanding their judicial powers in this manner, it was decided that tribal Shaikhs and courts should also be given certain administrative responsibilities to exercise simultaneously with their judicial functions—the separation of the two being considered, in the circumstances, both artificial and false.[5] Accordingly, the heads of a few selected tribes were given control over the pay of their retainers and subordinates, and at least one had his own tribal budget in 1928.[6] The clearest example of financial devolution in these days was that of Tokar, in Eastern Sudan, where a co-operative society, financed by the central government, was entrusted to the local tribal court to administer and to regularize the provision of funds

[1] MacMichael, *The Anglo-Egyptian Sudan*, p. 252.

[2] *Annual Report* for 1926, p. 6.

[3] *Annual Report* for 1927, Sudan, no. 1 (1929), Cmd. 3284, p. 7.

[4] Preamble of The Powers of Sheikhs Ordinance, 1928, in the *Sudan Government Gazette*, no. 505, 15 June 1928.

[5] MacMichael, *The Sudan*, p. 110.

[6] *Annual Report* for 1928, Sudan, no. 2 (1929), Cmd. 3403, p. 10.

for agricultural loans to cultivators in the Tokar delta.[1] The collection of direct taxes had been entrusted to tribal Chiefs many years previously, but they were now given powers of tax assessment as well.[2] In addition, Shaikhs were, in many provinces, made responsible for the maintenance of roads, wells, and schemes of water storage within their respective areas of jurisdiction. In certain cases they were also given charge of personnel for the provision of minor medical and veterinary services. Above all, whereas their authority and that of their courts had been securely established, Shaikhs (or 'Nāẓirs' as the more important among them are called) were entrusted with 'a very large or even preponderating share in the maintenance of public security'.[3]

By the end of 1929 no less than 72 courts had been established (under the Powers of Sheikhs Ordinance, 1928) throughout the Northern Sudan including the Jazīra, where urbanization and the consequent mixing of the population had most conspicuously resulted in the appearance of what the Governor-General preferred to call 'artificial and non-tribal'[3] communities. The extent of the activity of these courts can be seen in the fact that, by the end of the year, they had tried 10,205 cases—not including those heard by the 220 Shaikhs who had been authorized, under the Ordinance, to try cases 'sitting alone', that is, with unspecified assessors.[4] And, as we have seen, many of them were given financial and administrative powers to exercise in addition to their judicial functions.

7. *The politics of reaction: 'Southern Policy'*

In the Southern provinces (of Mangalla, Baḥr al-Ghazāl, and Upper Nile) where the process of 'pacification' had only recently been concluded, the first important step towards the establishment of Native Administration was taken in 1931 with the passing of The Chief's Courts Ordinance for that year. In the words of the Governor-General, in his Annual Report for 1931, 'Primitive negroid tribes are here affected, and the Ordinance marks the object at which we aim rather than the codification of heterogeneous existing practices.'[5]

[1] *Annual Report* for 1928, Sudan, no. 2 (1929), Cmd. 3403, p. 10.
[2] *Annual Report* for 1929, Sudan, no. 1 (1930), Cmd. 3697, p. 12.
[3] Ibid., p. 11.
[4] Ibid., pp. 9–10.
[5] *Annual Report* for 1931, Sudan, no. 1 (1932), Cmd. 4159, p. 12.

In order fully to appreciate that object and the administrative system designed for its realization we need to examine the two in the wider context of the 'Southern Policy' which was vigorously pursued by the British administration in the Sudan until 1947, with serious consequences for the whole country.

Generally speaking, it may be said that this policy passed through two main phases. Throughout the first phase, from 1899 to 1919, the policy of the Sudan Government towards the Southern provinces was—apart from the maintenance of law and order and the provision of different forms of assistance to Christian missionary societies—largely passive or *laissez-faire*. During the second phase, following the Egyptian Revolution, on the other hand, the Government became increasingly active and interventionist, especially—as was the case with regard to Native Administration in the Northern provinces—after the rising of 1924 (which was itself led by an officer of Dinka, i.e. Southern, origin). And although the geographical differences between the Southern and Northern provinces had always been an important factor, the basic considerations which dictated the Southern Policy were, in both its stages, the colonial interests of the British Empire in the Sudan and in East Africa.

With regard to the early days of the Anglo-Egyptian regime, Cromer was firmly convinced that the first requirement of 'the savages who inhabit this region'[1] was law and order, and that this could best be maintained by means of strong and direct military rule.

> I do not suppose that the most ardent advocate, whether of internationalism or of equality of freedom to all creeds and races, would seriously contend that it would have been possible in practice to have worked a system under which Kwat Wad Awaibung, a Shilluk who murdered Ajok Wad Deng because the latter bewitched his son, and caused him to be eaten by a crocodile, would have been tried by a procedure closely resembling that followed at Paris or Lyons. . . .[2]

In these circumstances, he maintained, the adoption of a civilized system of government would only result in the creation of 'very serious risks' for all concerned.

This being so, and since the Sudan Government was, in any case, short of money and dependent on the Egyptian Treasury for balancing its modest budget, no work of construction could be contemplated or service provided in the South beyond what was necessary for the

[1] *Annual Report* for 1904, Egypt, no. 1 (1905), Cd. 2409, p. 140.
[2] Ibid., p. 110.

maintenance of government personnel and hence law and order. With only limited improvement in the financial situation during the following decade, even the administration could not, except with difficulty, be extended beyond the limited objectives of defending government posts and putting down occasional tribal risings. Thus, when the Lado enclave reverted from the Congo to the Sudan, following the death of King Leopold of the Belgians in 1910, the work of garrisoning and administering the additional territory was viewed as 'a serious tax on the slender resources of the government' and the extra expenditure involved could only be met by increasing 'the Egyptian contribution on account of the Soudan military expenses' by £45,000.[1]

Under these circumstances, therefore, the best and the only thing that could be done by way of general improvement, it was felt, was to allow Christian missionary societies into the region in the hope that their activities would help in winning the confidence of the inhabitants for the new regime and also prove a civilizing influence.[2] The missionaries, however, had their own plans and, being ignorant of 'the great difference between the Soudan and those parts of Africa which are inhabited by non-Moslems',[3] wanted to proceed with proselytizing the whole country. In a private letter to Lord Lansdowne, Cromer described the situation in the following terms: 'I am being vigorously assailed on all sides to allow active proselytism in the Soudan. The Catholics backed up by the Austrian Government, the High Church Party, with various influential Bishops behind them, the Church Mission and other societies, all join in the cry.'[4] He then goes on to explain his own attitude: 'I have no objection to giving the missionaries a fair field amongst the black pagan population in the equatorial regions, but to let them loose at present amongst the fanatical Muslims of the Soudan would, in my opinion, be little short of insane.'[4]

This was, in fact, the basis of the final agreement reached on the subject—the main exception, during the first years, being the opening of mission schools and the building of an Anglican Cathedral in Khartoum which were justified by the existence of non-Muslims in the town. Having freedom of action in the Southern provinces, on

[1] *Annual Report* for 1910, Egypt, no. 1 (1911), Cd. 5633, p. 74.
[2] *Annual Report* for 1905, Egypt, no. 1 (1906), Cd. 2817, p. 125.
[3] Cromer to Salisbury, 22 Feb. 1900, P.R.O. FO/633/6.
[4] Cromer to Lansdowne, 9 Mar. 1900, P.R.O. FO/633/8.

the other hand, the missions, each Church or denomination working in its own defined zone, carried on with their work of prosyletizing the population and 'teaching these savages the elements of common sense, good behaviour, and obedience to Government authority'.[1] It was a measure of their success that the Governor-General, when he toured the region in 1908, was 'struck with the confidence now shown by the natives in Government'.[2]

In the meantime, the Government's policy of making each province 'as self-contained and independent as possible'[3] was being pursued throughout the country, but with particular success in the Southern provinces, where it was aided by the activities of the missionaries and the gradual introduction of a religion and an outlook different from those which were prevalent in the country as a whole. Another factor which is still (though to a much lesser and rapidly diminishing degree) evident today, but was of major importance in the early years of the regime, was the poor state of communications between the Southern provinces and the rest of the country. Thus, the general outcome of administrative policy, Christian missionary activity, and poor communications was to deepen and enhance the differences between the Southern and Northern parts of the Sudan.

But this fact, obvious though it had been from the beginning, did not acquire a definite political significance until the outbreak of the Egyptian Revolution of 1919 when, confronted by the realities of a new situation in Egypt, the British administration of the Sudan found it advisable, in its own interest, to revise its policy within the country as it had done with regard to the relationship of Egypt and the Sudan. Indeed, the two issues were directly connected in the memoranda submitted to the Milner Mission. One of these explained that 'the Government policy has been to keep the Southern Soudan as free as possible of Mohammedan influences. Black Mamurs are employed: where it has been necessary to send Egyptian clerks, Copts are, if possible, selected. Sunday is observed as a day of rest instead of Friday as in the North and missionary enterprise encouraged'. The memorandum then continues: 'The possibility of the Southern (black) portion of the Sudan being eventually cut off from the Northern (Arab) area and linked up with some Central African

[1] *Annual Report* for 1905, Egypt, no. 1 (1906), Cd. 2817, p. 125.

[2] Wingate to Gorst, 3 May 1908 (Wingate Papers).

[3] Memoranda on the Sudan submitted to the Milner Mission (Milner Papers).

system is borne in mind.'[1] Another memorandum on 'The Separation of the Sudan from Egypt' discussed 'Decentralization of Sudan Government with a view to the separation of the Negroid from the Arab Territories' in some more detail. Having made the realistic observation that 'it would be very difficult to make a clean cut between the two races', it nevertheless suggested that 'a line from East to West following the Baro, the Sobat, the White Nile and Bahr el Gebel rivers' might be a suitable frontier between the two.[2] A third memorandum was more definitive in tone:

The Government of the Sudan would have, eventually, to be assimilated to the government of other African possessions, such as Uganda and East Africa, as far as the Negroids are concerned. The Arab provinces would require different treatment. Therefore, consider the question of a central African Federation under British control, and lop the Negroids off the Sudan Government—in time of course.[3]

The Milner Report, however, did not make any formal recommendations about the Southern Sudan as such. But the policy of decentralization which it recommended 'with a view to the separation of the Negroid from the Arab Territories', as noted above, naturally tended in this direction. And, in conformity with this, it was decided that the Governors of the three Southern provinces should not, unless required, attend the annual meetings of Governors of provinces at Khartoum, but should have their own gatherings in the South and keep in touch with their opposite numbers in Kenya and Uganda. But the way in which this was expressed in the Annual Report is interesting and worthy of note. Having commented on the usefulness of the new practice of holding regular Governors' meetings in Khartoum, the Governor-General interestingly points out that:

a natural division has emerged between those provinces which are accessible and those which are not, in that it has only been possible to collect the former in Khartoum. This division has been found to correspond almost exactly between the Arab and the Negroid portions of the Soudan, for all the former provinces, Halfa, Dongola, Berber, Red Sea, Blue Nile, Sennar, White Nile, Khartoum, excepting only Kassala, are connected with Khartoum by railway, whereas the nearest of the negroid provinces is approached only by river and is not less than five days away. The Governors of the latter, therefore, meet separately at some convenient place on the river, south of Khartoum.[4]

[1] Khartoum, 14 Mar. 1920 (Milner Papers).
[2] The Governor-General's Office, Khartoum, 15 Feb. 1920 (Milner Papers).
[3] Sirdār, Khartoum, 25 Feb. 1920 (Milner Papers).
[4] *Annual Report* for 1920, Egypt, no. 2 (1921), Cmd. 1487, p. 125.

In order to exclude Egyptians, Northern Sudanese, and other Muslims who were likely to engage in activities contrary to the policy of separating the Southern provinces and giving them a different outlook from the rest of the country, the Passports and Permits Ordinance, 1922, was promulgated in October of that year. It introduced a rigorous system of permits in accordance with which permission to non-Sudanese to enter the Sudan could be refused or withdrawn 'without reason'.[1] In addition, the Ordinance empowered the Governor-General (and his authorized representatives) to declare any part of the Sudan a 'Closed District'. A Closed District could either be 'absolutely closed', in which case it was completely and unquestionably out of reach for Northern Sudanese and non-Sudanese alike, or it could be declared an ordinary 'Closed District', in which case 'ingress shall be permitted subject to such conditions and for such purposes as may be set forth in the said order and he (the Governor-General) may limit the application of such order or conditions to such persons or classes of persons as he may deem fit'. Furthermore, authorities that were competent to grant permits under this Ordinance had 'absolute power to refuse to issue a permit or to renew a permit on expiry for any applicant without reason assigned and, in like manner and without notice, to cancel any permits previously granted and thereupon the holder of the permit which has been cancelled or whose renewal has been refused shall, within a time reasonably sufficient to wind up his affairs to be notified to him, cease to trade in the district to which the permit applied'. Such person may in addition forfeit the deposit (of £50) which he will have been required to pay on applying for a permit.

The manner in which these aspects of the Ordinance were applied is best shown in a circular letter, containing a re-statement of the Government's Southern Policy, which was prepared, on the request of the Governor-General by the then Civil Secretary, Sir Harold MacMichael, and sent to the Governors of the three Southern provinces and the Directors of Departments in January 1930.[2] The letter, which continued to be the main statement of official policy until 1947, reads as follows:

It is the aim of the Government to encourage as far as is possible [Christian] Greek and Syrian traders rather than the Gallaba [i.e. Muslim Arabs

[1] *Laws of the Sudan*, i. 93 (1941 edition). All quotations are from the Passports and Permits Ordinance in this volume.

[2] 25 Jan. 1930, CS/I.C.I., Government Archives, Khartoum. See Appendix VI.

from Northern Sudan] type. Permits to the latter should be decreased unobtrusively but progressively, and only the best type of Gallaba, whose interests are purely commercial and pursued in a legitimate manner should be admitted. The limitation of Gallaba trade to towns or established routes is essential.

But the Passports and Permits Ordinance, 1922, was also aimed at stopping, or, at any rate, drastically reducing the number of Southerners who tended to look northward for employment and the prospects of a higher standard of living. The Ordinance, therefore, prohibited the engagement of labour in any part of the Sudan for employment outside or in any other part of the country except under permit. Besides, prospective employers were required, before a permit could be issued, to deposit the sum of £1 for each labourer permitted to be engaged by the terms of the permit with a maximum of £150. Where permits were granted, a breach of the conditions on which they were obtained could result not only in the loss of the deposit, but in punishment with imprisonment, which might extend to six months, or with fines, not exceeding £100, or with both. Finally, the Ordinance provides that a person who, in the judgement of the competent authority, contravened the provisions of the Ordinance or of any order issued under its terms, 'shall, in addition to any other penalty to which he is liable under this ordinance . . . be liable to be expelled from the district in which he held a permit . . . and to confiscation in whole or in part of the goods in his possession'.

Contacts between Northerners and Southerners, however, were not confined to the relationship of buyer and seller or worker and employer; they could also occur on a personal level between government officials and members of the public. Therefore, the Civil Secretary also directed that Northern officials should be gradually eliminated from the Southern provinces.[1] It is true, he said, 'local boys' were not fit to fill the higher posts in government offices and the supply of such boys depended on the speed with which the mission

[1] 25 Jan. 1930, CS/I.C.I., Government Archives, Khartoum. 'As the removal of Northern [people] may give rise to considerable repercussions of a political nature', however, the Civil Secretary was careful to point out that 'the greatest tact and care will have to be exercised in adjusting means to the end in view. . . . There can be no question of ejection *en masse* being applied to these people. The weeding out must be gradual, and in each case adequate cause must be shown, so that, should the necessity arise, we may be in a position to supply a complete answer to any complaints or enquiries from interested quarters here' (MacMichael to the Governor, Bahr al Ghazal Province, 11 May 1930, CS/I.C.I., Government Archives, Khartoum).

schools produced them. But since their employment in Government offices was a vital feature of the general policy, every encouragement was to be given to those in charge of mission schools to co-operate by sending boys into government service.

Sir Harold continued:

It is also recognized that in such places as Wau itself, Arabic is so commonly used that the local languages have been almost completely excluded . . . (Nevertheless) . . . every effort should be made to make English the means of communication. An official unable to speak the local vernacular should try to use English when speaking to Government employees and servants, and even, if possible, to chiefs and natives. In any case, the use of an interpreter is preferable to the use of Arabic, until the local language can be used. . . . In short, whereas at present Arabic is considered by many natives of the South as the official and, as it were, the fashionable language, the object of all should be to counteract this idea by every practical means.[1]

The introduction of such radical changes, however, was bound to meet with difficulties and give rise to doubts and uncertainties even in the minds of some of the British officials who were entrusted with its execution. For example, the District Commissioner of Raja, who was later on to condemn Southern Policy as 'ridiculously artificial' and 'one which no one, I think, could sincerely follow',[2] protested 'that it is not consistent that I should insist on them [Southerners] using their proper, tribal, names and dropping their foreign (Arabic) ones when the Missions are permitted to baptise them with another foreign (Italian) name.'[3]

But such protests only met with exhortations to abide by official policy, show greater zeal in combating Muslim-Arabic influences and urge people to persist with the English language and tribal customs. 'Please note', the Governor of Bahr al Ghazal wrote to his restive subordinate,

that in order to further the policy of encouraging local languages and tribal consciousness and English and of suppressing Arabic, everything which in the *smallest degree* may contribute to this should be done. The use of Arabic words—'sheikh', 'sultan', etc., should be discontinued and their native equivalents substituted (e.g. 'beng' in Dinka Districts). . . . Chiefs

[1] Ibid.
[2] D.C. Raja to D.C. Western District, 12 Feb. 1932, CS/I.C.I. (Archives, Khartoum).
[3] D.C. Raja to Governor, Bahr al Ghazal, 17 Jan. 1932, CS/I.C.I. (Archives, Khartoum).

and people should be dissuaded from changing their native names and those who have adopted Arabic names should be discouraged from using them.[1]

Commenting on this case, a few weeks later, the Civil Secretary intimated to the Governor that the matter was a delicate one and required considerable tact. However, ' . . . in friendly conversation with chiefs you might from time to time represent that "amour propre" demands the upholding of tribal custom with regard to clothing and similar matters'.[2]

Should it be protested that this meant that the Government was condoning or even encouraging, for example, nudity which was normal amongst tribes of the Southern provinces, the ready answer would be that 'the policy of the Government in the Southern Sudan is to build up a series of self-contained racial or tribal units with structure or organization based, to whatever the requirements of equality and good government permit, upon indigenous customs, traditional usage and belief'.[3] Where nudity was being deserted for clothing, however, every care was to be taken to see that European and not Arabic styles were used. In this case, even those members of the administration who, like the District Commissioner of Raja, were worried about consistency, could be relied upon to carry out government policy. He, as it happened, was prepared to be very firm with those Greek and other merchants who sold Arab clothing. In January 1935, for instance, he wrote to one of them:

I notice that in spite of frequent requests to the contrary, large quantities of 'Arab' clothing are still being made and sold. Please note that, in future, it is FORBIDDEN to make or sell such clothes. Shirts should be made short with a collar and opening down the front in the European fashion and NOT an open neck as worn by the Baggara of Darfur. Also tagias [i.e. skull caps] as worn by Arabs to wind emmas [i.e. turbans] round are not to be sold in future. No more Arab clothing is to be made as from today: you are given till the end of February to dispose of your present stock. This order applies to all outside agents and owners of sewing machines.[4]

[1] Governor, Bahr al Ghazal, to District Commissioner, Raja, 19 Mar. 1930, CS/I.C.I. (Archives, Khartoum).

[2] Civil Secretary to Governor, Bahr al Ghazal, 11 May 1930, CS/I.C.I. (Archives, Khartoum).

[3] Civil Secretary to Governors and Directors of Departments, 15 Jan. 1930, CS/I.C.I. (Archives, Khartoum).

[4] D.C. Raja to Mr. Emmanuel Lagoteris, Agent of Messrs. Papoutsidis at Raja, 21 Jan 1935, CS/I.C.I. (Archives, Khartoum).

Compared with those District Commissioners who by 1941 had been 'for ten years . . . burning Arabic clothes',[1] the District Commissioner of Raja was, at any rate up to February 1935, remarkably mild and accommodating. The common pursuit of all, however, was the elimination of all traces of Muslim and Arabic culture in the South, the substitution of Christianity and the English language and, above all, in the age of Lugard and Native Administration, the revival of tribalism as an instrument of government.

With this end in view, exploratory attempts at the establishment of Chiefs' courts (or *lukikos*) to deal with cases of minor importance were made early in 1922—the year in which The Powers of Nomad Sheikhs Ordinance was promulgated and first applied in the Northern Sudan. Four such *lukikos* were established during the course of the year in Mangalla Province and in the Upper Nile Province. The internal administration of the Shilluk was left as much as possible in the hands of tribal Chiefs under the supervision of their Mek and, beyond him the District Commissioner and the Governor of the Province. Reports of early and unqualified success were received at Khartoum,[2] and expectations of even greater success were thereby aroused.

Soon afterwards, however, it appeared that such unguarded optimism was not justified and the Governor-General found it necessary to caution all concerned that native institutions needed 'patient and careful nursing' before they could be made of practical administrative value.[3] There were two main reasons for this. The first was that, although in nearly every tribe 'traces of an ancient governing organization' could be found, such organizations had greatly declined in course of time 'due to constant feuds, migration or famine'.[3] The second obstacle was that the process of 'pacification' had not yet been completed in the South, and periodical tribal risings continued to engage the Government at least until 1928.[4] In these conditions, therefore the progress of Native Administration was necessarily halting.

In order to overcome the second of these two difficulties, and thus bring the recalcitrant tribes under control, it was emphatically

[1] Governor, Equatoria, to D.C. Western District, 29 Apr. 1941, CS/I.C.I. (Archives, Khartoum).

[2] *Annual Report* for 1922, Sudan, no. 2 (1923), Cmd. 1950, p. 8.

[3] *Annual Report* for 1923, Sudan, no. 2 (1924), Cmd. 2281, p. 7.

[4] *Annual Report* for 1928, Sudan, no. 2 (1929), Cmd. 3403, p. 11.

stated, in 1928, that periodic patrols—even when supported by bombardment from the air—were not sufficient. Roads, passable at all seasons, and the creation of neutral zones between tribes which were hostile to one another, such as the Nuer and the Dinka, had to be created and steadily maintained.[1]

As for tribal traditions and organizations, it was decided, also in 1928, that expert advice should be sought from trained specialists. Thus, with the help of Professor Westermann, director of the International Institute of African Languages and Cultures, the systematic study of the main-group languages in the South, was made possible,[2] and Evans Pritchard prepared the classic studies of the Nuer, the Azande, and other tribes of the Southern Sudan, which are still of great value for administrators and policy-makers in the Sudan—as well as for students of anthropology the world over.[3]

Equipped with better understanding, and supported by a rapidly improving system of roads and moto rtransport, the Government was able to extend the system of the *lukikos* to the Upper Nile Province during the following year,[4] and in 1930 the Chiefs' courts in the three Southern provinces heard and settled no less than 14,046 cases.[5] But these, it is needless to say, were of minor importance and the courts themselves were always kept under close supervision by the District Commissioners and the Governors. Even after the Chiefs' Courts Ordinance, 1931, had been passed, neither the findings nor the sentences of *lukikos* could be considered final until they had been confirmed by the Governor.[6] And when the Native Courts Ordinance, 1932, which consolidated the system of Native Administration throughout the Sudan, came into force, the provinces of the Upper Nile and Equatoria were excluded from its provisions.[7]

Whatever its limitations, however, a system of chiefs' courts had been effectively established. It relieved the District Commissioner of many elementary routine duties, and was, in general, popular with the inhabitants. *Lukikos* were, in fact, so popular in some areas that a

[1] *Annual Report* for 1928, Sudan, no. 2 (1929), Cmd. 3403, p. 11.

[2] Ibid., p. 94.

[3] Professor Seligman began his pioneering survey of *The Pagan Tribes of the Nilotic Sudan* in 1909 but it was not published until 1932.

[4] *Annual Report* for 1929, Sudan, no. 1 (1930), Cmd. 3696, p. 12.

[5] *Annual Report* for 1930, Sudan, no. 1 (1931), Cmd. 3935, p. 10.

[6] The Chiefs' Courts Ordinance, 1931, *Sudan Government Gazette*, no. 549, 15 July 1931.

[7] The Native Courts Ordinance, 1932, 15 Sept. 1932, vol. iv of *The Laws of the Sudan.*

small fee had to be charged to litigants in order to discourage the presentation of purely frivolous complaints.[1]

In administrative, as distinct from judicial, matters, however, native agencies in the Southern provinces, by contrast with those of the North, were far from successful. And by 1936, when numerous Shaikhs and Shaikhs' courts had, for many years, been exercising both judicial and administrative powers and no less than eight administrations were in full control of their own budgets, Chiefs and Chiefs' courts in the Southern provinces were still confined to the initial stage where only judicial powers were delegated[2]—and exercised under close supervision from District Commissioners and Governors.

A parallel contrast between the two regions during the preceding ten years or so is to be found in the difference of policy towards education (always, under the Anglo-Egyptian regime, closely linked with administration and suited to administrative purposes) in the two parts of the country. For whereas the intervening years since 1924 were, from the educational point of view 'a decade of utter stagnation'[3] in the North, the policy in the South, where the government had for the first time begun to take an interest in education, was one of rapid expansion which, as may be expected, was undertaken in close co-operation with the Christian missionary societies.

Two factors were prominent in bringing about the adoption of this attitude towards education in the South. The first was the policy of replacing Northern officials by 'local boys' which has already been described. The similarity between this and the substitution of Sudanese for Egyptian officials after 1919 is, of course, obvious. But there is one important difference: namely, that, whereas the expansion of education in the Northern Sudan (and hence employment in the governmental hierarchy) was soon called to a halt after the rising of 1924, the growth of education in the Southern provinces was not similarly interrupted. This was in large measure due to the intensification of efforts in the development and execution of Southern Policy which followed 1924, particularly in connection with the eradication of Muslim-Arabic culture and the substitution of the English language and Christianity. But it was also due to the inadequacy of native administration in the South, the second factor

[1] *Annual Report* for 1934, Sudan, no. 1 (1935), Cmd. 5019, p. 12.
[2] *Annual Report* for 1936, Sudan, no. 1 (1937), Cmd. 5575, pp. 11–12.
[3] P. M. Holt, *A Modern History of the Sudan* (London, 1961), p. 132.

making for the expansion in Southern education after 1924. For, in the absence of a reliable system of administration through tribal agencies, there was no alternative to bureaucratic government, and this depended on the educational system for providing the initial training for its recruits. In the words of the Governor-General in his Annual Report of 1925, it was then 'recognized that increasing economic and administrative development in the Southern Sudan demands additional educational facilities'.[1]

Until then, education in the Southern provinces, such as it was, had been exclusively provided by missionary societies, and the subject did not, as such, appear in the Annual Reports. It was only mentioned in the course of statements on the condition of missions. But the situation was transformed from 1925 when, for the first time, a comprehensive scheme of education in the South was prepared by the government, in co-operation with the missions[1] which received 'considerable grants',[2] by way of subsidy, for the execution of the scheme. The hope was then expressed that 'the happy combination of missionary enterprises and experience on the one hand, and of government aid, on the other, should afford sure ground and opportunity for the development of these negroid and pagan peoples'.[2] In 1926, an Inspector of Southern Education was appointed, and he began his work with a visit to Uganda 'in order to study the methods adopted there, among a population somewhat similar' to that of the Southern Sudan.[3]

The system of education which finally emerged was based on two types of schools—elementary vernacular schools, with four-year courses which were simple and directly linked with the practical needs of the people, and intermediate schools, in which English was the language of instruction, and the courses of study, extending for six years, were aimed at producing teachers, clerks, and other minor officials.[4] The problem presented by 'the infinite variety of local languages and their orthography'[5] was tackled at the Language Conference held at Rajjāf in April 1928. This was attended by the Director of Education, Uganda, the Provincial Commissioner, Northern Province, Uganda, a representative of the Belgian Congo

[1] *Annual Report* for 1925, Sudan, no. 2 (1926), Cmd. 2742, p. 47.
[2] *Annual Report* for 1926, Sudan, no. 2 (1927), Cmd. 2991, p. 8.
[3] *Annual Report* for 1926, Sudan, no. 2 (1927), Cmd. 2992, p. 73.
[4] *Annual Report* for 1927, Sudan, no. 1 (1929), Cmd. 3284, p. 80.
[5] *Annual Report* for 1927, Sudan, no. 1 (1929), Cmd. 3284, p. 81.

Administration, and 'many representatives of mission schools in the Sudan, the Belgian Congo and Uganda'—as well as Professor Westermann. As a result of this conference, certain group languages were selected for development for educational purposes and a uniform orthography was adopted.[1]

Thus equipped with money and expert advice, the missionaries, under the general supervision of the government, proceeded with the work. Several schools were opened in subsequent years and, in 1930, there were three intermediate schools with 177 boys (in addition to 15 at the Stack Memorial School at Wau) and 32 elementary vernacular schools with 2,024 pupils.[2] By 1936, the number of pupils at the intermediate schools rose to 246 (it had reached 261 in the previous year); and the number of elementary schools for boys was 36 with an attendance of 2,977. In addition, there were 18 girls' schools with 760 pupils and 3 trades schools with 100 boys. Textbooks were already being produced in the vernacular languages as well as in English and the general standard of education was gradually being raised.[3] In the meantime, Islam and the Arabic language were not only totally excluded from the schools, but were also being systematically erased throughout the Southern provinces.

By the mid thirties, then, Southern Policy was in full flood and Native Administration, its counterpart in the North, was still thriving.

8. *Winds of change*

In the meantime, however, new forces, both domestic and inter-international, had been gathering momentum. The immediate consequences were the partial restoration of Egypt's position in the Sudan and the ending of Native Administration as the fashionable philosophy of government in the country. Ten years later, the same forces led to the reversal of Southern Policy and all that it stood for, and by the end of the next decade, they brought about the end of the Anglo-Egyptian regime.

With regard to the first of these changes—relations between Egypt and Britain had never completely recovered from the shocks of 1919. The unilateral British declaration of Egypt as an independent

[1] *Annual Report* for 1928, Sudan, no. 2 (1929), Cmd. 3403, p. 94.
[2] *Annual Report* for 1930, Sudan, no. 1 (1931), Cmd. 3935, p. 94.
[3] *Annual Report* for 1936, Sudan, no. 1 (1937), Cmd. 5575, p. 90.

monarchy in 1922 did not reconcile the nationalists. For these, the reservation of certain subjects (including the Sudan and the defence of Egypt) which accompanied the declaration constituted a complete negation of independence and the exclusion of Egyptians from the Sudan after 1924 was a particularly unpopular measure. The Depression increased discontent and political unrest in Egypt and to that extent frustrated renewed efforts to settle outstanding questions between Britain and Egypt. But the Depression also paved the way for the rise of Nazism and Fascism in Europe. And this gradually inclined the British and Egyptian Governments to seek an acceptable form of accommodation with one another. The invasion of Abyssinia by the Italians (who had been in Libya since 1911) in 1935, and the consequent threat to British interests in East Africa on the one hand, and to Egyptian interests in the Nile on the other, made agreement an immediate requirement of both. A Treaty of Alliance was, therefore, duly signed on 26 August 1936.[1]

The Sudan was dealt with in Article 11 of the Treaty. The question of sovereignty over the country, which had constantly bedevilled Anglo-Egyptian negotiations in the past, was not touched. It was similarly agreed that the existing administration in the Sudan should continue as before. In order to give Egypt some satisfaction, however, it was provided that Egyptian troops might, once more, be stationed in the Sudan and that Egyptian immigration into the country should be unrestricted 'except for reasons of public order and health'. A further limitation was implied in another section which provided that no person of either Egyptian or British nationality should be appointed to new posts for which qualified Sudanese were not available—except with the approval of the Governor-General.

A Note which was attached to the Treaty allowed an Egyptian Economic Expert to serve in Khartoum and also provided that the Inspector-General of the Egyptian Irrigation Service in the Sudan be invited to attend the Governor-General's Council when matters relating to his department were brought before the Council.

It is apparent that none of these (or the other) provisions of the Treaty constituted a substantial gain for Egypt. But, in the circumstances, and especially after the humiliation of 1924, the Treaty was hailed, in Egypt, as a great national victory.

In the Sudan, where the negotiations leading up to the Treaty

[1] *Treaty of Alliance between H.M. Government in the United Kingdom and the Egyptian Government* (*1936*), Cmd. 5360 (1937).

had been watched 'with keen interest and some apprehension'[1] a different attitude prevailed. The Sudanese had not been consulted about the Treaty and the main reference which it made to them was that Britain and Egypt were agreed 'that the primary aim of their administration in the Sudan must be the welfare of the Sudanese'. This was greatly resented by the Sudanese both for its paternalism, and because they felt that they should have been consulted about matters that concerned them. A nationalist ferment had already been in evidence. The signing of the Anglo-Egyptian Treaty of 1936 proved a turning-point in its development.

[1] *Annual Report* for 1936, Sudan, no. 1 (1937), Cmd. 5575, p. 7.

PART TWO

THE ROAD TO INDEPENDENCE

CHAPTER IV

The Rise of Sudanese Nationalism

1. *Resistance: Mahdist and non-Mahdist styles*

PROFESSOR Wilfred Cantwell Smith, in his classic study, *Islam in the Modern World*, gives an admirably perceptive description of the sense of loss and utter disarray which a Muslim people experiences when it is subjected to alien rule. In the process of soul- and heart-searching which follows such a catastrophe, the situation, he finds, is viewed not merely as one in which sovereignty has been lost or the body-politic put in chains, but rather as one in which history itself has gone wrong and the governance of the universe has been upset.[1]

This is a fitting description of the feeling of the Sudanese people after the decisive battle of Omdurman. The Mahdi's own 'Anṣār' (or Supporters) who formed the backbone of the regime which had then perished, no doubt had a more intense experience of this feeling than the rest of the people, some of whom had been disappointed or otherwise alienated by the Khalīfa's rule and were, therefore, driven to react differently from the Anṣār. Like the Wahhābis in Arabia the Mahdists had hoped to conquer the Muslim world—as well as other areas[2]—and regenerate Islam. These hopes however had been severely checked at Toshki in 1889, and numerous set-backs were suffered afterwards. But now that the Mahdiyya had been crushed in its own homeland and the Mahdi's tomb shattered by the shells of the infidels, the agony was unbearable and a series of

[1] W. C. Smith, *Islam In The Modern World* (Princeton University Press, 1957). The same point was expressed in the Report of the Milner Mission as follows: 'That a Mohammedan should occupy a position of political subordination to a Christian is opposed to the essential spirit of Islam, and the sentiment which this spirit has engendered survives long after strong religious feeling has been greatly attenuated . . . There is in the East a patriotism of religion which is an even more fundamental sentiment than the patriotism of home and tradition' (*Report of The Special Mission to Egypt*, Cmd. 1131, 1921).

[2] The Khalīfa 'Abdullāhi sent letters to numerous people, Muslims and non-Muslims, asking them to accept the Mahdiyya and follow him. Among these was Queen Victoria, to whom he offered, not only salvation, but the prospect of becoming his wife.

desperate risings took place. They were all poorly organized and hopelessly ill-equipped to withstand the superior arms and forces of Egypt and Britain. Nevertheless, frustrated by their recent experience on the one hand and inspired, on the other, by the messianic belief that, after the Mahdi, al-Nabi 'Isa (or Prophet Jesus) was bound to come, deliver the faithful and 'fill the earth with justice even as it had been filled with iniquity', Mahdist risings continued to occur at least once a year for well over twenty years. The fact that, materially speaking, they were no match for the new regime did not deter these men from seeking 'either of the twin excellences: victory or martyrdom'[1]—and the latter was their usual lot either in the battlefield or by hanging.

The most serious of these risings, that of 'Abd al-Qādir Wad Ḥabboub in the Jazīra in 1908, was no exception, and the villages of his supporters, moreover, were burnt down.[2]

Wingate's opinion on the subject (and he was probably influenced in this by the Inspector General, Slatin Pasha, who was his personal friend) was that 'it will be kinder in the end to deal severely'[3] with the insurgents. 'The long and the short of the matter', he wrote to Gorst, 'is that Mahdiism in this country is not really dead; it has been stifled but there is still plenty of vitality in it and only the occasion is needed to bring it to the surface; nor is it to be wondered at when one remembers that most of the present generation have been born and brought up in the faith.'[4] '. . . it behoves us therefore never to relax for a moment our precautions to guard against the spread of such movements and the only means of doing this, with our meagre sources, is to crush them—almost mercilessly—in their inception.'[5]

Under these conditions it is not surprising that none of these risings was a success. The Anṣār were treated as an obvious security

[1] A saying of the Prophet regarding Jihād.

[2] In an interesting private letter dated 10 Mar. 1908, Wingate wrote to Gorst: '. . . in the present political situation both in Egypt and at home, I think the less said in official reports about burning insurgents' houses, putting them in chains etc. the better; so I shall cut out references of that sort when sending it on officially, and I shall accompany it with a further explanatory note which I hope will have the effect of silencing all this twaddle about the Dervish Prisoners, Ali Yousef's nonsense & Co.' ('Ali Yūsif was the editor of *al-Mu'ayyid*, the organ of the Egyptian Nationalist Party). A fortnight later Wingate thanked Gorst for his favourable response to this suggestion adding: 'The silence of the F.O. is satisfying and I hope it will long continue!' (Wingate Papers, School of Oriental Studies, Durham).

[3] Wingate to Gorst, 24 May 1908 (Durham).

[4] Wingate to Gorst, 10 May 1908 (Durham).

[5] Wingate to Gorst, 3 May 1908 (Durham).

risk. The sale and circulation of al-Mahdi's *Rātib* (a selection of Daily Readings which also served as a political manifesto) was forbidden. And his posthumous son, 'Abd al-Raḥmān, was kept under close watch. In order to counteract popular forms of Islam—represented by the semi-mystical 'Ṭariqās' (or religious fraternities) in which the Mahdi had himself been nurtured—an official organization of seven 'ulamas (i.e. Muslim scholar-jurists) was established in 1901. On that occasion Wingate wrote to Cromer that Ṭariqās had been rather on the increase—'but I hope with the aid of the Council [of 'ulamas] to quietly but firmly deal with them'.[1] Cromer who, as we have seen,[2] was fully aware of the relationship between the religious feeling of the people and their resistance to the new regime, was equally concerned to prevent subversion from within government institutions. 'Some one', he wrote to Wingate, 'told me that the historical textbooks in schools were all of a nature to encourage Moslem feeling. If so, they should be changed.'[3]

Ironically, however, the most important of government institutions, and the one which constituted its main support, i.e. the army, was also imbued with a similar spirit. The Sudanese battalions in the Egyptian Army were certainly no Mahdists. They belonged to other, normally rival Ṭariqās, such as the Khatmiyya—whose leader was Sayyid 'Ali al-Mirghani[4]—or to no Ṭariqās at all; but they were also, in different degrees, resentful of the British presence in the Sudan. Typically, as it was to become increasingly clear in subsequent years, the anti-British sentiments of these non-Mahdist, or anti-

[1] Wingate to Cromer, 13 Jan. 1901 (Durham).

[2] In connection with the control of the activities of Christian missions in the Northern provinces. See p. 71 above.

[3] Cromer to Wingate, 3 Feb. 1904 (Durham).

[4] al Sayyid 'Ali al-Mirghani was decorated with the C.M.G. in December 1900. Lord Cromer then wrote to Queen Victoria: '. . . Lord Cromer in Your Majesty's name, decorated Colonel Jackson with the C.B. and Major Peake and Sheikh Morghani each with the C.M.G. Your Majesty may remember that it was due to Colonel Jackson's judgement and to the influence which he possesses over the black troops, that the subordination which showed itself about a year ago in the native army, did not develop into a serious mutiny. Major Peake underwent great handicaps and performed admirable service in cutting through the mass of vegetation on the Nile known by the name of the Sudd. Sheikh Morghani is the head of the leading religious sect in the Sudan. He possesses great local influence, and the fact that he should have been the recipient of a decoration conferred by Your Majesty has, Lord Cromer hopes and believes, produced an excellent effect. He is a young man, very intelligent and well mannered. He appears highly gratified at the distinction which Your Majesty has been pleased to confer on him' (Lord Cromer to H.M. The Queen, 29 Dec. 1900, P.R.O. FO/633/8, p. 304).

Mahdist, elements were nursed and developed in close co-operation with Egyptian officers and troops or Egyptian civilians in the Sudan. The first manifestation of this spirit was the mutiny of 1900—when the new regime was less than one year old. As Cromer told Salisbury: 'It is next to impossible to obtain direct evidence of the origin of the mutiny . . . but by degrees enough leaks out to form a pretty fair idea of what happened. It seems that there has been great discontent and a talk of combined action for a long time.'[1] The discontent was in large measure due to Kitchener's stern discipline and harsh treatment of the troops. In so far as the Egyptian officers and troops were concerned there was the added resentment of the British occupation of Egypt and the recently signed Anglo-Egyptian Agreement which put the administration of the Sudan in the hands of the British. Egyptian views on the matter were clearly, if somewhat inaccurately, expressed in *al-Liwāʿ*, the organ of the Egyptian Nationalist Party of Mustafa Kāmil:

> The officers and soldiers exhibited great feats of courage in the re-occupation of the Sudan—such as the English themselves admired. They were however soon greatly insulted—an insult which no other army in the world has expected, for they saw the British flag flowing over Khartoum . . . It was further seen that an agreement was passed between England and Egypt which made the Sudan a common possession of both . . . The regret was greater when it was further noticed that the Governor General was English and not Egyptian . . .[2]

In addition it was rumoured that arrangements were being made to send the Sudanese and Egyptian troops to the Transvaal in order to fight the Boers. The eleventh and fourteenth battalions mutinied in January 1900, and the mutiny assumed serious proportions before it was finally put down. Cromer reported:

> The idea was not to kill the English officers—except perhaps Kitchener—but either to keep them in confinement at Omdurman or to send them to Cairo. The whole army was to join, and then one of two programmes was to be adopted—either the Khedieve was to be informed that there were 20,000 men at his disposal, and his orders requested, or else, without waiting for an expression of the Khedieve's views, the whole force was to move on to Egypt.[1]

[1] Cromer to Salisbury, 27 Apr. 1900, P.R.O. FO/633/6.

[2] Official translation of an article in *al-Liwāʿ* of 7 Feb. 1900, which was forwarded by Cromer to Salisbury on 8 Feb. P.R.O. FO/78/5086.

There are remarkable similarities between the 1900 mutiny and that of 1924. Both were inspired by a vision of an independent Nile Valley under the leadership of Egypt. Both were staged by Egyptian and Sudanese army officers and troops working together—and both ended in failure. Also the reactions of the Sudan Government in 1900 compared remarkably with those adopted a quarter of a century later. For example, after the mutiny of 1900, Kitchener suggested that an Imperial Service Corps of purely Sudanese units should be formed[1] to replace Egyptian battalions in the Sudan. For the same reasons the Sudan Defence Force was established in 1925 following the evacuation of Egyptian units from the country. But although Kitchener's suggestion was seriously considered at the time no mass evacuation of Egyptian forces was effected, it was decided that the army should be reduced and Sudanese should replace a number of Egyptian officers.[2] Salaries were, in due course, increased; grievances considered legitimate were redressed and the importance to the regime of keeping British battalions in the Sudan was more fully realized. A few years later Wingate wrote to Gorst: 'I have ample proof that the Nationalist spirit has taken deep root in the Army, though, so far, beyond taking a keen interest in the personal questions of pay and allowances and pensions, they have done nothing to call down reproof on them.'[3] In these circumstances, therefore, it is not surprising that with the exception of the Mahdist rising of Wad Habboub of 1908 (which was, significantly, crushed by Sudanese, as well as British and Egyptian, troops) no serious armed conflict took place until 1924.

Politics, however, continued to engage the more thoughtful and enlightened sections of the population. And as the country gradually recovered from the devastation which it had suffered during the later days of the Khalīfa's rule and as a result of the conquest[4] and 'pacification', more and more people began to take an interest in national questions and the spirit of nationalism gradually spread. Improved economic and living conditions greatly facilitated the

1 Cromer to Lord Lansdowne, 28 Nov. 1902, P.R.O. FO/633/6.

2 Cromer to Salisbury, 25 Feb. 1900, P.R.O. FO/633/6.

3 Wingate to Gorst, 8 May 1908 (Durham).

4 The greatest disaster of the Khalīfa's reign was the famous famine of 1306 A.H., now part of Sudanese folklore. The number of those who were killed during the reconquest is not known, but the number of casualties during the battle of Omdurman alone has been estimated at 11,000. The battle started at dawn and ended by about noon of 2 Sept. 1898 (W. Churchill, *The River War* (London, 1899), ch. xvi).

growth of national consciousness especially after the Gash Delta, the Jazīra and other parts were turned into cotton-growing areas on a scale large enough to meet the needs of Lancashire and enable the Sudan Government to carry on after the cessation of Egyptian subventions in 1913. But the gradual expansion of modern education and schools, though they were closely geared to purely administrative purposes,[1] was perhaps the most important factor in the development of this process. Besides the influence of Egypt contined to be felt—through her Arabic papers and publications, her personnel working in the Sudan and Sudanese traders, students (especially of al-Azhar University) and visitors in Egypt and, above all, through the example of the Egyptian nationalist movement.

2. *The impact of the First World War*

The First World War marked a turning-point in the growth of Sudanese nationalism. It stimulated the younger generation which had been through government schools and had acquired some idea of modern methods of administration by working in government offices. Their interest was also aroused by the outbreak of the Arab Revolt in 1916. But the greatest stimulant was perhaps that of President Wilson's fourteen points which were widely discussed in the Egyptian press. In 1918 the graduates (i.e. former pupils of the Gordon College) opened the Graduates' Club at Omdurman. In an often-quoted speech on the occasion Mr. Simpson, the Deputy Director of Education who was appointed first President of the Club, said that the Club was destined to play an important role in the future development of the country.

The outbreak of the war was also a turning point for the leaders of the Ṭariqās, especially the Ansār.[2] Until then 'Sayed Ali El Mirghani stood alone as the only great religious leader in whom the Government placed confidence, Sayed Abdel-Rahman El Mahdi and Sherif Yousef El Hindi[3] were even under the eye of suspicion—and were very well aware of it.'[4] But the war put the Anṣār and Sayyid

[1] Above, p. 41 n. 1.

[2] Strictly speaking the Anṣār, who are essentially a revivalist orthodox movement rather than a mystically oriented fraternity, are not a 'Ṭariqa' as such, though the word is commonly used with reference to them as well as to the Ṭūrūq al-Sūfiyya proper.

[3] The leader of a third, smaller, Ṭariqa.

[4] Intelligence Report dated 19. 12. 1921 (P.G.R., Durham).

'Abd al-Raḥmān in a different light. The main factor that occasioned the change was Turkey's declaration of war on Britain and the allies, and her subsequent attempts to persuade Sultan 'Ali Dinār of Darfur to attack the British Government of the Sudan simultaneously with a similar proposed attack on Egypt by the Sanousi of Libya. The anxiety of the Government about the possible effects on the Sudan of Turkey's call to the Muslims of the world to rise against their infidel oppressors, was clearly demonstrated in a speech which the Governor-General delivered to 'Mashaikh el Din,[1] men of education and intelligence', who were specially summoned to the Palace. 'God is my witness', Wingate told the gathered dignitaries, 'we have never interfered with any man in the exercise of his religion. We have brought the Holy places within a few days' journey from Khartoum. We have subsidised and assisted men of religion . . .' Britain had nothing but goodwill and friendship to the Muslims of the world. She had no quarrel with Islam or with its spiritual leaders and did not enter the war with the object of gaining territory at the expense of any Muslim state—'Her anger is directed solely against the Germans and their Turkish allies'. The Government of the Young Turks had not only overthrown Sultan 'Abd al-Ḥamīd and—through their reckless maladministration—created discontent amongst the non-Turkish races of the Ottoman Empire; but, like broken gamblers, they were now staking their last coin by going to war against Britain,

> the one Power who, by her actions and the sentiments of her people, has ever been a true and sympathetic friend to the Moslems and to Islam . . . You in the Sudan have had the bitter experience of the evils of Turkish rule and can judge better than those people who have been fortunate enough never to be under the Turkish Empire. But you may feel—and believe me I sympathise with you truly in this matter—a certain sorrow at this war. You may feel, some of you, that the result of this war may in some way affect the situation of Mohammedans in other parts of the world. I assure you before God that your fears are groundless, that in the British Empire the position of no single Mohammedan will be changed one iota and no single privilege granted to Islam will bc repudiated.

The Governor-General concluded his speech by appealing to his audience to give humble and wise counsel to the people and thus save their followers from being misled by rash and irresponsible suggestions: 'for here in the Sudan, as elsewhere in the world, the

[1] 'Leaders of the faithful', literally 'Shaikhs of religion'.

fools will listen to the wise, the ignorant to the learned, and the common people to men of wisdom and education'.[1]

It is clear the Government was intensely anxious about the situation and was straining to win the support—or at any rate the neutrality—of the Muslim population through their leaders. In these circumstances, therefore, Sayyid 'Abd al-Raḥmān and the Anṣār were naturally seen in a more favourable light. For the Mahdists were the traditional enemies not only of the Turks but also of the Egyptians. Both, in the eyes of the tough and puritanical Anṣār, were soft, corrupt, and decadent. They were held responsible for the general decline of Islam in recent times and for numerous iniquities in the treatment of their Sudanese subjects during the Turco-Egyptian regime of Muhammad 'Ali and Ismā'īl. Moreover the Egyptians were held guilty for bringing the British into the Sudan and wrecking the Mahdist regime there in the hope of, one day, re-establishing their own authority in the land. It is true the British were infidels and themselves guilty of unspeakable enormities.[2] But, it was felt, they were bound to leave the country one day or, perhaps, be forced out of it. But the Egyptians, if only because of the proximity of their homeland, would be infinitely more difficult to dislodge once they were established in the Sudan. From a Mahdist point of view, therefore, a tactical alliance with the British authorities, who were in any case in control of the Sudan and Egypt, was, for the time being, acceptable.

A tacit agreement was thus reached whereby Sayyid 'Abd al-Raḥmān—in order to be able to counteract the Pan-Islamic propaganda of the axis powers—was, for the first time, allowed to visit and live in Jazīra Aba, from which his father's revolt had started and was generally considered to be the cradle of Mahdism. He was also allowed to consolidate his position and that of his followers by engaging in large-scale farming and cotton cultivation. The tight

[1] The Governor-General's speech to the 'ulama on 8 Nov. 1914 (Durham and Milner Papers, New College, Oxford).

[2] The British and Egyptian press reported that, following the battle of Omdurman, troops under Kitchener's command committed certain atrocities, including the disinterment of the body of the Mahdi. 'I thought', Kitchener wrote to Cromer, 'it was politically advisable, considering the state of the country, that the Mahdi's tomb should be destroyed . . . When I left Omdurman for Fashoda, I ordered its destruction. This was done in my absence, the Mahdi's bones being thrown into the Nile. The skull only was preserved and handed over to me for disposal. No other bones were kept . . .' (quoted in a letter from Cromer to Salisbury, 12 Mar. 1899, P.R.O. FO/78/5022).

restrictions hitherto ruthlessly imposed on the Anṣār were gradually relaxed. And for them things became generally brighter after the disappearance from the scene of Slatin Pasha, the Inspector-General. By 1916 the intelligence department reported that Sayyid 'Abd al-Raḥmān was 'gaining considerable influence with the people', and 'was regarded by many as the Khalīfa of his father'. It was, therefore, necessary 'for this man to be watched daily'.[1] It was also considered necessary to watch and control, not only the son of the Mahdi, but all other leaders, both tribal and religious—even in the wake of the Egyptian Revolution when their support was needed most. To quote another Intelligence Report:

the length of the rope which it is possible to give to the religious or the tribal sheikhs must be regulated with due regard to ignorance and inflammability of the peoples among whom they desire to expand their influence and the means at the disposal of the Government to deal with the possible infringements of law and order which may be anticipated as the process develops. The middle way is not easy to find. Undue suppression of what may be held to be the legitimate expansion of the power of either the religious or secular leaders can only result in antagonising them. Too free a hand may lead to serious trouble, either because the individual gets an exaggerated idea of his own importance and is tempted to try to throw off control to a degree which is not permissible, or because (and this is the more probable difficulty) his motives, harmless in themselves, are misrepresented by his agents and misinterpreted by his followers.[2]

Within such limits as the Government wished to impose, the three Sayyids, tribal Shaikhs, and other influential persons were to be allowed full freedom of action—and where their views happened to coincide with those of the Government—even encouraged or actively supported by the administration.

The first important success of this policy was the neutralization of the Pan-Islamic sympathies of the population during the war—except, for a while, in Darfur which was finally annexed to the Sudan in 1916. 'The actual outbreak of hostilities with Turkey caused no excitement, and messages were received from all over the country affirming the loyalty of the people and their trust in the Government.'[3] The fact that Pan-Islamism had such little effect during the war was all the more interesting, as Stack wrote, with obvious satisfaction,

1 Secret Intelligence Report, Khartoum, 10 Sept. 1916 (Durham).
2 Political Situation, Khartoum, 19 Dec. 1921 (P.G.R., Durham).
3 *Report on Egypt and the Sudan, 1914–19*, Egypt, no. 1 (1920), Cmd. 957, p. 93.

'because the outstanding result of the war in the neighbourhood of the Sudan has been the establishment of an Arab Kingdom just across the Red Sea . . . the movement has aroused in the Sudan nothing but a friendly interest in spite of distinct efforts on the part of King Hussein himself to court the sympathy of the Arabs over here'.[1]

In the immediate post-war period, the most important question facing the Sudan Government was how to implement its policy[2] of separating the country from Egypt and, at the same time, demonstrate to Egypt and the world that this was in accordance with the wishes of the Sudanese people. It can be safely assumed therefore, that official encouragement was not withheld when the three principal religious leaders expressed, in informal conversation,

> a keen desire that the Government should take a stronger line than is taken at present (February 1919) to emphasise the fact that the Sudan is under the British Empire and that its future is with British control [and especially when] Sayed Ali Morghani in particular spoke of his ambition to see the people of the Sudan grow up under the influence of Great Britain a united people with their own laws, customs and administration, capable of both governing and fighting for themselves.[3]

For, a few weeks later, the Governor-General received the following letter:

> We beg you to convey to His Excellency the High Commissioner in Egypt, and the Government of His Majesty the King in London the following:
>
> We read daily the news contained in the Egyptian papers about the demonstrations in Egypt directed against the British Authorities there, and about the demands of the Egyptians that the British occupation should leave the Valley of the Nile, and we have throughout been confident that, through the wise counsel of the British officials in Egypt and the Egyptian Officials, everything will be settled satisfactorily.
>
> Yet, in order that nothing should reach the hearing of the British Authorities in Egypt and in London which may tend to make them believe that we are here in agreement with the movement now in progress in Egypt, we, the undersigned, on behalf of ourselves and of the whole population of the Sudan have hastened to express to the British Government the following:
>
> Firstly, that we are extremely grateful for all that the British officials in the Sudan have done for the welfare of the Sudan, which has resulted in the country's advancement and progress.

[1] Stack to Wingate, 23 Feb. 1919 (Durham). [2] Above, pp. 58 ff.

[3] Stack to Wingate, 'Note on the Growth of National Aspirations in the Sudan', 23 Feb. 1919 (Durham).

Secondly, our great loyalty and sincerity to the British Government which is unalterable.

Thirdly, our perfect and complete assurance that we have no hand in, or connection with the movement which is now in progress in Egypt, nor is the movement in accordance with our desires.

In conclusion please accept our highest esteemed respect.

(Sgd.)
Sayed Ali El Mirghani
Sayed Abdel-Rahman El-Mahdi
El Tayib Hashim—Mufti of Sudan
Abu El Gaseem Ahmed Hashim (President of the Board of 'Ulema)
Ismail El Azhari (Grand Kadi, Darfur)
Sayed Mirghani El Sayed El Mekki (Head of the Ismaelia Tarika in the Sudan)

Omdurman 23.4.1919.[1]

Sharīf Yūsif al-Hindi sent a similar letter dated 21 April.[1]

At the same time it was agreed that a deputation of Sudanese notables, including tribal Shaikhs and Government officials as well as the leaders of the religious fraternities,[2] should be sent to England in order to present officially their congratulations to the King on the signing of the peace.

The delegation, led by Sayyid 'Ali al Mirghani, arrived in London in July 1919, and was duly received by the King. The consummation of this historic occasion, as Wingate viewed it,[3] was the presentation by Sayyid 'Abd al-Raḥmān al Mahdi of his father's 'Sword of Victory' to King George V 'as a sure token of my fealty and submission to your Exalted Throne'.[4]

This, Wingate felt, was 'a solemn justification for and the highest tribute to our rule in the Sudan'.[4] But the most important business of the occasion was, no doubt, the confirmation 'both by H.M. The King and the High Officials of Government of the policy adopted ever since the reconquest of the Sudan in 1898–9'—namely, that Egypt would never again be allowed to rule the country.[5] This was common ground between British policy in the Nile Valley after the

[1] Official translation, Milner Papers, Oxford.

[2] It was feared, at first, that 'sentimental objections might make Sayed Abdel-Rahman an unacceptable visitor to England' (Stack to Wingate, 8 May 1919, Oxford). But these fears were eventually overcome by Wingate and Curzon (Graham to Wingate, 16 June 1919, Oxford).

[3] Wingate acted as translator.

[4] Wingate's translation (Durham).

[5] Wingate to Lord Hardings, 1 Mar. 1920 (Durham).

Egyptian Revolution and the interests of the Sudan as visualized by the members of the delegation. This, Wingate concluded, 'is the bedrock of our position in the Sudan—but the delicacy of the situation caused by the Cromer–Boutros declaration of January 1899, establishing a joint Anglo-Egyptian Control and the use of both Flags, necessitates the utmost caution'.[1]

Five months before their departure to Britain the two Sayyids, together with Sharīf Yūsif al-Hindi, had asked the Governor-General to give them permission 'to institute among their followers a kind of propaganda which will endeavour to foster loyalty and co-operation with the British Imperial Idea, with the ultimate object of cultivating a spirit of national unity among the Sudanese'.[2] But permission was not granted at the time. This was partly due to the Government's cautious attitude towards any increase in the power and influence of the leaders of the principal Ṭariqās. The main reason, however, was that, until then, the Government considered the granting of permission to engage in active propaganda for

> a national policy of the Sudan was hardly desirable . . . it would be out of keeping with the spirit of our administration and unfair to the Egyptians, who would be sure to attribute our action to a desire to intrigue against them and undermine their influence. If the sense of nationality is to grow, it will do so naturally, and to cultivate it by means of propaganda would be a false move.[2]

A fortnight after the three religious leaders had made their request, the Egyptian Revolution broke out and the logic of the Sudan Government with regard to Sudanese nationalism was therefore reversed.[3] The visit of the delegation of Sudanese notables to London in July was a direct result of this reversal of policy, and the visit in turn led to the establishment of closer relations and understanding between the Sayeds and the British Government. As the Governor-General had foreseen, however, this unholy alliance between Britain and the delegates became the object of violent attack and criticism by the Egyptian nationalists, and the wave of indignant abuse rose to a particularly high pitch after the return of the delegation

[1] Wingate to Lord Hardings, 1 Mar. 1920 (Durham).

[2] Stack to Wingate, 23 Feb. 1919 (Durham).

[3] On 3 Apr. 1919, Wingate wrote to Curzon that 'it was soon apparent that racial antagonism between the Sudanese and the Egyptians . . . was far too deep seated to be easily eradicated and it became clear that the gradual introduction of a policy of the "Sudan for the Sudanese" was that best suited to the conditions of the country' (Durham).

to the Sudan.[1] To rebut these attacks and, more importantly, to propagate the case for a separate identity for the Sudanese, the three religious leaders were allowed to launch the first political newspaper in the history of the Sudan. *Ḥadārat al-Sūdān* (or *al-Ḥadāra* for short) had been established as a literary paper by Sayyid Muḥammad al-Khalīfa Sharīf, a nephew of Sayyid 'Abd al-Raḥmān al-Mahdi, in 1919. In its issue of 24 June 1920, however, it was announced that *al-Ḥadāra* had become a political newspaper, jointly owned and directed by Sir Sayyid 'Ali al-Mirghani, Sayyid 'Abd al-Raḥmān al-Mahdi, and Sharīf Yūsif al-Hindi.[2] The Editor of *al-Ḥadāra*, Sayyid Muḥammad al-Khalīfa Sharīf (one of the ablest writers and orators of his day), then published a series of articles under the general title 'The Sudan Question'. The theme of the articles was that Egypt and the Sudan were indeed sister countries held together by many bonds. But each had certain rights and interests which must be respected and rationally maintained without reference to sentimental considerations. For the time being the Sudanese were unable to govern themselves and required outside assistance. This could indeed be provided, after a fashion, by the existing 'condominium' regime. But the 'condominium' was an anomalous and cumbersome arrangement which was also harmful to the Sudanese because it made them a bone of contention between two conflicting forces. The 'condominium' should, therefore, be ended and the country should, instead, be governed by one power. Egypt was no doubt one of the most sophisticated countries in the Orient, but she was still far from capable of governing herself, let alone ruling the Sudan or helping its people. 'We are therefore left with the English. And they are undeniably the most able and efficient of all colonial powers.' They should, therefore, be the guardians of the Sudan. When the Sudanese had learnt to administer their own affairs properly the need for paternal guidance would cease and the Sudan would be for the Sudanese. The same argument was used by Sayyid 'Ali al Mirghani, Sayyid 'Abd al-Raḥmān al-Mahdi, Sharīf Yūsif al-Hindi, Shaikh al-Ṭayyib Hāshim, Shaikh Ismā'īl al-Azhari, and Shaikh Abul-Qāsim Aḥmad Hāshim.[3]

[1] Hasan Najīla, *Malāmiḥ Min al-Mujtama'a al-Sūdāni* (Khartoum, 1959), p. 20.

[2] Ibid., p. 19. Sayyid 'Ali was knighted in 1919 before the return of the delegation to the Sudan.

[3] Their joint letter to Mr. Willis, the Director of Intelligence, dated 11 Feb. 1927 (Archives, Khartoum).

3. *The Revolt of 1924*

Today, 'The Sudan for the Sudanese' is, naturally, taken for granted. But in 1920 (and for the next thirty-five years or so) it was the subject of bitter controversy, both in Egypt, where it was strongly felt that the Sudan was an inseparable part of Egypt, and in the Sudan itself. In so far as the Sudanese were concerned there were two main reasons for doubt and controversy. The first was that most graduates (both of the Gordon College and the Military College) were convinced that 'The Sudan for the Sudanese' was not a genuine nationalist motto, but one inspired by the British in order to exclude the Egyptians from the Sudan and leave Britain a free hand in running the country for her own ends. The very fact that the Sudan Government had allowed the propagation of this view, while suppressing or, at any rate, opposing propaganda for the opposite view, was enough to condemn it in the eyes of the majority of the enlightened sections of the population for some of whom suspicion of everything official or favoured by the Government, was a first principle of sound nationalist thinking.[1]

The second reason for the opposition of the majority of the graduates was that they felt that independence, even if it was sincerely desired by its protagonists, could only be achieved by allying the Sudan with Egypt, which was not only a Muslim and Arabic-speaking neighbour, but one which was also suffering the same experience of alien rule at the hands of British Imperialism. Once the common enemy was expelled, it was argued, Egypt—which was, after all, only a nominal partner in the regime—could easily be persuaded to leave the Sudan for the Sudanese.[2]

Accordingly open propaganda of *al-Ḥaḍāra* for 'co-operation with the British Imperial Idea, with the ultimate object of cultivating a spirit of national unity among the Sudanese'[3] was met by secret, but determined, propaganda for 'The Unity of the Nile Valley'. Thus in November 1920, for example, 'A Faithful Advisor' sent

[1] Aḥmad Khair, *Kifāḥ Jīl* (Cairo, 1948), p. 22.

[2] Interview with Sayyid Ismā'il al-Azhari, Omdurman, August 1960. Also Dirdiri Muḥammad 'Uthmān, *Mudhakkirati*, Khartoum, 1961, p. 50. In 1924 the Department of Intelligence reported that 'the attitude of the Sudanese towards Egyptian politics is subservient to national self interest. The "Unity of the Whole Nile Valley" is at most but a temporary expedient to get rid of the British before turning on the Egyptians' (Archives, Khartoum).

[3] Stack's report (on an interview with the three religious leaders) to Wingate, 23 Feb. 1919 (Durham).

copies of a famous circular letter to hundreds of addresses all over the Sudan. The letter, of which a rather poor translation was sent by Stack to Lord Allenby in Egypt and thence to Britain, where it was circulated to the Cabinet, is a good example of the pro-Egyptian and anti-British feelings of that period. Beginning with a quotation from the Holy Qur'ān ('And hold fast, all of you together to the cable of Allah, and do not separate'), it goes on to say:

. . . The aim of this [British] policy is to create divisions between the different tribes and to gain the help of one against the other. . . . It aims also at creating divisions between the leading religious notables. At one time they draw one nearer to them and send away the other, and at other times they support one with money and imprison the other. . . . They [the English] have expropriated your lands which you possess by legal rights and which have come down to you from your fathers and grandfathers, in order to give them to English companies for their benefit.[1] They deprive you of your liberty and your rights, forcing you to sell your products to their English companies at the lowest prices. . . . They have enslaved the high and the low. . . . They have blocked the way of advancement and education. . . . If the Government were a Mohammedan one, it would not enforce regulations which are against the Mohammedan law. . . . Look at their schools in Khartoum and Omdurman where students are forced to attend the preaching of the Gospel. The Government is also introducing Christianity throughout the Southern Sudan. What more proofs do you wish of their bad institutions than the fact that in Khartoum itself there are six Churches and only one mosque, which has not been completed in twenty years. . . . Now they have started a new policy to create divisions between us and them [our brothers the Egyptians]. For the execution of this policy they have published a paper called 'El-Hadara' in order to serve them to attain aims which are evident to everybody. What we deeply regret, however, in the matter is the utilisation of the names of three religious leaders who are respected throughout the land. God knows that the policy of the paper is enforced on them, but they are obliged to keep quiet owing to the military rule prevailing in the Sudan. My brethren! The English have adopted for a long time the policy of creating dissension between Mohammedans and Copts in Egypt, causing continual intrigue and bringing misery to both. When, however, the two elements appreciated this and united they attained their object and God helped them. Put this before your eyes: unite with your brethren the Egyptians and work for your independence. . . . Your brethren the Egyptians are now working for themselves and for you. If they attain their objects you will be on the same level as they. . . . Do not let the British enslave you for ever, as they had done in their other colonies, which are unable to find a way of escape. You are still outside the net, so do

[1] This is a reference to the Jazīra, where land had been bought at nominal prices for the purpose of establishing the scheme.

not get into it. Consider other countries such as Canada, Australia, New Zealand, South Africa, etc. See how the original inhabitants have been extinct and have been replaced by the English colonisers. . . . Rise and claim independence for Egypt and the Sudan, and may the Almighty grant us victory for our religion and for Islam.[1]

Anonymous articles expressing similar views and sentiments were secretly smuggled into Egypt, where they were published in the daily press. In 1921 various Leagues and Societies were formed in the principal towns of the Sudan. 'To some extent the methods of all secret societies' were used: groups of 'five' were formed, each member heading a subsidiary 'five', each group being intimate within itself but ignorant of and unknown to subsidiary or parallel groups—the whole system being so organized as to ensure an adequate replacement of casualties from arrest.[2] The most influential of these groups, The League of Sudanese Union, was formed in 1922. By concentrating on teachers at the village-school level, the League of Sudanese Union made a substantial contribution to the organization of opposition especially among the young.[2] Through their rapidly increasing circle of contacts the critics of the regime were better able to spread hostile propaganda up and down the country. 'The employee was told he deserved better pay and prospects. The merchant was told that the Traders Tax was an unjust imposition. The English were accused of robbing the peasant to enrich their own companies.'[3] A turning-point was reached in May 1922, when 'Ali 'Abd al-Laṭīf (a Sudanese ex-officer of Dinka origin who had been dismissed from the Army following a personal clash with an English officer, who, he felt, had treated him arrogantly) sent an article entitled 'The Claims of the Sudanese Nation' to the editor of *al-Ḥaḍāra* requesting the publication of the article in the newspaper. Sayyid Muḥammad al-Khalīfa Sharīf (who was greatly respected by his opponents and believed by them to be sincere, though mistaken, in his attachment to the policy of the Sudan for the Sudanese)[4] thought the article was 'very good' but felt that the time had not come for its publication.[5] A few days later both he and 'Ali 'Abd al-Laṭīf were arrested.

[1] Official translation, Milner Papers, Oxford. Extracts from the original letter, written in an elegant Arabic style, have been reproduced in Najīla.

[2] Intelligence Department's Report on 'The History of Politics and Political Agitation in the Sudan, 1919–24' (Archives, Khartoum).

[3] Ibid., appendix 7.

[4] Najīla, pp. 21 and 32.

[5] Extract from the Memoirs of Ahmad Fahmi al-Rayaḥ, first director of *al-Ḥaḍāra*—in Najīla.

After a brief trial the editor of *al-Ḥaḍāra* was discharged, but 'Ali was sentenced to a year's imprisonment. It is interesting to note that, in the words of the Director of Intelligence, 'the document for writing which he was convicted contains no word in favour of Egypt, it advocates the Government of the Sudan by the Sudanese and the ending of foreign rule. In this respect and in view of its inflammatory phraseology the document was actionable.'[1]

On his release from prison during the following year Ali 'Abd al-Laṭīf, as may be expected, was generally acclaimed as a national hero and became the acknowledged leader of the opposition to the British Government of the Sudan. His recent experience moreover convinced him of the necessity of having closer relations with Egypt and finally led him to the formation, in close co-operation with Egyptian officers and officials working in the Sudan, of an organization which, though in some respects identical with the League of Sudanese Union, was much more militant in character. The new organization was called 'The White Flag League' and was formally inaugurated on 20 May 1924.[1]

Four days before the inauguration of the White Flag League the central committee (consisting of 'Ali 'Abd al-Laṭīf and, it is worth noting, one postmaster, Ḥasan Ṣharīf, two postal clerks, Ṣāliḥ 'Abd al-Qādir and Ḥasan Ṣālih, and one ex-postal clerk, 'Ubaid Ḥāj al-Amīn) sent a telegram to the Governor-General protesting that the Sudanese people, for whom they spoke, had not been invited to the forthcoming Anglo-Egyptian negotiations during which the Sudan question, which had been declared a reserved subject in 1922, was to be discussed. In the meantime the Sudan Government, acting through Governors and District Commissioners, had asked certain 'leading natives in the provinces . . . to express their wishes. This signal produced a number of addresses to the Governor General protesting the desire of the signatories and those they represented to remain under British tutelage until such time as they were able to govern themselves.'[1] To counteract this move Sudanese army officers and civilians who were members of the League of Sudanese Union and the White Flag League toured the provinces urging the people not to express a too wholehearted desire for purely British rule or, better still, to throw their weight behind the movement for the unity and independence of the Nile Valley.

[1] Intelligence Report.

Their arguments were mainly to the effect that the English and Egyptians acted as checks on each other and that the idea of 'The Sudan for the Sudanese' would be better served by the continuance of the Condominium than by the sole dominion of either party. Their activities were not without effect on the tone of some of the later addresses presented to the Governor General and led to stories gaining currency in Egypt and in the Sudan as to the methods alleged to have been employed in stimulating pro-British declarations which did much, it must be admitted, to minimize the effect of these declarations.[1]

In addition petitions of loyalty to Egypt were collected by members of the White Flag League, including Muḥammad al-Mahdi, a son of the Khalīfa 'Abdullahi. Furthermore, Muḥammad al-Mahdi and another colleague, acting as a Sudanese 'Wafd' (Delegation), proceeded to Egypt, where they proposed to meet the leaders of the Egyptian Wafd Party and present them with the petitions of loyalty to Egypt which had been collected in the Sudan. But they were arrested at Ḥalfa and sent back to Khartoum. Their arrival in Khartoum on 17 June triggered off the first political 'demonstration' in the history of the Sudan.[1] A series of demonstrations, constantly fed and popularized through anti-British speeches in the mosques, took place during the following weeks. On 4 July 'Ali 'Abd al-Laṭīf was once more arrested and, after another trial, during which he was defended by an Egyptian advocate, was sentenced to three years' imprisonment. The general excitement which followed the trial and imprisonment of 'Ali 'Abd al-Laṭīf induced the cadets of the Military College to joing the growing wave of demonstrations in August. On 9 July they held arms and ammunitions and marched with the Egyptian flag to 'Ali 'Abd al-Laṭīf's house where they presented arms. The performance was afterwards repeated outside the prison where 'Ali and other members of the White Flag League were kept—thus raising the already mounting enthusiasm to a still higher pitch. The cadets (fifty-one in number) were eventually arrested and sent to prison, where further demonstrations finally led to a mutiny of the prisoners. Outside the prison walls, in the meantime, the members of the White Flag League—especially the postal clerks with their numerous telegraphic contacts all over the country—spread the news and the spirit of insurrection throughout the Sudan, as far as Talodi and al-Fashir in the West and Wau and Malakal in the South. The fact that a number of clerks and military officers had been posted to

[1] Intelligence Report.

these distant places 'on account of disloyalty' only served to spread anti-Government feeling and propaganda. The Director of Intelligence subsequently wrote:

This method of dealing with troublesome people by transfer has nothing to commend it. The postal clerk [Ṣālih 'Abd al-Qādir] sent to Port Sudan promptly organized an active branch of the White Flag there. . . . Few things are more striking in a study of the records of sedition in the Sudan from 1922 onwards than the way in which some half dozen individuals have been able to spread disaffection all over the country owing to being transferred on duty from place to place.[1]

However, a far more serious situation was precipitated when, on 19 November, Major-General Sir Lee Stack, the Governor-General of the Sudan and Sirdār of the Egyptian Army (and a personal friend of Lord Allenby, then the British Consul in Egypt) was shot and fatally wounded in Cairo. Allenby promptly, and without previous consultation with the British Government, delivered a strongly worded ultimatum to the Egyptian Government requiring them, among other things to 'order within twenty-four hours the withdrawal from the Sudan of all Egyptian officers and the purely Egyptian units of the Egyptian Army', and to note that 'the Sudan Government will increase the area to be irrigated in the Gezira from 300,000 feddans to an unlimited figure as need may arise. . . . Failing immediate compliance with these demands,' the ultimatum concluded, 'His Majesty's Government will at once take appropriate action to safeguard their interests in Egypt and the Sudan.'[2]

The Egyptian Government under the leadership of Sa'ad Zaghlūl refused to order the withdrawal of her troops from the Sudan. The troops, for their part, refused to obey orders to evacuate the country unless they were issued by the Egyptian Government. In order to demonstrate their solidarity with the Egyptian troops and because, as men and officers of the Egyptian Army, they had taken an oath of allegiance to the Egyptian crown, the Sudanese battalions also mutinied. The mutiny involved various battalions all over the country, including Wau and Talodi. But it was in Khartoum, while on their way to join the Egyptian battalion in Khartoum North on 27 November, that Sudanese troops were involved in a direct clash with British forces who wanted to prevent them from crossing the bridge to

[1] Ibid.

[2] Quoted in J. Marlowe's *Anglo-Egyptian Relations 1800–1953* (London, 1954), pp. 268–9.

Khartoum North. A pitched battle ensued, during which many were killed on both sides and the Khartoum Military Hospital, where some of the mutineers took cover during the night and continued to fight to the last man, was shelled and partly destroyed. Rifa'at Bey, the Commander of the Egyptian battalion in Khartoum North, had promised to open fire on the British troops if they attacked or tried to stop the Sudanese platoons from crossing the bridge to Khartoum North. This promise, however, was not honoured, and orders to evacuate having been issued by a new Government in Cairo, the Egyptians proceeded to evacuate 'without other delay than that imposed by the incompetence of their officers'.[1] The bitter disappointment at thus having been let down by their friends and fellow men-in-arms had a great disillusioning effect on some of the Sudanese officers and civilians who had hitherto been staunch advocates of close co-operation with Egypt.[2] Some, like Sayyid 'Abdalla Khalīl, who until then, as a young officer, had been an active member of the League of Sudanese Union and a close associate of 'Ali 'Abd al-Laṭīf, became staunch protagonists of the opposite view—'The Sudan for the Sudanese'. Sayyid 'Abdallah Khalīl himself eventually became the secretary of the Anṣār-dominated Umma Party, which was hostile to having any form of close association with Egypt.

4. *Challenge and response: the aftermath of the Revolt*

The Revolt of 1924 having collapsed, those of its leaders who were still alive and had not managed to escape were arrested, on 29 November, and brought to trial. Four (on three of whom the sentence was carried out) were condemned to death by firing squad and others were given long terms of imprisonment.

Politically, the reactions of the Government to the mutiny, as has been shown in the previous chapter, were to accelerate the process of mitigating Egypt's influence in the Sudan, though relations between the two countries were not formally severed; to hasten the separation of the Northern from the Southern provinces of the country, making special use in this connection of the Christian missions; and, thirdly, to substitute as far as possible tribal organization for bureaucratic methods, which necessitated the educa-

[1] J. Marlowe, *Anglo-Egyptian Relations 1800–1953* (London, 1954), appendix 11.

[2] Interview with Sayyid 'Abdallah Khalīl, summer 1960; also Aḥmad Khair, p. 28.

tion and training, however limited, of Sudanese people in the administration of the country.

Four years before the outbreak of the mutiny, the Governor of Barbar Province had warned his colleagues, in the Annual Conference of 1920, of the consequences for the British regime in the Sudan of repeating the mistakes made in India and Egypt by creating an educated and, almost by definition, dissatisfied class of Sudanese people.[1] In his final assessment of the political developments which led to the rising of 1924, the Director of Intelligence made similar remarks. 'It must be recognized' he wrote, 'that there is now in the Sudan a class, small but vocal and inevitably possessing influence out of all proportion to its numbers, which has ideas and aspirations whose growth has been "forced" so that they are now at a stage, the attainment of which would have taken a generation of more normal growth. Forced growths from shallow roots', he continued, revealing a somewhat surprising misunderstanding of the nature of Sudanese nationalism, 'cannot result in a healthy plant, but the seed was sown deliberately by the British Administration, which has a peculiar responsibility for its after care.'[2]

The small class of educated Sudanese being regarded in this light, it is not surprising that not a single school was opened during the decade following 1924 except in the three Southern provinces, where the prevention of the growth of a common Sudanese nationalism in accordance with the Government's 'Southern Policy' necessitated the opening of many non-Arabic and non-Muslim schools. The Military College was closed down. The courses for training Sudanese administrators were discontinued. The sending of students to Beirut (as an alternative to Cairo, to which many had fled from the Gordon College,[3] and in order to replace Egyptians by a cadre of Sudanese teachers, officials, etc.), which had been started in 1922, was stopped.

[1] Civ. Sec., 1/9 L.F.I., vol. i, Archives, Khartoum. Mr. Brown's actual words are: 'I think there is now general agreement based on what has happened in India and Egypt . . . [that] . . . we must have a definite policy unless we wish to have the same phenomena repeated in countries like the Sudan, the moment they awaken to some rudiments of national self consciousness. . . . It is . . . our business to strengthen the solid elements in the country, sheikhs, merchants, etc. before the irresponsible body of half-educated officials, students and town riff-raff takes control of the public mind.'

[2] Int. Dept. Report of the History of Politics and Political Agitation in the Sudan, 1919–24 (Archives, Khartoum).

[3] The feelings and attitudes of these young adventurers and their admiring friends in Khartoum are well reflected in their poems, some of which have been published in Najīla's *Malāmiḥ*.

The attitude of the Government towards the educated class became generally hostile, and students who went to the Gordon College during the decade following 1924 retain memories of unusually harsh treatment by their British masters at a time when the cane was an integral part of the teacher's equipment.[1] Mr. Edward 'Atiyah, a young Oxford graduate, who was then appointed to the staff of the Gordon College (which, however, he soon deserted for the Intelligence Department), gives us a telling 'outsider's' impression of the College in those days.

> The British Tutors . . . exercised a kind of military authority, and the discipline they enforced savoured strongly of the barracks. This is why I disliked the Gordon College the moment I walked into it. It was a military not a human institution. It was a Government School in a country where the Government was an alien colonial government. The tutors were members of the Political Service. They were there in the dual capacity of masters and rulers, and the second overshadowed the first. The pupils were expected to show them not the ordinary respect owed by pupils to their teachers, but the submissiveness demanded of a subject. . . . Even if the master was individually kind and human, there stood behind him, in the eyes of his pupils, the Director of Education, the Civil Secretary, the Governor-General, the Union Jack, and the power of the British Government. Behind him there also stood the District Commissioner who ruled their village homes. The master himself, indeed, would one day be a District Commissioner and rule over them and their fathers.[2]

Finding themselves at the mercy of a powerful and hostile Government the nationalists found it expedient to lie low for the time being. The pressure imposed on them by the Government on the one hand, and the dramatic happenings of the recent past on the other, required an effective outlet. Since organized political and, of course, military action were out of the question, the required outlet had to be social and literary in character. The dominant form of literary expression, in the immediate post-1924 period, was the anonymous patriotic poem or song,[3] often containing allusions to Egypt—'the beloved one who had been taken away'—but usually given to the expression of more virile and robust sentiments. That poems should be the chosen vehicle of national feelings in an Arabic-speaking

[1] The joint autobiography of M. A. Maḥjoub and Dr. 'Abd al-Ḥalīm Muḥammad, *Mawt Dūnya* (Khartoum, 1946), pp. 26 and 76; Aḥmad Khair, pp. 33–4. This point was emphasized by all those whom I interviewed in Khartoum during the summer of 1960.

[2] Edward Atiyah, *An Arab tells His Story* (London, 1946), p. 138.

[3] Najīla has collected a number of these in his book.

country, where poetry has traditionally played a social role not unlike that of newspapers in modern society, and where almost everything of public importance, from the opening of a national bank to the celebration of the anniversary of the Prophet's birth, is greeted with a spate of poems, is by no means unusual. The most famous author of such song, as it afterwards became known, was 'Ubaid 'Abd al-Nour, a teacher, who, like Ismā'īl al-Azhari, subsequently the leader of the 'extremist' Ashigga Party and the first Sudanese Prime Minister, had been sent to Lebanon to study at the American University of Beirut—away from Cairo and the infectious nationalism of the Egyptians. The most popular singer of the day, Khalīl Faraḥ, whose memory is still greatly cherished by the Sudanese, did not receive any form of advanced or higher education. This, coupled with the fact that he was educated enough and sensitive enough to read and appreciate some of the classical Arab poets, enabled him to be at home both with the 'graduates' and the multitude. The type of patriotic song which he popularized, half-way between literary and colloquial Arabic in style, was 'designed' primarily to articulate the former to the latter—a function of considerable importance in a predominantly illiterate society. Almost ideally suited to play this part, Khalīl Faraḥ became the singer of patriotic songs *par excellence*. Since most of the hostile references to Britain and the 'loving' allusions to Egypt were allegorically expressed and could be interpreted in more than one way, Faraḥ, it was felt, was personally safe *vis-à-vis* the Intelligence Department. For the same reason, and because it was not easy to trace the origins of popular songs composed in a basically colloquial form of Arabic, the authors remained practically anonymous and equally safe.[1]

Considering its obvious limitations as a means of political education, mobilization, and general advancement of the nationalist movement, it is not surprising that this form of expression soon began to fade into the background, its place being gradually taken by the serious discussion and study group. Having been brought up in an orthodox Muslim society, which traditionally attached great importance to learning, considered it a sacred pursuit, and urged the faithful to 'seek knowledge even if it were in China',[2] the nationalists, especially the young post-1924 generation who considered they had a peculiar responsibility towards the country at that difficult juncture

[1] Najīla, p. 171.
[2] An often-quoted saying of the Prophet.

in its development,[1] came to the conclusion that the failure of 1924 was primarily due to lack of knowledge and general political maturity on the part both of the leaders and the rank and file of the nationalist movement. In order to educate the masses and groom the leaders for the proper execution of their duties, it was necessary that all efforts should, for a while, be directed to learning and serious thinking. Special emphasis had to be given to the study of international politics and the history of other nationalist movements.[2] Above all Sudanese society had to be thoroughly and 'scientifically' studied with a view to establishing close links between the people and the new generation of educated young men.[2] Since this type of education was not provided by any of the existing Government institutions, young men had either to go to Egypt and other Arab countries, or seek to attain cultural maturity by means of personal effort. Provided they were willing to make the necessary effort, their knowledge of the English language enabled them to improve their understanding of the modern world and its thought, while through Arabic, they rediscovered their own roots, developed their national character and formed closer links with like-minded people in Egypt and other parts of the Arab world.[3]

Study groups of earnest young men began to appear almost wherever a 'group of five' of the League of Sudanese Union or the White Flag had previously been convened. It can safely be assumed that there was a somewhat high mortality rate among these study groups once the novelty of the idea had worn off, but many, especially in Omdurman and Wad Madani, survived and in due course produced recognizable types of political and social attitudes which proved important in the development, at a later stage, of national political parties. Judging by the calibre of some of the products of these study circles it is obvious that they were also successful agents of advanced general education. The short-lived but lively journals which

[1] Maḥjoub and 'Abd al-Ḥalīm, pp. 41–2 and 86–8, and MacMichael's Memorandum no. 222 (36/G/1/81) on 'The Attitudes of The Sudanese Towards Egypt' (Khartoum, 10 Sept. 1933, Durham). 'Our generation', wrote the editor of *al Fajr* in 1935, 'is the living articulated position of Young Sudan. We aspire to distinguish ourselves by having an outlook on life political, social and literary. We stand at the cross roads and we shall either follow the right road or go astray' (p. 1019, no. 21, 1 June 1935).

[2] Ahmad Khair, p. 25.

[3] This theme was best developed by Maḥjoub in an interesting lecture on *al-Ḥaraka al-Fikriyya Fi-l-Sūdān* ('The Intellectual Movement in the Sudan') which will be mentioned below. Also Aḥmad Khair, pp. 35–9 and 50–4.

they pioneered, under difficult circumstances, such as *al-Sūdān*, *al-Nahda* (The Renaissance), and, more important, *al-Fajr* (Dawn), 1934–7, testify to the vigour and earnestness of that generation. *al-Fajr*, established and edited by 'Arafāt Muḥammad 'Abdalla, an ex-postal clerk and member of the White Flag League, who was rightly described by the Director of Intelligence as 'very capable',[1] has set a standard of literary journalism in the Sudan which has scarcely been surpassed even today. The poems, short stories, and purely literary materials published in *al-Fajr* were sometimes unconvincing, structurally weak, and infected with a pathetic form of romanticism which, under the circumstances, is perhaps understandable; but with poets like al-Tijāni Yūsif Bashīr and writers like Muḥammad Ahmad Maḥjoub they often reached impressive standards. Foreign affairs—from Sino-Japanese relations, communal strife in India, and European re-armament to T. E. Lawrence and Arab unity, Italian imperialism in the horn of Africa, and Ataturk's exciting victories *vis-à-vis* the West and his saddening policies at home—were eagerly followed and commented upon. Articles were written on Greek mythology, Lord Nuffield and his Morris Works, the nature of living things, the co-operative movement, nationalism and internationalism, Aldous Huxley and Anatole France, Shakespeare and al-Firdawsi, Muḥammed 'Abdu and G. B. Shaw, and a host of Eastern and Western themes and persons. Most of these writings were, naturally at that stage, heavily dependent on second-hand sources in Arabic or on secondary literature in English. Nevertheless, taken as a whole (and some of them were excellent) they clearly demonstrate the determination of that generation to deepen its understanding of Arabic-Muslim culture, to widen the scope of its education as far as available means permitted, and to develop some appreciation of universal thought and literature. This, Maḥjoub said (in a debate on the theme 'Sudanese culture is independent and should be separate from Egyptian culture', which took place in the Graduates' Club at Omdurman and was subsequently reported in *al-Fajr*), was the diet on which a revitalized but distinctly Sudanese nation, firmly based on Islam, Arabic culture, and African soil, should be brought up. As such it would have close friendly relations with the neighbouring Egyptian culture but would be independent from it, it would retain its own distinct character but learn from the culture and thought

[1] Intelligence Department's Report on the History of Politics and Political Agitation in the Sudan, 1919–24 (Archives, Khartoum).

of all other nations both ancient and modern.[1] As one of its most outstanding leaders, Maḥjoub, who alone among the writers of his generation showed a constant and clear-minded concern with the question, made yet another attempt to clarify the goals and character of the nascent literary movement in the Sudan in a remarkable pamphlet, based on a public lecture, which he published in 1941.

The objective towards which the literary movement in this country should be directed is to establish an Islamic-Arabic culture supported and enriched by European thought and aimed at developing a truly national literature which derives its character and its inspiration from the character and traditions of the people of this country, its deserts and jungles, its bright skies and fertile valleys. . . . By giving an increasingly more prominent place to political studies of a kind more directly concerned with our problems and ambitions, this movement should then be transformed from a cultural to a political movement whose final goal should be the achievement of the political, social and cultural independence of this country.[2]

This is indeed the attitude which, consistent with nationalist tenets, eventually prevailed. It had been gradually, but fitfully, gathering momentum since 1924 when many pro-Egyptian Sudanese nationalists, having been bitterly disillusioned by the course of events of that year, either retired from politics altogether, or began to think that the best way of achieving their final objectives was to rely on their own efforts, using whatever help they could get from Egypt but without reliance on the permanent support of any outside forces. In May 1926 the Egyptian Wafd Party, which was greatly admired by the young men of the Sudan as the embodiment of vigorous nationalism, won an overwhelming majority in the elections, but Zaghlul was nevertheless debarred from the premiership, and the Wafd, tamely in the views of Sudanese spectators, accepted the humiliation of forming a coalition government with other groups. Each new disappointment added to the impression that Egypt was but a 'broken reed'.[3] In 1929 moreover an Anglo-Egyptian Nile Waters Agreement was signed which gave the Sudan less than one twenty-second part of Egypt's share, which was (because the Sudanese had

[1] *al-Fajr*, no. 18, 1 Apr. 1935, pp. 857–64; also his rejoinder on correspondence on the subject, in *al-Fajr*, no. 22, 16 June 1935, pp. 1040–5.

[2] *al-Ḥaraka al-Fikriyya Fi-l-Sūdān*: Ilā 'Aina Yajib 'An Tattajih (Khartoum, 1941).

[3] Memorandum on the Attitudes of the Sudanese Towards Egypt, 1905–32 (no. 222/36/6/1/21) Khartoum, 10 Sept. 1932 (Durham).

not been consulted) resented in the Sudan, especially by the Anṣār. By 1932 Egypt seemed finally to have withdrawn and it was officially reported that 'for the last four or five years' Egyptian interest in the Sudan had virtually disappeared.[1] The Sudanese nationalists, for their part, had 'few, if any illusions left concerning Egypt. They would no doubt welcome any development calculated to hasten the day when the destinies of the Sudan would be entrusted to its *jeunesse dorée* . . . but they feel that Egypt, save as a field for intrigue [against Britain], has little of value to offer.'[1] Moreover, many who had visited Egypt (among them Mu'āwiya Muḥammad Nour, a bright young man who had a high reputation as a literary journalist in Lebanon and Egypt, where he was much encouraged and admired by the eminent writer Abbas Mahmoud al-Aqqād, and who was also associated with *al-Fajr* group in the Sudan) had had unpleasant personal experiences there, and were no longer enthusiastic about the Sudan having close political relations with Egypt.[2]

Nevertheless, as long as Britain remained in control of the Sudan and, for reasons of its own, continued to favour the policy of the Sudan for the Sudanese (which for the bulk of the educated Sudanese at that time meant: the Sudan nominally for the Sudanese but actually under British control and without interference from Egypt or the outside world), the call for independence, despite the obvious sincerity and logical consistency of Maḥjoub and his friends, was bound to have a limited appeal outside the circle of the Anṣār and a few educated men. Besides, the educated class as a whole, including Maḥjoub and others who shared his views with regard to the future of the Sudan, had many grievances against the British administration of the Sudan and, for most of them, these, more or less automatically, offset any possible disadvantages of alliance with Egypt. Egypt, after all, was a neighbour and a Muslim-Arab country which, despite its formal independence since 1922 was, like the Sudan, still under the effective (and humiliating) control of British imperialism. It was, therefore, a natural ally against the common enemy; it was, in fact, the only possible ally with whom the Sudanese nationalists could associate themselves with any hope of effecting support.

The grievances which the nationalists held against the regime could not publicly be ventilated in the Sudan at that time, and were only

[1] Ibid.

[2] Political History of the Sudan, 1924–31 (Public Security), Archives, Khartoum.

obliquely referred to in, for example, *al-Ḥaḍāra*, *al-Nahda*, and *al-Fajr*, at any rate until the end of 1934, when a newly appointed Governor-General, considering, amongst other things, the impact of the mounting Nazi–Fascist campaign to woo the colonial peoples of the British and French empires on the growing nationalism of the Sudanese, decided that it was expedient to reduce pressure. In about April of the following year the editor of *al-Fajr* was informed that censorship on journals and newspapers had ceased to exist and that editors could publish whatever they wished on their own responsibility.[1] Accordingly the editorial issue of 1 May 1935, announced that *al-Fajr* was, from then onwards, making 'a called-for departure in objectives and subject matter'. Whereas it had previously been devoted to the arts and literature *al-Fajr* was to be 'mainly concerned with the social and political life of the country'. The editorial (which was entitled 'Our Policy') then continued:

> Obviously we are not entirely satisfied with the present run of things, and we definitely wish to stand for a new order of intelligent reform, and a steady progressive life, along our own lives.... We wish to see the young enlightened generation taking an active part in the affairs of this country, certainly not in the notorious, facile, negative and irresponsible way; but in a truly civic temper and with real responsibility.... We ought to have a share in the moulding of our destinies. This is a task, we are sufficiently aware, that is neither easy nor smooth, nor clear. It needs to be all that. And in this precisely lies our duty, our hope and our policy.[2]

The article then goes on to say that *al-Fajr* did not identify itself with any existing group or class of people—be it religious, political, or social. It was certainly not the mouthpiece of the 'Effendi' (i.e. Sudanese government officials) class but stood 'for the whole people of the Sudan', especially 'the toiling millions of the land'.[2]

[1] Maḥjoub and 'Abd al-Ḥalīm, p. 146. They record that people were so unaccustomed to criticism of the Government and the public expression of nationalist views at that time that some suspected that *al-Fajr* published such articles with the consent, or even the backing, of the Government. Since the Government did not look with disfavour upon the 'Sudan for the Sudanese' as opposed to the Unity of the Nile Valley—a similar position to that of *al-Fajr*—it is not unlikely that there was some truth in the allegation. Aḥmad Khair makes some critical remarks about the *al-Fajr* group for associating with Edward 'Atiyah of the Intelligence Department in social and cultural matters (*Kifāḥ Jīl*, p. 45). Since he was a Unionist, however, his remarks in this connection were probably not impartial.

[2] *al-Fajr*, no. 19, 1 May 1935, pp. 925–6. From this issue onwards the editorial article was always translated into English and published at the back of the journal. The above quoted extract is taken from the published translation.

A month later the Government was reminded of its responsibility for training the Sudanese people for self-government.

We demand the second place in office, next to the senior British officials in order that we might get in direct contact with the difficult problems of the government and have a share in moulding our destiny. . . . The following question may be asked: 'Is not native administration the right basis for self government?' But our answer to that is that native administration is liable to be a failure so long as it is in the hands of the ignorant, whereas we see in it but a counterfeit of the Feudal System. If native administration is to survive, it must be in the hands of the educated generation.[1]

As it was then practised, moreover, native administration based on tribalism had tended to create a form of religious sectarianism which was as pregnant with dangers as was the situation in India. The educated class could not, on principle, be reconciled to it.[1]

The same point was repeated a fortnight later when, under the title 'Give Us Education', the Government was also attacked for the steady reduction of intake at the Gordon College, especially as from 1932, 'because the government offices need no more officials'; for altering the curriculum so that it was now limited to 'a short study of commerce and business correspondence'; and for discontinuing the practice of sending selected teachers to Beirut, which was the only source of higher education for the nation, though 'limited to a certain class'. The article then continues to warn that

once education is started in a country it must be continued and developed; failing this the people will cry and ask for more education, because it becomes to them as essential as food, water and light. Mr. J. H. Oldham, as quoted by Professor Julian Huxley in his book 'African View', says that the fundamental business of Governments in Africa is education. Our Government is surely in favour of such a saying and would not fail to carry out its fundamental business. . . . 'Give us education and leave us alone' is our slogan![2]

5. *The Graduates' Congress: its rise, development, and demise*

Whatever their feelings about the Anglo-Egyptian regime or their views on the tactics and strategy of the nationalist movement, the Sudanese did not, after 1924, attempt to organize themselves on any sort of nation-wide political basis until after 1936. The nearest they came to this during the intervening twelve or thirteen years was in

[1] *al-Fajr*, no. 21, 1 June 1935, p. 1018.
[2] *al-Fajr*, no. 22, 16 June 1935, pp. 1065–6.

1931 when, still in the grip of the Great Depression, the Sudan Government introduced a retrenchments scheme in accordance with which the salaries of the graduates of the Gordon College, who were employed in the Government Departments, were reduced from £8 to £5½ per month—a cut of 30 per cent. But the starting salaries of British and other non-Sudanese officials (all fixed at higher rates than those of Sudanese staff) were not touched by the retrenchments, though salaries above the starting rates were to a lesser extent affected. The students of the Gordon College, feeling that the Government's decision was both severe and unfair, decided to strike in protest. The general effects of the Depression, the fact that the Government was by far the most important employer of 'graduates', and the existence of the extended family system—which meant that many more people were affected by the retrenchments than the graduates themselves and their immediate relations—helped to win the sympathy of the general public for the students' point of view. The graduates for their part suspected that this decision, unfair as it was in their eyes, had not been dictated by purely administrative considerations, but was also aimed at reducing their status as a class *vis-à-vis* the class of tribal shaikhs and chiefs, who were then being built up by the Government as important agents in the execution of its new policy of Native Administration. Since they were the leaders of the nationalist movement, the graduates also felt that the Government's retrenchments scheme was a blow to Sudanese nationalism in general. Thus what started as a relatively minor issue soon became a political question of national importance. Sayyid 'Abd al-Raḥmān al-Mahdi, among others, tried to persuade the students to end the strike and return to their classrooms. But they refused to accept what was, in their view, a defeatist suggestion. A 'committee of ten' was then formed from among the graduates in order to mediate between the Government and the students. Negotiations eventually led to the acceptance of a compromise solution whereby the starting salary of graduates newly appointed in Government Departments was to be £6½ instead of £5½ per month.

While the dispute was still unsettled and negotiations were in progress 'the committee of ten' was viewed by the graduates as their representative body and thus became an important focus of national sentiment. The class of educated Sudanese rediscovered the importance of unity and organized action. But the fact that the final solution accepted by the committee was a compromise solution, coupled with the use by the committee of what appeared to some graduates as 'devious methods' involving the humiliation of 'begging' the Government to change its decision,[1] paved the way for the first serious split within the ranks of the graduates. There is no evidence to suggest that either of the two camps which emerged had any particular political programme or that the split was basically anything more than a clash of personalities which had been augmented by the failure, in the eyes of some graduates, of the committee of ten. But it is known that the Fīlists and the Shawgists—so called after their leaders, Shaikh Aḥmad al-Sayyid al-Fīl and Muḥammad Afandi 'Ali Shawgi—tended to identify themselves with Sayyid 'Ali al-Mirghani and Sayyid 'Abd al-Raḥmān al-Mahdi respectively. This, apart from its obvious sectarian significance, implied a certain division over the question of co-operation with Egypt and Britain. But no proper parties were established and no political programmes were formulated. Matters were simply allowed to drift and get lost in the cross currents of endless rivalry and competition between the Ṭariqās. As has already been suggested, however, some graduates—mostly from among those who left the Gordon College after 1924 (the so-called post-1924 generation) turned their backs on the sterile feuds of these factions, and coalesced around one or other of the journals that appeared in the early and mid thirties and continued to attack sectarianism and division, concentrating their efforts on advocating the cause of national unity. From the point of view of direct and organized political action, however, the period from 1924 to 1936 was mainly sterile. The bulk of the older generation had either been disillusioned by the turn of events in 1924 or subsequently cowed by the Government's reactions to the mutiny. The younger generation was still fumbling in its attempts to restore confidence and give an effective lead to the masses. The Government was, as yet, not prepared to allow an adequate measure of freedom of expression and political action except to the leaders of Ṭariqās and favourable opinion. But these only helped to split the graduates and reduce their already limited chances of effective action. Finally, the international scene—though becoming increasingly pregnant with possibilities for growing national movements—had not yet had any direct effect on the local conditions of the Sudan.

[1] Maḥjoub and 'Abd al-Ḥalīm, pp. 108–10; also Aḥmad Khair, *Kifāḥ Jīl*, p. 42. Formal expressions such as 'we beg to' and 'your obedient servant', when translated into Arabic, do sound somewhat submissive.

The turning-point was the signing of the Anglo-Egyptian Treaty of 1936. The negotiations which led to the conclusion of the Treaty were keenly followed by the politically conscious public in the Sudan. The resultant Treaty however was disappointing both to the pro-Egyptian Sudanese and to their opponents. The former were dismayed to see the Egyptian (Wafd) Government endorse the Agreement of 1899 and publicly announce their approval of the existing regime in the Sudan. Still more disappointing to them was the fact that Egypt—far from behaving like an ally against the common British enemy—was only too pleased to be re-admitted as a nominal co-ruler of the Sudan and, to that end, sent a token force to be stationed there.[1] The protagonists of the Sudan for the Sudanese, especially the Anṣār, were perturbed by the fact that, according to the provisions of the Treaty, the all-important question of sovereignty over the Sudan was to be shelved for twenty years. For the Anṣār and their political allies this implied that Egypt could—in theory at any rate—still claim to be legally sovereign over the Sudan. Hoping to obtain the reassurance of the British Government on this question Sayyid 'Abd al-Raḥmān al-Mahdi made another journey to London, but did not get a satisfactory response.[2] For the politically conscious Sudanese in general, irrespective of political or sectarian considerations, the 1936 Treaty appeared offensive not only because they had not been consulted—a fact which was greatly resented—but also because the only reference made to the future of the Sudan and its people in the Treaty was that 'the primary aim of the administration in the country must be the welfare of the Sudanese'. In the eyes of the nationalists this was a most obtuse affront because it appeared to treat them as less than human and certainly not as responsible adults.[3]

These feelings of resentment and discontent however were mixed with a certain delight in the relative freedom and increased opportunities which followed the restoration of Egypt's position in the country

[1] Aḥmad Khair, pp. 46–50 and 72.

[2] 'Abd al Raḥmān 'Ali Ṭāha, *al-Sūdān Li-l-Sūdāniyyīn*, p. 30. The author who was a confidant of Sayyid 'Abd al Raḥmān says that when the Sayyid questioned the British Government about sovereignty he received the usual evasive answers: 'sovereignty over the Sudan is represented by the two flags' and 'it is described in the Condominium Agreement'.

[3] In the summer of 1960 I interviewed about twelve outstanding Sudanese political leaders representing different shades of opinion. They invariably singled out this clause for special condemnation. The notion that 'animals may aspire to, and be content with, so-called welfare, but free men will not be satisfied with less than freedom' was uniformly expressed by almost every one of them.

and the return of the old competition between Egypt and the British Sudan Government to win the sympathy and support of the Sudanese. Thus commenting on the fraternization which took place between the Egyptians and the Sudanese during the first year of the 'New Era', the Director of Intelligence wrote:

The Egyptians (chiefly in the persons of Nahas and Omer Toussoun) have seized every opportunity not only for entertaining, but for honouring and flattering the Sudanese in a manner which, in English eyes at least, must seem crudely fulsome. I refer particularly to the treatment accorded to the party sent to Cairo to attend King Farouk's Accession celebrations, and more still to the entertainment by the Egyptian Government of the London Coronation party on their way back through Egypt. . . .

The Director's assessment of the situation and his further comments on it are interesting:

Our surest way of nullifying any harm that might be done by this Egyptian flattery of the Sudanese is to give the Sudanese frequent opportunities of visiting and forming contacts with England. In Egypt the Sudanese are overwhelmed with flattery, but they see very little in Egyptian life that impresses them. They enjoy themselves; some of them may even have their heads turned; they may feel really grateful to their hosts; and one or two may get excited over 'the common bonds of religion and language'. But I have not yet seen a single Sudanese return from Egypt with anything like admiration of the Egyptians, or a desire to emulate them.

With regard to England, it is quite different. The results of the Coronation party's visit to England were most gratifying. The members of this party were profoundly impressed by England and the English people; they were impressed not only by the outward manifestations of material progress, but also, and more deeply, by the moral qualities which they were able to see behind this progress. They came back feeling both grateful for what had been done for them, and convinced that they had a lot to learn from the English people. . . . This, of course, should not blind us to the generally still considerable pull of Egyptian influence over the Sudanese, but it would seem that in this genuine appreciation shown by the Sudanese visitors to England this summer, of the values of English life and culture, we have a new force which, if skilfully developed and canalised, might exercise a powerful check on the hitherto unchallenged operation of Egyptian influence.[1]

Being fully aware of the advantages of the new situation, the Sudanese tried, with varying degrees of subtlety and success, to play off Egypt and the Sudan Government against one another. Thus in a

[1] Sudan Monthly Intelligence Summary, no. 43, August 1937, Appendix (*b*), Notes on the Near East (Archives, Khartoum).

leading article dated 19 October 1937, and headed 'The Need for Sending Educational Missions Abroad', the Acting Editor of *al-Sūdān* eulogized the Egyptian Government for accepting forty-four Sudanese students free in its schools and then went on to say that the Sudanese hoped that England, as the other partner in the dual administration, would do something similar for the Sudan. The Gordon College was no doubt a useful institution but unless Sudanese students were given a chance of receiving higher education in England itself their theoretical priority for Government employment given them in the Treaty would not be realized.

In its issue of 5 October 1937, *al-Nīl* carried an article pointing out that 'England has already raised several monuments in the Sudan . . . The Gordon College, the Kitchener Medical School, the Stack Laboratories . . . from all of which a large number of trained Sudanese leave every year to serve the country'. Egypt, of course, had done a lot, but mostly of a general and transient nature. 'The Egyptians should also raise in the Sudan a permanent visible monument; a Farouk Institute, a Nahas College, a Toussoun Orphanage.'[1]

Under these conditions of more or less open rivalry between Egypt and the Sudan Government (and at a time when the axis powers were intensifying their efforts to woo the Muslim subjects of the British Empire) it was natural that the British administration of the Sudan should change some of its established practices. In the field of education for instance flogging was abolished—a 'reform' which was warmly commended by *al-Nīl* in an article headed 'A New Spirit in Education'.[1] More important, the Gordon College, which had so far been a secondary school, was—on the recommendation of the De La Warr Commission on Education in the Sudan and of 'Ali Bey al-Jārim's report on the teaching of Arabic and the training of Arabic teachers in the Sudan[2]—transformed into a group of 'higher schools' which, among other things, taught law for the first time in the Sudan. Elementary education was expanded and the intermediate and secondary system was improved. The publication of the three Local Government (Municipalities, Townships, and Rural Areas) Ordinances, 1937, showed that Native Administration was no longer the dogma that it had become since 1924. The creation

[1] Quoted in Sudan Monthly Intelligence Summary, no. 45, October 1947 (Archives, Khartoum).

[2] The reports of 'Ali Bey al-Jārim (of the Egyptian Ministry of Education) and of the De La Warr Commission were published on 29 Dec. 1937.

of the post of Assistant District Commissioner especially for the Sudanese showed (though the A.D.C. was strictly an executive officer who did not share in the political duties of his seniors) that the Government was, slowly, beginning to move from traditional 'paternalism' to the more flexible and fashionable idea of 'partnership' in colonial rule.

But these improvements, significant though they might have been when viewed against the background of the previous thirteen years, fell far short of the growing expectations of the forward looking nationalists. As might have been expected they were impressed, not so much by what had been done, but by what had not been done. Particularly shocking in their view was the fact that far from changing its policies in the Southern provinces, the Government openly declared that its aim was to create two entities in the Sudan: one Northern, the other Southern.[1] In the eyes of the nationalists furthermore, the necessarily limited gains which accrued to them were merely the windfall of Anglo-Egyptian (or Anglo-Nazi) rivalry, and though they were no doubt willing and determined to use to the full those opportunities which were thereby bestowed upon them, the nationalists were equally convinced that their ultimate salvation lay in their own hands, and that they needed to organize themselves to achieve that end.[2]

[1] 'Note on Administrative Purposes in the Anglo-Egyptian Sudan', Appendix IV to the Annual Report of 1937 (Sudan, no. 1 (1938), Cmd. 5895). For Sudanese reactions: Maḥjoub and 'Abd al-Ḥalīm, pp. 152–3. The editor of *al-Sūdān* published an article, on 25 Dec. 1936, headed 'Religious Freedom; The Necessity of Removing the Restrictions on Islam in the Southern Sudan', which strongly criticized the Government for subsidizing the Christian missions in the Southern provinces while putting restrictions on the propagation of Islam in that part of the country. The article was widely publicized by the Egyptian press and, for a while, created a considerable wave of agitation, especially on the part of students of al-Azhar University in Cairo.

[2] Summing up Sudanese reactions to the return of Egyptian troops to the Sudan in 1937, the Director of Intelligence wrote: 'The masses were mildly excited over an unusual event, involving what is always popular with the crowd, a military display. The *mualledin* [i.e. Egypto-Sudanese] expressed a natural sentimental pleasure. Retail merchants and petty tradesmen welcomed the troops as a new source of revenues, but the intelligentsia were, on the whole, unsympathetic. Many of them, particularly the young intellectuals, looked upon the returning troops as another *alien* army of occupation, whose arrival stressed the subjection of the Sudanese to foreign dominion. The explanation of this attitude is that Sudanese nationalism has really divorced itself from Egypt and developed an autonomous identity of its own. 'We are pleased', say the intelligentsia leaders, 'that England and Egypt have become friends, and above all that they have pledged themselves to work together for the good of the Sudanese. If we welcome the Egyptian troops, it is because their return symbolises the new era from which we hope to get certain benefits, and not because we regard it as in itself an occasion

Accordingly a number of suggestions, all aimed at the creation of some national body which would act as a spokesman for the Sudanese people were put forward during 1937—each version reflecting the attitudes of a particular brand of political opinion in the country. Thus Sayyid 'Abd al-Raḥmān al-Mahdi, arguing that Egyptian propaganda was turning the heads of the Sudanese and that it was, therefore, imperative that something should be done to preserve the separate political identity of the Sudan, suggested that an Advisory Council of representative Sudanese should be established in order to define the position and aspirations of the Sudanese under the new regime.[1] In a leading article entitled 'The Enlightened Class and the Prosperity of the Sudan', which appeared in the issue of 16 August, the editor of *al-Fajr* said that the 1936 Treaty left the Sudan in the same state of poverty and misery that resulted from the Condominium Agreement. In spite of British assurances that they would take every opportunity of promoting the welfare of the Sudanese, and in spite of the Egyptians' delight that they and the Sudanese would one day govern the Nile Valley together, the position of the Sudanese was still unsatisfactory and could not be improved unless the needs and demands of the Sudanese were ascertained. This could only be done through the enlightened class. The editorial then appealed to all graduates to join the Sudan Schools Club (i.e. the Graduates' Club, Omdurman), call a graduates' congress, and form a united front for the formulation and enforcement of a progressive programme. 'Thus the natural guardians of the interests of the Sudanese will form a united, authoritative body and will be the link between the Government and the people.' It was correctly understood in Government circles that the object of *al-Fajr* and the class for whom it spoke was '*inter alia*, to oppose to Sayed Abdel Rahman an organised and independent body of graduates as leaders and representatives of the Sudanese people'.[2] A few weeks later Sharīf Yūsif al-Hindi suggested a compromise. He proposed that 'a council should

for Sudanese national rejoicing' (Sudan Monthly Intelligence Summary, no. 47, December 1937, para. 1180, Archives, Khartoum).

[1] Sudan Monthly Intelligence Summary, no. 43, August 1937, para. 1059 (Archives, Khartoum).

[2] Ibid. The Club had previously declined to accept an offer of financial help which had been made by Sayyid 'Abd al-Raḥmān al-Mahdi. And rather than lose their independence by accepting such offers the promoters of *al-Fajr* (Maḥjoub and 'Abd al-Ḥalīm, after the death of 'Arafāt) preferred to run their journal at a loss met from their own private pockets and then chose to close down altogether towards the end of 1937.

be formed of ten persons, including the two Sayeds, the Mufti, Sheikh el-'Ulema, and six members to be elected by the graduates, to co-operate with the British government in working for the good of the country both internally and outside the Sudan, especially with Egypt, whose assistance we expect'.[1] In the meantime, however, the graduates, 'particularly members of the Sudan Schools Club, Omdurman, led by Ismail El Azhari and Makki Shibeika' (both graduates of the American University of Beirut and, at the time, teachers at the Gordon College) were actively pursuing their own independent path.[1] The upshot of their collective efforts and deliberations was the foundation of the Graduates' General Congress in February, 1938.[2] The name of the new organization, as may be expected, was inspired by the example of the Indian Congress.[3] The question whether the Congress, representing all the 'graduates' of Sudanese schools (the great majority of whom were Government employees) should, like its Indian model, begin by acting as a kind of officials' trade union and then move into politics, or whether it should, from the start, assume the role of a national representative body speaking for the whole nation, was the subject of prolonged discussions among the founder members.[4] It was finally agreed that the object of the Congress, as stated in its constitution, was 'to serve the public interest of the country and of the graduates'. The vagueness of the formula (which it is difficult not to think was deliberate) was necessary not only to guarantee the unity and solidarity of the graduates in supporting their new organization, but also in order to ensure the approval of the Government, whose attitude in the meantime was aptly described as one of being 'on the fence . . . by no

[1] Ibid.

[2] The idea of a Graduates' General Congress was first explicitly formulated by the Wad Madani literary society, one of the study groups which flourished in the twenties and thirties (Aḥmad Khair, p. 59, and Maḥjoub and 'Abd al-Ḥalīm, pp. 159–60 and 174–5; also Aḥmad Khair, p. 59). It is generally agreed that Aḥmad Khair was the first to make the suggestion.

[3] In 1931 the Intelligence Department reported: 'There is no doubt that especially the younger element of the intelligentsia have a great admiration and sympathy for Gandhi, and that when the movement in India was at its height, they followed the news with keen interest. In private assemblies they discussed the efficiency of the boycott weapon and agreed that Gandhi had discovered in it the only weapon which the poor and ignorant East could employ effectively against imperialism. The influence of Gandhi and Indian politics can be unmistakably seen in the Gordon College strike (of 1931) and attempted boycott of sugar by pupils' (Political History of Sudan 1924 to 1931, Archives, Khartoum).

[4] Ibid., pp. 60–1, and Sudan Monthly Intelligence Summary, no. 47, December 1937 (Archives, Khartoum).

means hostile, but not too sympathetic'.[1] Eligibility for membership of the Congress was likewise defined in a flexible manner. It was agreed that any former pupil of Sudanese schools above the elementary level was entitled to join while 'Sudanese educated elsewhere' could, with the approval of the Executive Committee, also be admitted.[2] Viewing themselves as an embryonic Sudanese Parliament the founders of Congress also agreed that a Council of sixty—later divided into specialist committees on the model of parliamentary committees—should be elected, by means of secret ballot, at an annual general meeting of the graduates. The Council was then to elect, from among its own members, an Executive Committee of fifteen who, like a cabinet, would be accountable to the Council and the annual general meeting. The first Council and Committee were elected, on non-sectarian basis, in February 1938. On 12 March they notified their proposed constitution to the Provinces Authorities, and in May this was followed by a letter to the Civil Secretary asking that 'in matters of public interest involving the Government or lying within the scope of its policy and concern the Government should give due consideration to the views and suggestions which we may submit from time to time'.[3] The Government accepted this on the understanding that the Congress should regard itself as 'a semi-public organisation interested in philanthropic and public affairs and competent to hold and express opinions on such matters as come within its purview' and not seek formal recognition as a political body or claim to represent the views of any but its own members.[3] The difference between Government and Congress over the proper role of the latter in Sudanese affairs which was thus made explicit was to become increasingly greater in the days ahead. For the time being however relations between them went on more or less smoothly. Congress submitted two memoranda, one on the expansion of education, the other on the reform of the Institute of Islamic studies

[1] Sudan Monthly Intelligence Summary, no. 46, November 1937.

[2] It is interesting to compare the ways in which Aḥmad Khair and K. D. D. Henderson regard this point. While the former suggests that the qualifactory position was deliberately introduced in order to suit the nationalist strategy of the Congress (i.e. enlisting wide support among the Sudanese), Henderson says that membership was 'confined' to former pupils of schools above elementary standard, 'but there was an unfortunate proviso allowing the committee to admit "Sudanese educated elsewhere" which left a loop-hole for subsequent manipulation of the electoral roll' (*Kifāḥ Jīl*, p. 65, and *The Making of the Modern Sudan*, p. 536).

[3] Quoted in Henderson, pp. 536–7.

(al-M'ahad al-'ilmi) at Omdurman. Both were welcomed by the Government and, for a while, there was even a show of friendship between Government and Congress. A third note, on the leave regulations of Government officials, was, however, considered by the Government to constitute an unwarranted interference in what she regarded as her own business. A further clash was thereby precipitated.

When the war broke out the Graduates' Congress declared its support for the cause of democracy versus the axis powers, but later declined to accept the Government's invitation to lead the campaign for the conscription of Sudanese in the Sudan Defence Force. When the Omdurman broadcasting station was established in 1940, Congress accepted the Government's invitation to participate in its management and, after some wrangling, involving a boycott of the station, members were allowed in 1942 to broadcast certain news items in the name of Congress.[1]

Encouraged by its successes and increasing popularity[2] on the one hand, and by the Atlantic Charter and the Sudan Government's decision to send Sudanese troops to Libya on the other, the Congress decided—on the occasion of a short visit to the country by Sir Stafford Cripps on his way back from India—to submit, on behalf of the Sudanese people, a Memorandum making the following demands:

1. The issue, on the first possible opportunity, by the British and Egyptian governments, of a joint declaration granting the Sudan, in its geographical boundaries, the right of self-determination, directly after this war; this right to be safeguarded by guarantees assuring full liberty of expression in connection therewith; as well as guarantees assuring the Sudanese the right of determining their natural rights with Egypt in a special agreement between the Egyptian and Sudanese nations.
2. The formation of a representative body of Sudanese to approve the Budget and the Ordinances.

[1] Henderson, pp. 537–8 and Khair, pp. 65–6.

[2] Henderson and Khair are agreed that the number of subscribing members reached a record figure in 1942. But, whereas Henderson says that it was then 1,390 (p. 538), Khair says that membership, the same year, rose from 1,400 to 5,280 (p. 79).

3. The formation of a Higher Educational Council, in which Sudanese would constitute a majority, and the devoting of a minimum of 12 per cent of the Budget to education.
4. The separation of the Judiciary from the Executive.
5. The abolition of ordinances on 'Closed Districts' and the lifting of restrictions placed on trade and on the movements of the Sudanese within the Sudan.
6. The promulgation of legislation defining Sudanese nationality.
7. The stopping of immigration, except within the limits agreed upon in the Anglo-Egyptian Treaty.
8. The termination of the Sudan Plantations Syndicate contract at its expiration.
9. The carrying out of the principle of the welfare of the Sudanese and their prior claim to government posts as follows:
   (*a*) By giving the Sudanese an opportunity to share effectively in ruling the country; this is to be attained by the appointment of Sudanese in posts of political responsibility in all the main branches of the Government.
   (*b*) By limiting the appointments to government posts to Sudanese.

   As regards posts for which it is necessary to appoint non-Sudanese, they shall be filled with persons serving on definite term contracts; in the meantime Sudanese to be trained to fill the posts at the expiration of the contract.
10. The Sudanese to be enabled to exploit the commercial, agricultural, and industrial resources of the country.
11. The promulgation of an Ordinance imposing on companies and commercial firms the obligation of reserving a reasonable proportion of their posts for the Sudanese.
12. The cancellation of subventions to missionary schools and the unification of syllabuses in the Northern and Southern Sudan.

On 16 April the Civil Secretary, Sir Douglas Newbold, discussed the matter with Sir Stafford Cripps: 'I told him about our difficulties, Congress manifesto etc. He said we must have a Sudanese Advisory Council and not wait on events.'[1] Sir Stafford Cripps's suggestion was accepted and the Advisory Council which was accordingly established in 1943 will form the subject of the next chapter. In handling

[1] Quoted in Henderson, p. 542.

the present situation the Civil Secretary chose to return the Memorandum to the President of Congress together with a stiff letter in which he was told that

in claiming to represent all the Sudanese and in attempting to turn itself into a political national body, the Graduates' Congress not only could not retain the co-operation of Government but could not hope for continuance of recognition. By the very act of submitting the Memorandum which is the subject of this letter, and by its wording, the Congress has fallen into both these errors against which I warned it and has accordingly forfeited the confidence of Government. There can be no restoration of that confidence until the Congress has so re-organized the direction of its affairs that the Government can rely on having its wishes respected and its warnings observed.

For the above reasons His Excellency [the Governor-General] finds himself unable to accept your Memorandum which is, therefore, returned to you herewith.

His Excellency desires me to add that he and his advisors are fully aware of the needs of the Sudan and of the natural and legitimate desire of the enlightened Sudanese for an increasing participation in the Government and development of their country. To this end the Sudan Government is constantly studying and carrying out plans for the closer association of the Sudanese with the direction of their affairs and for the general welfare and orderly development of this country and its people.

The Congress, however, must realise that it is the duty and business of the Sudan Government alone, having paramount regard to its tutelary obligations to the people of the Sudan, and in consultation if need be with the Governments of the two partners in the Condominium, to decide the pace at which this association and this development shall proceed. It is the earnest wish of the Government that the educated classes of the country should show themselves fitted and able to take their proper share in the administration of internal affairs, but any advance to such a position must be most seriously embarrassed and delayed unless the Congress realise clearly once and for all that the Government must and will insist that the Congress confine itself to the internal and domestic affairs of the Sudan and renounce any claim, real or implied, to be the mouthpiece of the whole country.[1]

This sharp rebuff, together with the 'individual consultations' which the Civil Secretary subsequently held with certain members of the Congress, precipitated a major crisis in the Congress between (*a*) those of its members (habitually referred to as 'reasonable' men—a term of abuse in the jargon of their opponents, who were, in their turn, dubbed 'hotheads', 'extremists', etc.) who wanted to come to

1 Arabic text in Khair, appendix III; English text in Henderson, pp. 542–3.

terms with the Government and co-operate with it, and who, generally, stood for the independence of the Sudan—from Egypt as well as from Britain, but through co-operation with Britain; and (*b*) those who felt that to mistrust the Sudan Government was the first principle of sound nationalism,[1] preferred co-operation with Egypt as against Britain, and, generally, favoured the cause of the Unity of the Nile Valley. This difference of opinion (as indicated in the preceding pages) was deep rooted, and had in fact dominated Sudanese politics since the early twenties. It was enhanced by the clash of personalities which played such an important part in the splits of 1931, from the after-effects of which the older graduates, at any rate, had never completely recovered. The internal difficulties of the Congress were made greater still by the fact that, from its inception, it had been subjected to heavy pressure by the two major Ṭariqās—al-Anṣār and al-Khatmiyya—each of which tried to control the new organization and use it for its own ends and against the other. The establishment of the Graduates' Congress, of course, had in itself been a victory for the new nationalism of the young, post-1924, generation which wanted to break away from the authority of the Ṭariqās and create a non-sectarian nationalist movement in the country. To this end, and in order to forge strong links between itself and the people, the Congress had launched a number of popular projects—notably the Education Day—for which nation-wide support was mobilized in the name of the Congress and the Sudan. Slowly but surely the Congress began to emerge as a new focus of nationalist sentiment. It was particularly popular amongst the literate and 'de-tribalized' sections of the population in the towns and the larger villages. But in 1942 the Sudan as a whole, including the majority of the townspeople, was very much under the influence of the Ṭariqās. Indeed many graduates, including some of the most eminent members of the Congress itself, openly showed allegiance to the Ṭariqās. To these graduates however the attraction of the Ṭariqās was not wholly religious or mystical in character. For, since the Ṭariqās still held the allegiance of vast sectors of the population and were themselves divided over the question of Independence versus the Unity of the Nile Valley, it was obvious that they could either be used or be co-operated with, in the furtherance of particular views with regard to the future of the Sudan. For reasons which have already been discussed the Anṣār were, of course, committed to the cause of

[1] Aḥmad Khair, p. 22.

the Sudan for the Sudanese. The same objective was, in principle, also accepted by the Khatmiyya, and Sayyid 'Ali al-Mirghani and Sayyid 'Abd al-Raḥmān al-Mahdi had identical views on the matters, at least until after their return from London in 1919.[1] However, the rise in power and prestige of Sayyid 'Abd al-Raḥmān al-Mahdi in subsequent years[2]—especially from 1924 onwards—gradually estranged the two leaders from one another. And when rumours began to spread that Sayyid 'Abd al-Raḥmān aspired to the position of crowned monarch[3] over the Sudan (and they were not immediately denied by Sayyid 'Abd al-Raḥmān) it was natural that Sayyid 'Ali, who had had to live as a refugee in Egypt during the Mahdiyya, and his followers, who had suffered persecution under the Mahdist regime, should oppose the call for independence and seek, instead, some form of union with Egypt.[4]

Thus motivated by strong traditional rivalry on the one hand, and the desire to win the greatest possible support for their political programmes on the other, the two Ṭariqās were only too willing to support those members of the Congress who subscribed to their respective views. By 1942 sectarian-political differences within the ranks of the graduates had assumed such proportions that it had

[1] Above, pp. 98 ff.

[2] Above, pp. 99 ff. Sayyid 'Ali al-Mirghani was created a C.M.G. in 1900, awarded a K.C.M.G. in 1916, and further honoured with a K.C.V.G. in 1919. In 1926 an Honorary K.B.E. was conferred upon Sayyid 'Abd al-Raḥmān al-Mahdi.

[3] In an interview on 15 Apr. 1967 Sayyid 'Ali al-Mirghani stated that several attempts had been made to persuade him to accept the position of a monarch in the Sudan but that, for many reasons, he had himself rejected the offer and opposed its implementation by 'others'. After all, he pointed out, kingship cannot be *given* to anyone; and if it were it wouldn't be a genuine kingship: instead the 'king' in question would merely become the 'cats-paw' of those who installed him in office.

[4] When the Khatmiyya-dominated National Front was formed in 1949 its object was defined as 'Dominion status under the Egyptian crown with the right to secede'. It is interesting to note in this connection that the formation of the Umma Party in February 1945, with the supposed object of imposing a Mahdist kingship on an independent Sudan, was seen by the Governor-General to have had 'the double effect of driving many moderates into the Ashigga camp and of assuring wholehearted Khatmia support for the Ashigga. As a counter-blast to kingship the Congress Committee of sixty [took] a snap decision to announce that their policy was to be union of the Sudan with Egypt under the Egyptian crown' (*Annual Report* for 1945, Sudan, no. 1 (1948), Cmd. 7316, p. 139). As we shall see in Chapter VIII, Sayyid 'Abd al-Raḥmān's public declaration, in 1953, that he was not interested in monarchy, but favoured the establishment of a democratic republican regime in the Sudan, was an important factor in facilitating the country's progress to independence.

become normal practice to contest elections to the Council of Sixty and the Executive Committee on sectarian, as well as political grounds. Given the tensions which had been built into the political life of the Sudan by the Anglo-Egyptian Agreement and the internal peculiarities of the country, it was inevitable that this should be so and that the Graduates' General Congress, unlike its Indian model, should, therefore, begin to disintegrate before it was five years old. Considered in the light of this, the Civil Secretary's rebuff and subsequent consultations with individual members of the Congress appear to be no more than the *coup de grâce* which occasioned the final split between (*a*) those who subsequently formed the Independence Front under the leadership of the Umma (meaning 'nation'—with strong Islamic overtones) Party which, established in February 1945, was supported by the Anṣār, and (*b*) the Unionists, of whom the most important was the Ashigga (or 'brothers'—literally brothers by the same mother and father) Party which, established in 1943, was led by Ismāil al-Azhari and, for many years, enjoyed the support of the Khatmiyya.

* * * * * *

It is not necessary to trace here the development of these two groups or of the other numerous parties and factions that were formed after the break-up of the Graduates' Congress; some were splinter groups with a handful of members, who (while continuing to uphold the same objectives) broke from other factions for personal reasons, but (like the rest) were in effect satellites of one or other of the two main groups. It is important to note however that whereas the Umma Party, operating under the patronage of Sayyid 'Abd al-Raḥmān al-Mahdi, continued to be supported by the Anṣār, the alliance of the Ashigga and the Khatmiyya was of a more fragile and tentative nature. On several occasions—beginning in 1949, when the Khatmiyya formed the National Front which stood for dominion status with Egypt while the Ashigga continued to advocate the Unity of the Nile Valley under the Egyptian crown—it broke down and gave way to open rivalry and hostility. The nearest parallel to this in the pre-Independence history of the opposite camp occurred in 1951 when—at the prompting of the Government for reasons which will be discussed below[1]—a group of tribal leaders broke away from the Independence Front and, though without a socialist programme

[1] Below, pp. 187 and 218.

of any sort, formed the Socialist Republican Party which, during its short life, was bitterly hostile to the Umma Party, accusing it of harbouring secret plans for imposing a Mahdist monarchy on the country. In the meantime the most important development was the emergence of the Southern Sudanese, who after 1947 made their debut in national politics, finally emancipated from the restrictions of 'Southern Policy', though still suffering from its effects. As may be expected, they were primarily concerned with regional interests and—like the people of the Northern region in Nigeria—came to oppose self-government and independence until 'backward areas . . . which had been neglected in the past fifty years . . . reached the standard of the North in civilization'.[1] Meanwhile Sudanese students in Egypt, hundreds of whom had been sent under the auspices of the Congress and the Ashigga, were being exposed to wider and more diverse influences. This experience, coupled with the sense of frustrated nationalism which they (in common with their compatriots back home) felt in the difficult years following the war, stimulated the appearance among them of ideas and groupings which, consciously at any rate, were based, not so much on interest, whether of religious or traditional allegiance—though this continued to be important—but on ideology and questions of general principle. The result was the birth of the Sudanese Communist Party in 1946 followed, shortly afterwards, by the Muslim Brotherhood of the Sudan.[2]

[1] Sayyid Benjamin Lwoki in the debate on self-government which took place in the Legislative Assembly in December 1950 (*Proceedings of the First Assembly*, second session, no. 14, 6–16 Dec. 1950, p. 610).

[2] It is interesting to note that the great majority of Sudanese communists and left-wingers are of non-Mahdist, mainly Khatmiyya, background. This may, in part, be due to the fact that whereas the Mahdists—mostly concentrated in the Western Sudan and the Jazīra area—have a more rigid system of religious allegiance and are almost impervious to outside influence, the Khatmiyya and other non-Mahdists, who are dominant in the Northern Province and the Eastern Sudan—and, especially, in the towns—are less tightly organized and have greater contact with the outside world. It is also partly due to the fact that the non-Mahdists, especially the Khatmiyya, have historically regarded the dominant Mahdists in a way similar to that in which the Shī'a and non-Muslim minorities have regarded the Sunni Muslim majorities in Syria and Iraq—and just as these (and other religious and racial) minorities have provided the Syrian and Iraqi communist and left-wing parties with the bulk of their following so have the Khatmiyya and other non-Mahdists in the Sudan. In this connection it is also interesting to note that, though the Sudanese Communist Party has in the past allied itself with the Umma Party, a more enduring and by far more effective tactical alliance has been with the Khatmiyya after the Revolution of October 1964. By contrast, the Muslim Brotherhood—though seeking to transcend the traditional divisions of the Ṭariqās and, as an Islamic movement, having followers of both Khatmiyya and Mahdist

Both were destined to play fairly important parts in the history of the independent Sudan, but neither was of considerable political weight before 1956. Until that time the main preoccupation of politically conscious Sudanese continued to be with the ways and means by which the Anglo-Egyptian regime could best be brought to an end and the future of the Sudan safeguarded.

backgrounds—has had cordial relations with the Khatmiyya (though not close ones because of the latter's alliance with the Communists), while, on the other hand, it has, in some respects, been associated with the Umma Party—or that section of it which is led by Ṣādiq al-Mahdi. It seems that there is in fact a high degree of correlation between traditional patterns of allegiance and modern-type movements and associations not only in the Sudan but throughout the Middle East.

CHAPTER V

The Advisory Council

1. *From paternalism to partnership*

THE reaction of the Sudan Government to the rise of nationalism at home and changing conditions abroad was, gradually, to move from the traditional notion of paternalism as the guiding principle of colonial government to the more fashionable ideal of partnership. The 'Arcadian Period'—as Sir Douglas Newbold designated it[1]—of comparatively simple administration, based on the personal rule of the British District Commissioner, the Shaikh, and the tribal chieftain, gave way to a period of accelerated economic, social, and political development, which necessitated the creation of more sophisticated forms of administration and, at the same time, made it imperative that the Sudanese, especially the educated classes, should be more closely associated with the government of their country.

In the sphere of local government, the effect of this new outlook was the gradual displacement of Native Administration, with its emphasis on tribalism, by a modern system of local self-government based on the idea of representation and territorial, instead of tribal, association. The first landmark in the development of this process was the passing, in 1937, of The Local Government (Municipalities, Townships, and Rural Areas) Ordinances to which reference has already been made and which, together with subsequent developments in local government, will be discussed in Chapter VII.

The promulgation of the Advisory Council for the Northern Sudan Order—together with supporting legislation—in 1943 was officially described as 'the most far-reaching step yet taken'[2] in associating the Sudanese with the central government. That such a Council should be established without delay had been urged on the Civil Secretary by Sir Stafford Cripps on his way back from India during the previous year.[3] But Newbold had been thinking along similar lines, even

[1] K. D. D. Henderson, *The Making of the Modern Sudan* (London, 1953), p. 553.

[2] Explanatory Note, *Proceedings of the First Session of the Advisory Council*, Khartoum, 1945, p. 1.

[3] Above, p. 128.

before the Graduates' Congress submitted their Memorandum in April 1942.[1] The submission of the Memorandum and subsequent events, however, finally convinced Newbold, and the Sudan Government, that, despite their preoccupation with the war, steps should be taken to reassure the Sudanese people, especially those of the educated class who could reasonably be expected to want to collaborate with the Government, by giving them a greater say in the administration than they had hitherto been allowed. The timing of the decision was determined, above all, by the Government's desire to create an institution which, it was hoped, 'would take the place of Congress as a national medium of consultation'[2] during a period when the popularity of the Congress, as the only effective outlet for the frustrated patriotism of the politically conscious, was rapidly increasing under conditions of war, rationing, and rising prices. A formal request that 'a system of advisory councils for the Northern Provinces . . . be considered [and that] a small special committee be instructed to investigate the expediency of forming a central Advisory Council for the Northern Sudan' was made by Newbold to the Governor-General's Council in a Note,[3] dated 10 September 1942, which also asked the Council to approve a number of other suggestions aimed at the closer association of the Sudanese with the Government. Accordingly, a high-powered committee, of which the three (Civil, Financial, and Legal) Secretaries were members, was formed.[4] The Committee examined Sir Douglas Newbold's proposals and finally reported to the Governor-General's Council on 16 March 1943.[5] Its recommendations, as outlined in a letter from Newbold to R. C. Mayall,[6] were approved by the Council and this became the basis of the three major acts of the year: The Local Government (Province

[1] Henderson, p. 554.

[2] Henderson, p. 553. The special committee which was set up by the Governor-General to consider the formation of the Advisory Council 'was impressed with the urgency of issuing legislation establishing the Council and . . . recommended that the opening meeting of the Council should take place before the end of 1943, and should not necessarily await the formation of Province Councils' from which the members of the Advisory Council were to be elected (ibid., p. 562). And when the Advisory Council was set up, the Governor-General hastened, in his opening speech of the first session, to describe it as 'the first concrete expression of a Sudanese nation' (*Proceedings of the First Session* from 15 to 18 May 1944, Khartoum, 1945, p. 18).

[3] Reproduced in Henderson, pp. 553–60.

[4] Newbold to R. C. Mayall, 30 Jan. 1943 (ibid., p. 293).

[5] Newbold to R. C. Mayall 17 Jan. 1943 (ibid., p. 303).

[6] Dated 4 Mar. 1943 (ibid., p. 302).

Councils) Ordinance, 1943; The Advisory Councils Ordinance, 1943; and The Advisory Council for the Northern Sudan Order, 1943.

The first of these, as is shown in its title, was essentially a local-government instrument enabling the Governor-General to create, in any province, an Advisory Council to assist the Governor in co-ordinating the policies and activities of the various local authorities established in the province under the three Local Government Ordinances of 1937. But the provincial Advisory Councils thus established were also to act as links between local authorities in the provinces and the central Advisory Council particularly, as will presently be seen, in the election of province representatives on the central Council.

The Advisory Councils Ordinance, 1943, on the other hand, enabled the Governor-General to establish 'one or more Councils in the Sudan advisory to the Governor-General in respect of the good government either of the whole of the Sudan or of any specified part thereof'.[1] And it was under the terms of this Ordinance that the Advisory Council for the Northern Sudan Order, 1943, was passed.

2. *The structure and functions of the Council*

The Advisory Council for the Northern Sudan Order, 1943, provided that the Council should consist of a President, a Vice-President, and twenty-eight ordinary members. The Governor-General assumed the Presidency of the new Council and the Civil Secretary, Sir Douglas Newbold, became its first Vice-President[2] and—since the duties of the President were confined to the ceremonial opening and closing of sessions—the effective leader of the Council.

Of the twenty-eight ordinary members, the Order provided that eighteen were to be appointed by the Governor-General: three from each of the six Northern provinces—Blue Nile, Darfur, Kasala, Khartoum, Kordofan, and the Northern Province. Normally the three representatives of a province were to be appointed from among the members of the Province Advisory Council, either upon the direct recommendations of the Governor or after election by the members of the Council. Considering the urgency[3] of the matter, however,

[1] The Advisory Councils Ordinance, 1943, published in the *Proceedings of the First Session of the Advisory Council* (Khartoum, 1945), p. 4.

[2] Sir Douglas Newbold died in office in 1944 and was succeeded, as Civil Secretary and Vice-President of the Advisory Council, by Sir James Robertson.

[3] Above, pp. 128 and 136.

the Governor-General was advised[1] that the Council should be established as soon as was practicable and without necessarily awaiting the formation of the Province Councils. Accordingly, the Order provided that, where a Province Council had not been established previous to the date on which appointment to the Advisory Council at Khartoum were to be made, the Governor-General was to appoint, on the recommendation of the Governor, three members from among those who were already active in local government in the province or who were likely to be appointed members of the Province Advisory Council.

Of the remaining ten members (to be appointed at the discretion of the Governor-General) the Order stipulated that two, of whom 'at least one' was to be 'a person of Sudanese origin', were to be drawn from amongst the members of the Chamber of Commerce, while eight represented 'the more important social and economic interests including Agriculture, Education and Health as he (i.e. the Governor-General) may think desirable'. And since the overwhelming majority of educated Sudanese capable of representing these interests were serving officials of the Sudan Government, the Order allowed the Governor-General to appoint 'one or more' such officials as ordinary members of the Council.

In addition to ordinary members, the Order provided for the appointment of honorary and extraordinary members of the Council. In the first category 'distinguished Sudanese Notables' could be appointed, while any person whom the Governor-General wished to give his views to the Council upon (or explain to the Council) an item of Government policy could attend Council sittings as an extraordinary member. Under these provisions, Sayyid 'Ali al-Mirghani and Sayyid 'Abd al-Raḥmān al-Mahdi were appointed honorary members, while heads of Government Departments, or their representatives (all British), were, from time to time, invited to act as extraordinary members. Neither honorary nor extraordinary members had the right to vote, but, whereas the latter, of course, took part in the deliberations of the Council, the two Sayyids, like the Governor-General, did not, and were only present during the ceremonial openings and closings of sessions.

The powers of the Council were entirely advisory; advice, however, could only be given within certain limits and in accordance with strict rules which were set out, in considerable detail, in the Order.

[1] See p. 136.

To begin with, the determination of the agenda of each session was a complete monopoly of the President. Individual members had no right to suggest that any particular subject should be included in the agenda. The inclusion of subjects, other than those introduced by the President, in the agenda could only be considered if requested by five members 'by notice in writing delivered to the Secretary to the Council at least two clear months before the opening date of any session'. Whether such a request was accepted or not depended on 'the entire discretion of the President'. Should he decide to allow the subject to be included in the agenda, it could not be debated by members, but the Government's policy with regard to it was 'explained to the Council'. This restriction, however, was not confined to subjects brought before the Council through this procedure, but was normal practice in dealing with all other items included in the second part of the agenda. On these items, the opinion of the Council was neither sought nor allowed, but the Government's point of view was explained and questions asked 'for the sole purpose of elucidating any point arising in the course of the explanation' were answered.

On the other hand, matters (set out in part one of the agenda) on which the President wished to take the advice of the Council could be debated. But debates were firmly controlled by the Civil Secretary who, as Chairman of the Council, was authorized to close, at any time, the debate or discussion upon any subject before the Council. Besides, the Council was not free to determine the form of its own conclusions and 'the manner in which each (piece of) advice is to be tendered' to the President was specified beforehand in the agenda. Thus, in certain cases, the Council was instructed to pass a resolution after debating a question, while in others, it was only allowed to debate a matter without adopting a resolution. Alternatively, it could tender its advice to the Governor-General by means of a report from a special committee—or a standing committee—or by report after reference to a committee of the whole Council.

The sessions of the Council were likewise severely circumscribed. The Order provided that they were to be held at least twice a year, and this number was never, in fact, exceeded during any year until the end of the Council's life. The duration of sessions was limited to four or five days each. Held in the Governor-General's Palace, it is inconceivable that any of the sessions of the Advisory Council could have got out of hand; nevertheless, the President was empowered to terminate any session of the Council at any stage of its development. 'In such event,' the Order stated, 'no business upon the agenda of that Session shall be carried forward to the following Sessions of the Council.' And, as if to guard against the remote possibility of the members of the Council emulating those of the Third Estate in 1789, it was also laid down that 'following the termination of any Sessions, the Council shall not meet again for any purpose, until duly convoked under the provisions' of its Order.

3. *The Council and the nationalists*

As may be expected, the excessive restrictions thus imposed on the Advisory Council by its constitution and regulations immediately became one of the main targets of criticism, especially by the Ashigga, the Congress (which they now controlled and in whose name they spoke), and other Unionist parties, all of which—by contrast with the Umma Party—boycotted the Council and did their best to discredit it in the eyes of the Sudanese and the world. Newbold himself privately thought that 'the safeguards . . . were overdone',[1] but as the spokesman of the Sudan Government, he undertook to defend them and the Advisory Council. Pointing out that some British as well as Sudanese people had expressed the view that there were too many restrictions, and that he sympathized with them, the Civil Secretary said that 'the legal safeguards' embodied in the constitution of the Council were 'not unusual' and that they were

> designed to facilitate the smooth and orderly running of the Council and not to prevent frank and free expression of views. If you study the rules of the British Parliament or of similar neighbouring countries, you will wonder at first sight how any business can ever be done. Laws are like that—safeguards have to be provided but it is always hoped to keep them in the background only to be used in emergencies. . . . It is, I think, true that the Englishman pays less attention to the written word than other races . . . he feels his way step by step without pledging the future and if his laws hamper his advance he leaves them in abeyance or rewrites them. It is in the light of this attitude that these laws should be read, and any fears of their working dissolved.[2]

It need hardly be said that Newbold's argument did not persuade the critics of the Council to change their views on the subject; for,

[1] Newbold to Ewen Campbell, 30 Sept. 1943 (Henderson, p. 340).

[2] From the text of a talk broadcast by Newbold from Omdurman Radio Station on 14 Jan. 1944, attached to the *Proceedings of the First Session of the Advisory Council*, pp. 12–13.

apart from the fact—privately acknowledged by the Civil Secretary—that the restrictions were obviously too heavy, Newbold's speech could not alter the basic psychological fact of the situation: that, just as the Congress had 'forfeited the confidence of Government',[1] the Sudan Government had, likewise, lost the confidence of the educated class as a whole. They simply could not believe that 'the Englishman' who ruled their country and enacted these restrictive regulations would leave them in abeyance or use them only in case of genuine emergency.

A more important reason for the Congress and Unionist parties boycotting the Council and for the criticism of its constitution by others is the fact that the functions of the Council were purely advisory. In the eyes of the nationalist opposition, this meant that the Council was at best useless, since it had no power even to choose the subjects of its deliberations or the time and manner in which advice could be tendered to the Government. By appearing to speak for the Sudanese and give them a real share in managing the affairs of their country, on the other hand, the Council, in the eyes of the opposition, did positive harm by misleading the politically innocent at home and giving the outside world the impression that some genuine representative institutions existed in the Sudan when, in fact, they did not. With regard to the first part of this argument, Newbold retorted that an advisory council could indeed influence decisions and was not necessarily a talking shop.

> The history and experience of most Governments including this Government proves that a very large part of the constructive work of a Government originates in advice and proposals put forward by an Advisory Committee. Most of our policy has actually been framed by Committees and Boards which do not have Executive Powers but whose proposals are more often than not approved and carried out by the Executive Government.

Examples of these were the Jazīra Advisory Board, the Higher Schools Advisory Committee, and the Board of Economics and Trade, all of which did useful work and 'on which we are steadily increasing the number of educated Sudanese'. As for the representation of the people in general, Newbold agreed that the Council did not satisfy the aspirations of the Sudanese. But the advisory state, he said, was not necessarily permanent and the Government regarded it as only one more step in the direction of self-government.

[1] The Civil Secretary's reply to the Memorandum of the Congress quoted above, p. 129.

However, he added, in a well-remembered and often-quoted phrase, 'the road of self government along which the Sudan is marching is a long and painful one'. The Advisory Council should be regarded as a school in which the Sudanese could be trained for undertaking that long march 'and the quickest way to pass through school is to work hard and learn hard, class by class'. In the light of this argument, suggestions that the Government should create a Legislative Assembly were premature and, therefore, unacceptable.

On the face of it, Newbold's argument—despite its unfortunate paternalistic tone—was basically sound and, as such, could reasonably have been expected at least to soften the opposition to the Council. This, however, it failed to achieve, the main reason being the conviction, generally held by members of the literate class, that, although the notion that self-government could only be achieved gradually was itself valid, the Sudan Government used it as an excuse for holding up the constitutional progress of the country and as a means of undermining the Congress movement—the true expression of Sudanese nationalism. Like the notion of 'the Sudan for the Sudanese', it was frequently—and rightly—said, the gradual training of the Sudanese for self-government was 'Kalimato ḥaqin orīda bihā bāṭil'—i.e. 'a truthful statement used to serve a false purpose'. Training was, indeed, desirable, but it could only be gained if people were given real power to exercise. That is why the Congress had, in their Memorandum, asked for the formation of a representative body of Sudanese to approve the Budget and Ordinances. But the constitution of the Council did not give its members any power whatsoever and even the advice they were allowed to give was so severely limited that the Council was, in the eyes of the critics, merely a talking-shop and in many ways positively harmful. The committees which the Civil Secretary mentioned were, of course, useful. But they were Government committees, formed by the Government, almost exclusively from amongst Government employees in order to advise the Government. As such they had no pretensions of the sort claimed for the Advisory Council. Since the Council, it was argued, was on the contrary supposed to be 'the most far-reaching step yet taken in the Government's declared policy of associating the Sudanese with the administration of their country'[1] it was only right and legitimate to expect it to be representative of the Sudanese people

[1] The Explanatory Note to the Advisory Councils Ordinance, 1943, and the Advisory Council Order, 1943.

and to have, at least in some specified field, the right and the power to act on their behalf. The fact that the Advisory Council had neither of these attributes automatically discredited it in the eyes or the nationalist opposition.

The third and, perhaps, most vigorously argued criticism levied against the Council was the fact that it sought to speak for the Northern Sudan to the exclusion of the Southern provinces. This conspicuous omission aroused the old-established suspicion that the Sudan Government was secretly plotting to sever the Southern from the Northern Sudan. The fact that the Explanatory Note stated that 'the ordinance . . . provides for the possibility of a separate Advisory Council for the Southern Provinces'[1] confirmed this suspicion. And when Newbold tried to allay these fears, he only succeeded in increasing them. The reason for excluding the Southern Provinces from the Council, he said, was practical and not political. 'It is simply that the Southern Sudanese have not yet, for historic and natural reasons, reached a degree of enlightenment and cohesion which enables them to send competent representatives to a Council of this kind. Nor are there any Northern Sudanese who can fairly claim to be able conscientiously to represent the Southern peoples.' Therefore, he continued,

it has been suggested that District Commissioners or even Missionaries might be nominated as Southern Representatives. A District Commissioner might with difficulty represent the Nuba Mountains but the diversity of tribes and customs and languages and the distances in the Southern Provinces are such that almost each district would have to have a separate representative and it is the Government's aim that this Council should be a predominantly Sudanese assembly.[2]

Given the prevailing psychological atmosphere, Newbold's statement—however sincerely it might have been made, could not but be taken as yet another illustration of the Government's determination to 'divide and rule'. Furthermore, the logic which, in Newbold's view, made it difficult for any Northern Sudanese to represent Southern constituents, while total aliens, such as the District Commissioners and missionaries whom he mentioned, could be considered as suitable candidates was, to say the least, unacceptable. And when he explained that the only reason why these could not in fact be allowed to represent Southern Sudanese was that there would have had to be

[1] Ibid. [2] Broadcast talk.

so many of them, Newbold's critical audience naturally concluded that their old suspicions regarding the intentions of the Sudan Government had been more than fully justified. It is a measure of the general disenchantment of the nationalists with this aspect of the Council that even the Umma party, willing though it was to participate in the Council, was equally convinced that the exclusion of the Southern Provinces from the Council was 'indicative of a lack of goodwill'[1] on the part of the Government.

Leaving aside the purely legal aspects of its constitution, the social structure and actual working of the Advisory Council did not help to win it the sympathy and the loyalty of the country, but were, on the contrary new targets for critics—especially in the towns and larger villages where the Congress and the Unionist parties were dominant and the influence of the Umma Party, by no means great at any time, continued to diminish.

TABLE 2

Ordinary Members of the Advisory Council

		SUDANESE											BRITISH
		Tribal leaders					Employees and pensioners of central government departments						
		Nāẓirs	Sultans	Maks	Wakil Nāẓir	Shaikhs	Religious affairs	Civil Servants	Army Officers	Teachers	Doctors	Merchants	Bank managers
Elected	18	4	1	1	1	4	..	4	..	1	..	2	..
Appointed	10	..	..	..	..	1	3	1	1	1	1	1	1
		4	1	1	1	5	3	5	1	2	1	3	1
Total	28				12				12			3	1

Considering the nature of the Province Councils[2] and the process whereby—advised by the Provincial Governors—they chose their representatives, it is not surprising that eleven out of the eighteen

[1] 'Abd al-Raḥmān 'Ali Ṭāha, *al-Sūdān li-l-Sūdāniyyīn* (Khartoum, 1955), p. 32.
[2] Chapter VII below.

elected members of the Advisory Council were tribal leaders—men whose outlook, rural, and traditional as it was, had been greatly influenced by Native Administration and the British Governors and District Commissioners under whom they worked. To these, another was added by means of direct appointment by the Governor-General, thus bringing the total number of Nāzirs and Shaikhs to twelve. An equal number—including five civil servants—was drawn from the various Departments of the central Government. Of the remaining four, three were Sudanese merchants of whom one was an appointed member of the Chamber of Commerce, the fourth being the British Manager of Barclays Bank, Khartoum Branch, who was also an appointed representative of the Chamber of Commerce. The Advisory Council, therefore, was almost entirely comprised of members of the administration, provincial and central. This fact, as may be expected, was readily seized by the Unionist parties and the Graduates' Congress (which boycotted the Council and expelled those of its members who were willing to sit on it) in order to characterize the Council as another 'Governmental institution', a term of abuse in nationalist usage, meaning that the Council, to paraphrase Aḥmad Khair once more, was an instrument for serving the imperialistic objectives of the British Government of the Sudan: by giving it an appearance of legitimacy which it did not and could not, in fact, possess; by seducing the weaker brethren among the intelligentsia and providing them with a semblance of justification for their 'collaborationism'; and by undermining the unity of the Congress and thus arresting the progress of the Sudan towards self-determination and genuine self-government.[1] The majority of the members of the Council, it was argued, were men of straw or 'yes-men' who—like Nūbār and others in Cromer's Egypt—merely did what they were told or were expected to do and who were, therefore, neither capable of nor interested in representing the Sudanese people. Newbold challenged this unfavourable image in the famous talk which he broadcast from Omdurman Radio Station on 14 January 1944.

I cannot repeat too often that the Sudan Government would not go to all the trouble of setting up Town Councils, Province Councils and a Central Council merely to fill them with Yes-Men. Are the members of the Town Councils Yes-Men? Are the Sudanese members of Government Committees Yes-Men? The Government has no use either for Yes-Men

[1] *Kifāḥ Jīl*, p. 81.

or No-Men. The Yes-Man is the man who *always* agrees with the Government, from motives of profit or cowardice or laziness. The No-Man is the man who *always* disagrees with the Government from motives of suspicion or pessimism or vanity. I hear reasonable criticism of Yes-Men in the Press and in conversation. I should like sometimes to hear a criticism of No-Men. The true Councillor is the man who agrees or disagrees from conscience and wisdom, but does not make a habit of either.[1]

For those sections of Sudanese opinion who generally favoured co-operation with the Sudan Government as the only practical way of breaking the then existing Egyptian Government's determination to make the Sudan a province of Egypt under the Egyptian crown,[2] Newbold's statement, no doubt, appeared as sensible as the assertions of the critics of the Council were senseless. But, from the point of view of those including the majority of the intelligentsia and the townspeople, who held the opposite view and felt that the British administration was the real enemy of the Sudan, the Civil Secretary's statement—though his personal integrity was much admired and he was personally liked by his numerous Sudanese friends irrespective of their political views[3]—was simply another 'Kalimato ḥaqin orīda bihā bāṭil'. Given the nature of the regime and the then existing attitudes of the British and Egyptian Governments to the Sudan question, the two points of view were irreconcilable. Every single issue of national import was, in the last analysis, seen and discussed in the light of the basic schism—and no amount of subsidiary argument could move either party from the position it held with regard to the future of the country, or induce it to soften its attitude to the other and the Power which supported it. For the Ashigga and many other Unionists, suspicion of all 'Governmental' projects and institutions, until it was established that they were harmless, was the first principle of patriotism, and willing co-operation with the British in them was tantamount to a betrayal of the cause of Sudanese nationalism.[4] The Umma Party and the Independence Front, on the other hand, maintained that 'selling out to Egypt' was an equally heinous offence, and that, so long as the Egyptian Government continued its efforts to impose Egyptian sovereignty and the Egyptian crown over the Sudan, participation in the Council, whatever its defects, was the only practical, because the only available, means of realizing the national aspirations of the Sudanese people.

[1] Printed in the *Proceedings of the First Session of the Advisory Council*, (Khartoum, 1945).

[2] Ṭāha, p. 32.

[3] *Kifāḥ Jīl*, footnote, p. 82.

[4] Ibid., p. 46.

Like the Legislative Assembly and the Executive Council afterwards, the Advisory Council was seen as giving the Sudanese a constitutional platform which enabled them to discuss issues with the Government at home and with the Governments of Egypt and Britain as well as the U.N.O., if necessary, abroad.[1]

In the resulting atmosphere of bitter controversy and recrimination, it was natural that Newbold—overworked and fully aware of the limitations of the new Council and the power of hostile comment—was nervous and worried about the way the Advisory Council was going to work.[2] It was indicative of this state of anxiety that the press was admitted only to the inaugural ceremony and the Governor-General's opening speech of the first session while members were reassured that 'the press will be kept informed of the results of your deliberations by the issue of an official summary without indicating the views of individual members'.[3] This was done, the Civil Secretary subsequently explained, not because the Government wished to keep the proceedings secret as critics hastened to say, but because the presence of reporters might have 'embarrassed' some members or prevented them from speaking their minds freely 'by the knowledge that (their) words may be the subject of hostile criticism in the Press or may be quoted apart from the context'.[4]

The subject, whether the Press should be admitted or not, was debated during the second session, seven months later. The following excerpt from the proceedings shows the views of the Councillors on the subject and also gives some indication of the calibre of the assembly as a whole. The discussions followed a statement by the Chairman, in which he mentioned the arguments for and against the admission of the Press; he declared that the Government did not wish to influence the opinion of the members in either direction and reminded them that, should they decide to admit reporters, it would be necessary to make provision against the issue of premature and possibly inaccurate accounts in advance of the official record. The debate, as recorded in the Proceedings, ran as follows:

2051. MUHAMMAD ALI EFF SHAWKI said that the Council represented the people of the Sudan but many councillors felt out of touch with public opinion. Public opinion on matters under discussion could only be formed by full ventilation in the press. No harm and much good would be done by wide publication. He moved that the Press be admitted.

[1] Ṭāha, pp. 32 and 65. [2] Henderson, pp. 371, 368, and 365.

[3] *Proceedings of the First Session*, p. 20.

[4] *Proceedings of the Second Session*, pp. 4–5.

2052. Mustafa eff Abu el Ela seconded the motion, mentioning the added advantage that a member of the public with a grievance would be satisfied if he knew that it had been voiced in the Council. He did not, however, consider that names should be published. Suggestions should be recorded as coming from a 'member'.

2053. Sheikh Khalil Akasha favoured admission on four conditions: (i) Anonymity, (ii) no distortion or quotation of remarks out of their context, (iii) no caricatures, (iv) press versions to be checked by the Council's secretaries or by a special committee of the Council.

2054. Abdel-Karim eff Mohammad said that the Sudan Press was still young and irresponsible. It was apt to try to please its public rather than to stick to the truth. None the less, he favoured admission, because members had nothing to hide or to be ashamed of. Their advice was given for the good of the public and it was well for the public to know of it. Secrecy means suspicion. He therefore favoured admission.

Asked by the Chairman if he would enforce conditions, he stipulated for anonymity and no sarcastic comment. They must publish the facts and nothing but the facts.

2055. Abdallah Bey Khalil said that if the Press could not be trusted they were better excluded. If the public wanted to know the truth it could get it from the official version. For the present he did not think the time was ripe for admitting the Press. The reasons given by the Chairman for excluding them from the first Session were equally applicable to the second, and he preferred to defer a decision for the present.

2056. Dr. Ali Bedri agreed with Abdullah Bey; there could be no secrecy so long as the official version was published and surely misrepresentation in the press was a much more likely ground for suspicion in any case. The Council was still young and must be nursed for a while.

2057. Mekki eff Abbas favoured unconditional admission. Members had nothing to fear if they spoke their minds honestly and they should be glad for the public to know what they had said. At present the public was ignorant of the good work done by the Council at its last Session. The Press Communiqués were colourless and failed to attract the public eye. The educated public had always resented private consultation and regarded the Council as merely an example of private consultation on a larger scale. Councillors were not children and should be glad to have their remarks reported under their names and as widely as possible, provided provision remained for secret sittings when necessary, and legal redress existed for any defamatory comment.

2058. Sheikh Ayube Abdel Magid favoured unconditional admission. Any other course would be cowardly. Any misrepresentation could be discussed at the next session.

2059. Sheikh Ahmed Osman el Qadi suported Mekki Eff Abbas in his plea for unconditional admission with legal action against personal or libellous criticism. A minority of the public considered the Council to be a retrograde step and must be convinced to the contrary. At present they regarded the official account as eye-wash. Publication without giving names would be valueless, and derisive criticism of the Council's debates as a whole would be most unlikely.

2060. SHEIKH SURUR MUHAMMAD RAMLI said that the public had great confidence in its representatives on their Council and accepted as true the official accounts of the debates. He was therefore against admitting the Press.

2061. SHEIKH FAHAL IBRAHIM agreed that the time was not yet ripe.

2062. NUH EFF ABDULLAH said that after listening to the arguments in favour he remained of the same opinion as Abdullah Bey Khalil. He was against admission.

2063. SHEIKH BABU NIMR thought that some members might be embarrassed by the presence of reporters and dissuaded from expressing themselves as they wished. He felt that representative councillors had the confidence of their people.

2064. ABDULLAH BEY said he wished to make it clear that his opposition was not permanent but that he did not think the time was yet ripe.

2065. MIRGHANI EFF HAMZA said that the real problem was not to inform the public of what had been said. This could be done by the Secretaries. What the public wanted to know was who had said what, so that it could assess the worth of the various councillors and discuss the arguments put forward. Public interest would thereby be quickened, which could only be an advantage. The Press was young like the Council and must be given the chance to prove itself, concurrently with the Council. The only condition he would impose was that the alleged statements of individuals should be checked against the official version.

2066. HASSAN EFF ALI SHEKELAWI said the Press was the voice of the nation. He supported Mirghani Eff Hamza.

2067. DR. ALI BEDRI, replying to these arguments, said that it was nonsense to say the public was not informed. The official account was very full. If the public had no faith in the Council was its faith likely to be increased by press reports? Did the councillors want to have their worth assessed by reporters? Would such an assessment, good will, be of any value to the Council or the assessed member? Why should the Press learn its job at the expense of the Council? Neither of them would be the better for a disastrous experiment.

2068. HAMID EFF EL SAYYID said that the proposal before the Council was for the immediate admission of the Press. Was the Council ready for this? It was proposed at this Session by way of experiment to check over each morning the official report to be published in advance. The minutes as read that morning did not in his opinion give a true picture of what happened at the last Session. This showed the need for careful checking to ensure accuracy. Many members were still ignorant of rules of procedure and methods of debate and the Chairman had already waived several of the rules in consideration of their inexperience. Under the new system it was proposed to produce an agreed version of the day's debate on the morning following. If this agreed version were handed to the Press would it not be sufficient? In any case he did not think the Press should be admitted until the Council had had an opportunity of seeing how the new system worked.

2069. MEKKI EFF ABBAS pointed out that he had not said that the public had no information at present but that the present press bulletins did not catch the public eye. What had Councillors to be afraid of? That they would be mocked at because of their ignorance of procedure? Everyone knew that the Council was new and inexperienced. That they would be too frightened to speak out? They had shown no such fear previously on this Council in the presence of the most senior members of the Government.

2070. SHEIKH ABDULLAH BAKR said that after all this argument he remained convinced that the Press should only be admitted after three or four sessions in camera. Many members had not spoken and were in their hearts nervous of premature admittance.

2071. SHEIKH ZUBEIR HAMAD EL MALIK said he was unreservedly in favour of admittance and did not think members would be afraid to speak their minds.

2072. MUHAMMAD ALI EFF SHAWKI after asking whether the motion was going to be put to the vote, and receiving an affirmative answer, said that members' one object was the truth and that they should hope therefore for the widest possible dissemination of their expressed sentiments. Everyone made mistakes from time to time but the wise could learn from their mistakes. He appealed to members who had spoken against the motion to reconsider their decision.

2073. Seven members having spoken in favour of unconditional admission, three in favour of admission on condition that no names were to be published, and eight against admission, the Chairman closed further discussion and called in turn upon each of the members who had remained silent to give his opinion. The remaining eight members present then signified that they had no objection to the admission of the Press and *the motion was carried, on a show of hands, by seventeen votes to eight.*[1]

[1] *Proceedings of the Second Session of the Advisory Council* held at the Palace, 5–10 Dec. 1944, pp. 5–7. The conditions on which the Press was finally admitted to the Council included the following:

'6. (A) Editors should not publish in their papers on the same day on which the discussions took place anything other than a general description of what happened in the Council. The description includes the time of the meeting of the Council, the members who attended, what subjects were discussed, and the kind of decision taken and the amount of opposition or otherwise which the propositions met. But such a description should not include the names of members and should not report what they said nor should it include any comments or criticism . . .'

'7. (B) Editors can publish on the next day the deliberations of the Council as reported by them and they are at liberty to comment on them and criticise them as they wish, *on condition* that the full official record, which will be sent to the Press by the Information Officer, be published in the same issue.'

(Quoted in the *Proceedings of the Fifth Session*, 17–21 Apr. 1946, p. 4. These conditions were gradually relaxed.)

Subsequent debates, on the whole, reflected the same tenor and quality as the discussion on the admission of the Press to the meetings of the Council. A considerable section of the members usually remained silent or, occasionally, raised minor points and queries. But there was a tendency for greater participation when matters of regional interest or subjects of general social significance were discussed—for example, the consumption of alcohol and, especially, female circumcision, both of which were introduced during the third session. On the other hand, subjects of a more specialized or technical nature, such as soil conservation and The Definition of 'Sudanese' and 'Sudan Denizen' Ordinance, important though they were, do not, on the evidence of the records of proceedings, seem to have aroused much interest among the members of the Council as a whole, active discussion tending to revolve around a small nucleus of teachers and civil servants in the Council. Since individual members within each of the three main professional groups—traders, tribal leaders, and employees of central Government Departments—varied a great deal in ability and training, it is not possible to make a rigid and unqualified generalization about their respective contributions as groups. It is nevertheless true to say that the employees of central Government Departments, all of whom, like a few members of the other two groups, had been students of the Gordon College, were the most active participants in the dealings of the Advisory Council, while the majority of tribal Shaikhs and Nāẓirs were mainly inactive.

Of the twenty-two debates held during the eight sessions of the Advisory Council, those that aroused the greatest wave of public interest were the two devoted to the pharaonic circumcision of females, a subject which has since become identified in the public mind with the Advisory Council. This form of mutilation, African and pre-Islamic by origin, had been, and still is, practised in certain parts of the Sudan, despite the fact that religious leaders—including the two Sayyids,[1] medical opinion, and various advocates of social reform have repeatedly condemned it as a cruel and barbarous custom. Apparently acting in response to a suggestion which had been made by the Governor-General that the time had come when the custom

[1] A pamphlet on the subject, with forewords by the Governor-General, the Mufti of the Sudan, Sayyid 'Ali al-Mirghani, and Sayyid 'Abd al-Raḥmān al-Mahdi, was prepared by the Government printers for the benefit of the Councillors and the public. The pamphlet was incorporated in the *Proceedings of the Third Session of the Council*, 23–28 May 1945.

should be finally abandoned,[1] the Advisory Council, itself a predominantly conservative body, decided to lead the country in the direction of radical social revolution. Rejecting a number of suggestions to the effect that a nation-wide propaganda campaign should precede legislation, it approved, by a majority of eighteen votes to nine, a resolution, introduced by Dr. 'Ali Badri, which requested the Government to prepare legislation making the practice of pharaonic circumcision a criminal offence punishable by law.[2]

As may be expected, however, the attempt to stamp out such a deeply rooted custom by legislative action proved abortive and had, instead, the exact opposite effect. For one thing, as Mirghani Ḥamza pointed out to the Council, pharaonic circumcision was practised *en masse*, even on girls of two or three years,[3] once it became known that legislation was being considered—and the process gained momentum after the adoption of the resolution. In addition, demonstrations were organized to protest against what was, not unnaturally, considered an unwarranted interference in the private affairs of the people and in at least one town, Rufā'a, a serious clash occurred between demonstrators and the police. Politically, the misguided zeal of the Advisory Council for social reform became an additional weapon in the hands of its opponents. Quoting Sayyid 'Ali al-Mirghani's statement[4] that pharaonic circumcision, like other bad customs, was bound to disappear with the spread of education and general enlightenment, they intensified their attack on the Council. In a country that was ridden by poverty, ignorance, and disease, it was pointed out, the Sudan Government's Advisory Council thought it fit to direct its urgent attention to trivial interference in the innermost affairs of the people and to the discussion of ways and means whereby wines and spirits could best be dispensed to the Muslim population of the Sudan[5]—a reference to the debate on the consumption of alcoholic liquor, which also took place in May 1945.

4. *The gathering storm: politics after the war*

In the meantime more important factors, both internal and external, were making for the heightening of the political tension of

[1] Pamphlet in *Proceedings of the Third Session of the Council* 23–28 May 1945, p. 28. [2] Ibid., p. 39. [3] Ibid., p. 38. [4] Ibid., p. 30.

[5] Cf. *Ma'āsi al-Injilīz Fi-l-Sūdān* ('The Tragedies of English Rule in the Sudan') —a collection of articles which was originally published, under the name of the Sudanese Delegation to Egypt, 1946, in the Egyptian paper *al-Wafd al-Miṣri* and subsequently served as a manual of nationalist criticism of British administration in the Sudan.

the Sudan in the immediate post-war period. The continued effect of the Atlantic Charter, the mounting tension in the Middle East, the march of India towards independence, the relaxation of war-time restrictions, the emergence of militant trade-unionism, and the inevitable frustration of hopes long cherished for a general improvement in living standards soon after the cessation of hostilities in Europe and the Far East—were all factors in the development of the new situation. Thus, while workers kept pressing for higher wages, the tenants of the Jazīra Scheme, for the first time, went on strike at the end of January 1946, demanding that £1,300,000 standing to their credit fund should be paid out. A special committee of the Advisory Council investigated the unrest and recommended the payment of £400,000 to the tenants. The recommendation of the committee was accepted and the tenants resumed work.[1]

An important landmark in the development of this situation was reached when it was announced, towards the end of 1945, that Egypt and Britain were to enter into negotiations for the revision of the 1936 Treaty. 'Abdalla Bey Khalīl, the Secretary-General of the Umma party, supported by four other members of the party and the Council, presented a letter, dated 3 September 1945, to the Chairman of the Council, asking whether the Government intended to enable members of the Advisory Council to discuss and give opinions about the future of the Sudan when the time came for such discussion by the Authorities concerned before any final new constitutional arrangement was made.[2] In reply, the Chairman read out the following statement during the fourth session:

> Should the question of the future status of the Sudan be raised by the Condominium powers in any revision of the Anglo-Egyptian Treaty, it would be the intention of the Sudan Government that the Advisory Council for the Northern Sudan should be consulted in order that its views should be at the disposal of the Sudan Government for transmission to the Powers. It is the opinion of the Sudan Government that the views of the Sudanese people should be obtained through constitutional channels in a matter of such vital importance to their future wellbeing.[2]

In addition, the Chairman declared that 'the Government would also give such weight to the opinion of other representative bodies as they may deserve'[2]—a reference to those parties and groups who had boycotted the Council and were not represented on it.

[1] *Annual Report* for 1946, p. 10.
[2] *Proceedings of the Fourth Session*, 3–8 Nov. 1945, p. 97.

Under these conditions it was obvious that, provided they could settle their differences, the Sudanese people and their spokesmen, would be at a considerable advantage *vis-à-vis* the British and Egyptian Governments. A group of independent graduates, backed by the students' union of the Gordon College, then a considerable pressure group in national politics, eventually succeeded in formulating a statement of political objectives which was acceptable to all existing parties. The statement envisaged the creation of a free and democratic Sudanese Government in union with Egypt and in alliance with Britain, the nature of the union and the alliance being left for the said Sudanese Government to determine.[1] Accordingly an all-party delegation proceeded to Cairo, amidst great jubilation, as from 22 March 1946. Once in Egypt, however, the component parts of the delegation, confronted by the unwillingness of the Egyptian Government to agree to anything other than the union of Egypt and the Sudan under the Egyptian crown, began to interpret the fragile compromise statement in their own particular way and the delegation disintegrated: members of the Umma Party and the Independence Front returning to Khartoum while the Ashigga and the representatives of other Unionist parties remained in Cairo. The Anglo-Egyptian negotiations themselves failed, the Sudan question and the diametrically opposed interpretations of the 1899 Agreement held by the Egyptian and British Governments being the stumbling-block, as they had always been since 1922.

However, in October of the same year a compromise agreement was reached by Ṣidqi Pasha, then the Prime Minister of the Egyptian Government, and the British Foreign Secretary, Mr. Bevin. The Ṣidqi–Bevin Draft Treaty, as it was called, included a 'Sudan Protocol', which stated that

> the policy which the High Contracting Parties undertake to follow in the Sudan (within the framework of the Unity between the Sudan and Egypt under the common Crown of Egypt) will have for its essential objectives to assure the well-being of the Sudanese, the development of their interests and their active preparation for self-government and consequently the exercise of the right to choose the future status of the Sudan. Until the High Contracting Parties can in full common agreement realise this latter objective after consultation with the Sudanese, the Agreement of 1899 will continue and Article 11 of the Treaty of 1936, together with its Annexe . . . will remain in force . . .[2]

[1] *Ṣawt al-Sūdān* (Khartoum Daily), 13 Oct. 1945 and 20 Mar. 1946. Also Ṭāha, p. 33.

[2] 'The Ṣidqi–Bevin Draft Treaty', attached to the *Verbatim Record* of the

Like the compromise agreement between the Sudanese parties, however, the 'Sudan Protocol' was subjected to different interpretations. Whereas Ṣidqi Pasha declared, on his arrival in Cairo, that—'I have returned with sovereignty over the Sudan', Mr. Bevin told the House of Commons:

After taking . . . the highest legal advice, I felt that, for the sake of an agreement which would have been as much in the interests of the Sudan as of either of the other parties, I should be justified in alluding, in the Sudan Protocol to the existence of a symbolic dynastic union between Egypt and the Sudan, provided always that no change was introduced into the existing system of administration. . . .[1]

Under the strain of the ensuing controversy, negotiations were finally broken off, and on 26 January 1947 Naqrāshi Pasha, the new Egyptian Prime Minister declared his intention to take the Anglo-Egyptian dispute to the Security Council. There the question was debated during nine sessions extending from 5 August to 10 September. In the course of the prolonged debate at Lake Success the two governments explained their respective points of view on the 1899 Agreement and the nature of the regime thereby established in the Sudan. In particular Naqrāshi Pasha insisted that the so-called Condominium Agreement did not, in fact, create a condominium regime in the Sudan but only an Anglo-Egyptian administration as its official title indicated. Sovereignty over the country, which the Agreement did not mention, therefore, belonged where it had been vested before the Mahdist 'rebellion'—i.e. in the Egyptian crown. Furthermore, he maintained, the Sudanese and the Egyptians were one people, united by history, race, religion, language, and common dependence on the Nile. Britain, having used Egypt's name, money, and men in order to establish its hold over the Sudan, decided to drive a wedge between the two peoples and was, similarly, scheming in order to sever the Southern provinces from the rest of the Sudan. Sir Alexander Cadogan, the British representative, on the other hand, insisted that the Anglo-Egyptian Agreement of 1899—though it did not refer to the subject by name—had constituted a condominium regime in which Britain and Egypt were jointly recognized as the co-rulers of the Sudan; that sovereignty over the country was vested in the Co-Domini; that the Sudanese people were

discussion of the 175th, 176th, 179th, etc., meetings of the Security Council covering the Anglo-Egyptian Dispute, 1947 (Government Press, Khartoum, n.d.).

[1] *The Times*, 28 Jan. 1947, quoted in MacMichael, *The Sudan*, p. 196.

different from the Egyptians and equally entitled to determine their own destiny; and that the Government of the Sudan was accordingly training them in the art of self-government, while the Egyptians were only interested in disrupting these efforts and imposing their own will over the Sudanese without consulting them. As regards the last of the charges made by Naqrāshi Pasha, however, Sir Alexander Cadogan was seriously hampered by a pamphlet entitled *The Sudan: A Record of Progress* which had been prepared by the Sudan Government and distributed to members of the Security Council. Referring to the fear of Sudanese nationalists that the ultimate result of 'Southern Policy' would be the splitting of the country in half with the possible attachment of the South to British Uganda, the pamphlet stated:

> The arguments whether such a course would be to the ultimate advantage of the southern Sudan or the rest of Africa are many on both sides and the whole question might at some date form a proper subject for consideration by an international commission. Meanwhile, the present Government . . . is proposing to associate sympathetic northern Sudanese with the implementation of a policy which aims at giving the south the same chances of ultimate self-determination as have been promised to the north.[1]

This, Naqrāshi Pasha was able to argue, not without effect, clearly demonstrated that Britain was not genuinely interested in helping the Sudanese to determine their own destiny, but only used the doctrine of self-determination as a pretext for justifying its own imperialistic policies of, first, separating the Sudan from Egypt and, then, separating the Southern from the Northern provinces of the Sudan.[2]

On 10 September rival resolutions (and amendments) were finally put to the vote. But none of them gained the requisite majority and the Security Council adjourned leaving the Anglo-Egyptian dispute unresolved on its agenda; the Egyptian and British Governments (backed, in the lobbies, by their respective Sudanese supporters), however, had the satisfaction of having made their respective points of view known to the world.

Meanwhile, the 'Sudan Protocol' had precipitated a difficult situation in the Sudan, where violent demonstrations, involving direct clashes between the supporters of the Independence Front and

[1] *The Sudan: A Record of Progress, 1898–1947* (Sudan Government, 1947), pp. 13–14.

[2] *Verbatim Record* of the discussions at the 175th, 176th, 179th, etc., meetings of the Security Council concerning the Anglo-Egyptian Dispute, 1947.

the Unionists, occurred, not only in the towns to which political activity had hitherto been confined, but also—through the involvement of the religious Ṭariqās—in the countryside as well.[1] At the same time, relations between the Sudan Government and the Anṣār, for whom the Protocol, implying as it did the recognition by Britain of Egyptian sovereignty over the Sudan, was an unexpected act of betrayal, were severely strained. The Umma Party threatened to withdraw from the Advisory Council, the sixth session of which therefore had to be twice postponed.[2] Not content with the reassurances of British officials at home, Sayyid 'Abd al-Raḥmān al-Mahdi flew to Egypt, and then to Britain, in order to discuss the matter with the leaders of their respective Governments.[3]

5. *The search for new policies*

Under the growing pressure of events at home and abroad,[4] the Sudan Government, determined not to let the initiative pass from its hands, decided to take further steps towards the closer association of the Sudanese—both Northerners and Southerners—with the government of their country. In his opening speech of the fifth session on 17 April 1946 (i.e. three weeks after the departure of the first members of the all-party Sudanese delegation to Cairo) the Governor-General reassured the Council that the objects of the Sudan Government, as Mr. Bevin had recently declared, were to build up the organs of self-government with the aim of eventual independence. 'I wish definitely to deny any suggestion that the Sudan Government is unsympathetic to Sudanese aspirations', he said. 'The Government is aiming at a free independent Sudan which will be able as soon as that independence has been achieved to define for itself its relations with Great Britain and Egypt.'[5]

[1] *Annual Report* for 1946, p. 139: and *Annual Report* for 1947, p. 9.

[2] *Annual Report* for 1946, p. 13.

[3] Ṭāha mentions that Ṣidqi Pasha refused to see Sayyid 'Abd al-Raḥmān in Cairo, while the Egyptian press continued to attack him, describing the Sayyid as a rebel against the crown who, therefore, deserved to be executed. In London, however, Sayyid 'Abd al-Raḥmān was met by Mr. Attlee, who reassured him that Britain would not accept the Egyptian view with regard to sovereignty over the Sudan (pp. 37–9).

[4] In his Annual Report for 1947, the Governor-General recorded that the events of that year led to an unprecedented external interest in Sudan affairs, which attained world-wide proportions and which was accompanied by a similar growing interest on the part of the Sudanese in world problems (p. 9).

[5] *Proceedings of the Fifth Session*, 17–21 Apr. 1946, pp. 1–2.

The Governor-General went further and specified that 'in twenty years' time the Sudanese will be governing their own country assisted and advised by a certain number of non-Sudanese specialists and technicians'. In order to plan the concrete steps by which this objective could be reached in the administration of Government Department, he added, a joint British-Sudanese committee of civil servants had recently been set up (on 11 March) to inquire into the existing plans for Sudanization and to make recommendations as to how they might be accelerated. With regard to the building-up of the organs of self-government with the aim of eventual independence, on the other hand, the Governor-General informed the councillors that it was his intention to call a conference forthwith to study the next steps in associating the Sudanese more closely with the administration of their country.[1]

The 'Sudanization Committee', as it came to be known, recommended that by 1962, 62·2 per cent of the total number of posts in Government Departments should be filled by Sudanese, most of whom were to be in Division II of the civil service.[2] The general plan for the progressive Sudanization of the Departments to this extent by 1962 was as follows:[3]

	Per cent			
	1948	*1952*	*1957*	*1962*
Division I	15·4	27·4	38·1	55·5
Division II	25·2	37·1	58·7	78·9
Both divisions	18·4	30·3	44·1	62·2

'The Sudan Administration Conference' on the other hand made a number of recommendations, the most important of which were concerned with the development of the Advisory Council—'so as to give it greater representative character and more responsible functions'.[4]

[1] *Proceedings of the Fifth Session* 17–21 Apr. 1946, pp. 1–2.

[2] Division I comprised the senior professional, administrative, and technical posts; Division II, the clerical, book-keeping, and junior technical posts; and Division III, the junior (unpensionable) technical, clerical, and book-keeping posts: *Report of the Committee on the Sudanisation of the Civil Service* (Khartoum, 17 June 1948), p. 5.

[3] Ibid., p. 19.

[4] *The First Report of the Sudan Administration Conference* submitted to His Excellency the Governor-General on 31 Mar. 1947 (Khartoum), p. 3.

CHAPTER VI

The Legislative Assembly

1. *The Sudan Administration Conference*

THE Governor-General convened the Sudan Administration Conference on 22 April 1946. Working under the general direction of the Civil Secretary, Mr. (later Sir James) Robertson,[1] the Conference was essentially a body of Sudan Government employees, of whom eight were British. To these were added sixteen Sudanese members: eight representing the Advisory Council, seven officials and Sayyid al-Ṣiddīq, the son of Sayyid 'Abd al-Raḥmān al-Mahdi. Political parties were invited to nominate representatives. Accordingly, the Independence Front, to which a majority of the sixteen Sudanese members belonged, sent five[2] more representatives. The Graduates' Congress, the Ashigga, and other Unionist parties were asked to nominate six, but declined the offer and boycotted the Conference.

Soon after the beginning of their first meeting, held on 24 April, the Conference decided to set up two sub-committees: one on central government, the other on local government.

The terms of reference of the central government sub-committee were:

(*a*) To consider the next steps for associating the Sudanese more closely with the Central Government and in particular to work out and recommend to the main Conference methods for developing the present Advisory Council so as to give them greater and more responsible functions;

(*b*) To survey the various other Central Government Boards, Councils, and Committees and to make recommendations for a larger Sudanese representation upon them; and

(*c*) To consider the possible creation of new Boards.[3]

[1] Afterwards the Governor-General of Nigeria.

[2] Of these five, three represented the Umma Party, one the Qawmiyyīn (i.e. National) Party, and another the Ahrār (i.e. Liberal) Party.

[3] *First Report of the Sudan Administration Conference*, 31 Mar. 1947 (Khartoum), p. 2.

The outcome of the Conference's deliberations based on the recommendations of the sub-committee, with regard to the last two points was simple: they recommended the creation of new Boards and the wide representation of Sudanese on every Departmental Board or Committee—provided that this was consonant with reasonable efficiency and that the number of Sudanese at that stage, did not, by sheer weight of numbers, influence the decisions of the Boards.[1]

By contrast, the expansion of the Advisory Council into a national, representative, and (it was hoped) responsible Assembly was a complex affair, the consideration of which engaged the Conference for many months and finally formed the bulk of its Report on the Closer Association of the Sudanese with the Central Government.[2] Endorsing the main criticisms which had been levied against the Advisory Council, namely that it 'was confined to the six Northern provinces; its functions were purely advisory and strictly limited in scope, and its members . . . could never really claim that they were fully representative of the people', the report summarized the main recommendation of the Conference as being 'the constitution of a Legislative Assembly of elected Sudanese members for the whole Sudan to exercise legislative, financial, and general administrative functions in conjunction with a newly-constituted Executive Council which would replace the present Governor-General's Council'.[3]

'After careful consideration' the Conference unanimously agreed that the Sudan should aim at a system of Parliamentary Government with a responsible Cabinet on the British model.[4] Accordingly, there were to be no honorary, *ex-officio*, or extraordinary members as had been the case with the Advisory Council, and the Chairman of the Assembly was to have the functions and perform the duties of the Speaker in the House of Commons.[5] In order to make it a more representative body, the Assembly was to have seventy members instead of the twenty-eight who sat in the Council. But, since the Sudan was not yet ready for a fully fledged parliamentary system, the Conference agreed that certain modifications were necessary. Thus, it recommended that ten out of the seventy members of the proposed Assembly should be nominated by the Governor-General, in order, it was argued, to ensure the presence in the Assembly of specially qualified Sudanese who might not otherwise find a seat.

[1] *First Report of the Sudan Administration Conference*, 31 Mar. 1947 (Khartoum), p. 11.

[2] The *Report* was formally submitted to the Governor-General on 31 Mar. 1947.

[3] Ibid., p. 3.

[4] Ibid., p. 4.

[5] Ibid., p. 8.

Again, although it was considered 'a truism that the same people cannot at the same time be Politicians and efficient Civil Servants' a point which the Government had repeatedly emphasized in dealing with the Congress[1]—the Sudan Administration Conference felt that the peculiar position of the Sudan, where the majority of the educated class were in the Civil Service, demanded a temporary modification of the rule that government servants might not take part in politics. Therefore, the report concluded, 'as long as the sessions of the Assembly last for no more than four months in each year we think that a government servant who is a member of the Assembly may still be able to retain his post'.[2] For the same general considerations, the report stated that, although direct elections were the best method of ensuring that the Assembly would speak for the Sudanese people, such elections could not, as yet, be recommended for rural areas. The Conference therefore recommended that these should be indirect elections outside municipalities and townships which had warranted local government councils.[3] And in the case of the South, where it was considered difficult to find representative individuals by means of elections, the Governors were to 'appoint such persons as they considered best fitted at the present time'.[4] Both in the South and in the North, however, the representation of the people was to be on a provincial basis, and the number of representatives from each province was to be determined in accordance with an Electoral Index based on factors of population, wealth, and education. According to the values given to each one of these factors by the Conference (50 per cent for population, 30 per cent for wealth, and 20 per cent for education) there were to be thirteen 'elected' members from the South and forty-seven from the North.[5]

The purpose of the Legislative Assembly which was thus to be created was, according to the Conference's report, to give the Sudan 'a voice of its own; some body which can speak with authority in the name of the whole Country'. 'The Sudanese', the report continued, 'will not be able to govern themselves unless they have

[1] Thus, writing to R. C. Mayall in 1942, the then Civil Secretary, Mr. D. Newbold, said: 'The majority of the members of Congress are government officials and we must not allow a politically-minded civil service to grow up' (Henderson, p. 244; also pp. 555–6).

[2] *Report*, pp. 6–7. [3] Ibid., p. 7. [4] Ibid., p. 3.

[5] Ibid., pp. 6–7. In addition to the sixty members who were to be elected in this manner, the Conference, it will be recalled, recommended that ten should be directly appointed by the Governor-General.

previously been trained in the art of Government and this in turn can be learnt only through the assumption of responsibility.'[1] But the nature and the extent of the responsibilities which the Conference recommended should be entrusted to the Assembly were by no means consistent with these declared objectives. Indeed, given the Agreements of 1899 and 1936, under which those responsibilities were to be discharged, they could not but be, in effect, advisory. For, in the last resort, the Assembly could not exercise any of the legislative, financial, or administrative functions assigned to it, except with the approval of the Governor-General, beyond whom there was no authority to whom the Assembly could appeal.

With regard to legislation, to begin with, the Assembly, according to the recommendations of the Conference, was to have the right to debate and the power to amend or reject Government Bills (which 'will be initiated by the Executive Council, as would be the case were they a Cabinet').[2] If a Government Bill was passed, it would receive the Governor-General's consent and become law. If, on the other hand, it was rejected or so amended as no longer to fulfil the Government's purpose, the Executive Council would either withdraw the bill or submit it again to the Assembly, stating the reasons for their action. Should the Assembly still feel unable to accept the bill in question, the Governor-General would, regardless of the wishes of the Assembly, give his consent to the Bill, which would thereupon become law.

Private Members Bills would only be introduced with the approval of the Business Committee which, in consultation with the Executive Council, would arrange the business of the Assembly. As in the case with Government Bills, however, legislation introduced in this way would not have the force of law except with the consent of the Governor-General.

From this angle, financial and non-financial legislation would receive the same treatment. The budget, which would be prepared by the Financial Secretary, a civil servant, in consultation with the Finance Committee of the Assembly, would be presented to the Assembly in the same way as other Government Bills. But the Assembly would not debate 'non-votable' expenditure, such as pensions and debt charges, and it would complete its deliberations on the budget within an allotted period of time in order to avoid holding up the government machinery through delay. It would criticize and

[1] *Report*, p. 3. [2] Ibid., p. 4.

reduce, but not increase, all items on the budget except those included in the category of 'non-votable' expenditure. As in the case of non-financial legislation, however, none of the resolutions of the Assembly in this respect would become law except with the approval of the Governor-General.

As the sessions of the Assembly were to last for four months a year, moreover, the Governor-General was to have the right to enact laws during the eight months when the Assembly was not in session, provided that such laws were afterwards submitted to the Assembly for ratification. Should the Assembly fail to ratify such legislation, the Governor-General would still have the power to give it his consent and thus make it law.

Besides, certain subjects were, on the recommendation of the Sudan Administration Conference, to be *ultra vires* the Assembly: e.g. 'legislation affecting the Constitution of the Sudan, of which the law constituting the Assembly will be part—and legislation to do anything contrary to the Constitution of the Sudan'.[1]

In an attempt to forestall the criticism and hostile comment which these provisions inevitably aroused—both in Egypt and in the Sudan—Mr. Robertson quoted the passage from the broadcast talk of his predecessor, in which Sir Douglas Newbold argued that the restrictive rules in the Constitution and Regulations of the Advisory Council were 'designed to facilitate the smooth and orderly running of the Council and not to prevent frank and free expression'.[2] Needless to say, the effect in 1948 was the same as it had been four years earlier—i.e. relentless hostility on the part of the Congress and the Unionists, and qualified acceptance on the part of the Independence Front.

The recommendations of the Sudan Administration Conference with regard to the Executive Council and the administrative functions of the Legislative Assembly, on the other hand, admittedly fell short of the ideal of responsible Cabinet Government at which the Conference felt the Sudan should aim. The main differences between the two were correctly summarized in the Conference's report as follows:

(*a*) Some of the members [of the Executive Council] will not be elected by the Assembly. They are members *ex-officio* and cannot resign.

(*b*) The Executive Council have no majority in the Assembly whereby they can influence the course of debates and voting in that body.

[1] Ibid., p. 5.

[2] *Proceedings of the Eighth Session of the Advisory Council*, 3–10 Mar. 1948, pp. 31–2.

(*c*) The Executive Council will not have the powers of dissolving the Assembly and of subsequently appealing to the country for approval of their policy.[1]

'Under the Constitution of the Sudan', the report continued, 'the ultimate authority is vested in the person of the Governor-General and any conflict between the Executive Council and the Legislative Assembly will have to be resolved by him.'[1]

Given this situation, the best way of training the Sudanese in the art of government was to give them enough responsibility 'to extend fully the capacity of the Sudanese to shoulder it successfully'.[2] Accordingly, the conference recommended that the Governor-General's Council (the place where 'the major decisions are made')[3] should be reconstituted so that not less than half its members should be Sudanese. The Conference considered it essential that the Sudanese members of the Executive Council (as the reconstituted body was designated) should have 'some definite responsibility to the Assembly' for administration, and it therefore proposed that they should be elected by the Assembly from among the Under-Secretaries.[4] These were themselves to be nominated by the Assembly, but could not be finally appointed as Under-Secretaries except with the approval of the *ex-officio* members of the Executive Council, i.e. the heads of the different branches of the administration to which the Under Secretaries, once confirmed, were to be 'attached'. From this point onwards, however, the position of the Under-Secretaries, as described in the report, becomes increasingly ambiguous. The nature of their 'attachments' is not explained, but the report states that 'they must be given the full confidence of the head of the Civil Service Department responsible for their particular subjects' and that, when a question is asked in the Assembly about, for example, the allocation of Nile waters, 'it will normally be the Under-Secretary for Irrigation who will convey to the Assembly the answer provided by the Director of Irrigation'.[5] Instead of elucidating the constitutional meaning of these expressions or clarifying the relationships of Under-Secretaries and Directors of Departments to one another and to the Assembly and the Council, the report of the Administration Conference concluded the discussion of the subject with a rhetorical statement:

. . . we have proposed a system which will ensure the greatest possible synthesis of views between the Assembly and the Executive Council before

[1] *The First Report of the Sudan Administration Conference*, p. 10.
[2] Ibid., p. 3. [3] Ibid., p. 9. [4] Ibid., p. 10. [5] Ibid., p. 6.

any measure is submitted for the Governor-General's consent. Given good will and a spirit of give and take, without which no system of Democratic Government can succeed, and given the presence of Under-Secretaries on both bodies, we think that the Executive Council and the Assembly should be able to work together in harmony.[1]

* * * * * *

The report of the Sudan Administration Conference was discussed, at an official level, by three main bodies: the Advisory Council, the Egyptian Government, and, more importantly, by leading Southern Sudanese and British administrators in the Southern provinces at the Juba Conference of June 1947.

The Advisory Council discussed the report during its seventh session which was held from 20 to 24 May 1947. Two main points were raised: the position of the Under-Secretaries and the method whereby Southern representatives were to be elected. In connection with the second point, the Chairman reassured the Council that there was no intention that Southern representatives should always be appointed—which would have raised the number of appointed members from ten to twenty-three, or to one-third of the proposed total.

With regard to the position of the Under-Secretaries, the Legal Secretary, who had been invited to attend the session as an extraordinary member, said that if the Head of a Department and the Under-Secretary expressed differing views, each would find himself in an impossible position. He proposed to leave the matter at that, but under closer questioning by Mirghani Ḥamza and Makki Abbās, probably the ablest members of the Council, he, in effect, agreed that the position of Under-Secretaries, as described in the report, was intolerably vague. The Legal Secretary told the Council that the most experienced constitutional advisor (Lord Hailey) with whom he had discussed the matter during his recent visit to Britain, began by saying that a bureaucratic system of government was a logical system, and a full parliamentary system, for example as in England, was also logical. But during the transitional period from one to the other 'there must inevitably be illogicalities and many difficulties requiring give and take on both sides'.[2]

[1] Ibid., p. 10.

[2] *Proceedings of the Seventh Session of the Advisory Council*, 20–24 May 1947, p. 78. Earlier on, the Legal Secretary had submitted a note which was read out to the Council. The note added that, during his visit to Britain, the Legal Secretary

Commenting on this, Mirghani Ḥamza said that, in his view, an Under-Secretary should combine the role of a permanent Under-Secretary with that of Parliamentary Under-Secretary: he had a duty to his Department and also to the Assembly. Mirghani Ḥamza felt strongly that both the Head of the Department and his Under-Secretary should be responsible to the Assembly.

Finally, the Advisory Council passed two resolutions, in the first of which it endorsed the recommendations of the report in general, while in the second it recommended 'that the Government give further attention to the position of the Under-Secretaries, which, in the opinion of the Council, requires further definition'.[1]

2. *The abandonment of 'Southern Policy'*

In the Southern Sudan, discussion of the report of the Sudan Administration Conference centred around its unanimously agreed recommendation that the proposed Legislative Assembly should, by contrast with the Advisory Council, extend over the whole country, including the South—a recommendation which clearly implied the negation of the traditional Southern Policy of the Sudan Government.[2] This, as has been indicated in Chapter III, was already being questioned by some of the British administrators who were responsible for its implementation. A few felt it was morally unjustifiable; some sensed that it was probably not going to succeed, while others were disappointed by the failure of Southern Policy to produce 'any Southern staff trained for executive work.... The highly-paid foreigner [i.e. District Commissioner]', complained the District Commissioner of Western District in 1941, 'is doing the job himself rather than

had dealt with no one as an official of His Majesty's Government. 'I saw these persons purely as technical advisers' (p. 75).

[1] *Proceedings of the Seventh Session of the Advisory Council*, p. 79.

[2] A majority wished to state this as the explicit object of their recommendations: 'There is no desire by the peoples of the North to dominate, or to exercise undue influence over the peoples of the South; but, if the advantages of a united Sudan are to be mutual, then the responsibilities of the different parts of the country to one another must also be mutual. And here although this is outside the terms of reference of the Conference, a majority of the members wish to record their opinion that the unification of the Sudanese people would be greatly assisted by the abolition of the Permits to Trade Order, 1928, the adoption of one educational policy for North and South, the teaching of Arabic in the Schools of the South, the improvement of communications between the two parts, the encouragement of transfers of Sudanese officials between the North and South and the unification of the system of establishment' (p. 4).

supervising Africans learning to help themselves. He is not only the motive-power but the whole government machine: if he stops everything comes to a standstill.'[1]

But no suggestion was made that the 1930 statement of Southern Policy needed to be re-examined until after the Graduates' Congress had submitted their Memorandum of 1942, in which they demanded, *inter alia*, 'the abolition of ordinances on "Closed Districts" and the lifting of restrictions placed on trade and on the movements of the Sudanese within the Sudan' and 'the cancellation of subventions to missionary schools and the unification of syllabuses in the Northern and Southern Sudan'. In August of the following year, the Governor of Equatoria, referring to the imminent publication of the Advisory Council legislation, wrote that Southern Policy required reaffirmation though he also felt that the political future of the Southern Policy could not, as yet, be determined; 'but whatever it may be', he continued, 'we should work to a scheme of self-government which would fit in with an ultimate attachment of the Southern peoples Southward or Northward. Northward cannot be excluded if we admit the principle of self-determination, but the policy that is being adopted makes political adhesion to the North improbable from the Southern Point of View.'[2]

The establishment of the Sudanization Committee in March 1946 gave greater impetus to the slowly growing awareness that a review of Southern Policy was overdue. The Sudanization Committee decided that a sub-committee should visit the Southern provinces in order to enquire into conditions there. The Civil Secretary informed the Governor of Equatoria on this occasion that 'the progressive Sudanisation of our governmental machinery is to-day a matter of the greatest political and administrative importance, and it is essential that we should give this sub-committee every opportunity of making realistic recommendations based on knowledge of fact'.[3] But the report of the sub-committee, besides recommending the ending of the differential system of pay which existed under Southern Policy and the unification of the system of establishment, turned out to be, in effect, an indictment of Government policy in

[1] District Commissioner, Western District, to the Governor, Equatoria, 30 June 1941 (CS/I.C.I., Archives, Khartoum).

[2] Governor, Equatoria, to District Commissioner, Western District, 14 Aug. 1943 (CS/I.C.I., Archives, Khartoum).

[3] Governor, Equatoria, to District Commissioners, Torit, Juba, Yei, Moru, Zande, Wau, Rombeck, and Tonj, 25 May 1946 (CS/I.C.I., Archives, Khartoum).

the Southern Sudan, which the Civil Secretary, therefore, refused to publish.[1] However, this was in itself a clear sign that the time had come when the reappraisal of Southern Policy could not, with prudence, be much delayed. Apart from the reports of the Sudanization Committee and the generally increased nationalist pressure for the abolition of Southern Policy and the consolidation of the Unity of the Sudan '. . . East Africa's plans regarding better communications with the southern Sudan have been found to be nebulous', wrote the Civil Secretary. He continued:

Besides the distinctions in rates of pay and other conditions of government service, the artificial rules about employment of Southerners in the North, attempts at economic separation, and all similar distinctions are becoming more and more anomalous as the growing demand for Northerners to be employed in Southern development schemes, the rapidly-growing communication and travel between north and south, and the very application of the policy of pushing forward in the South, break down the previous isolation of the Southern Provinces and strain these distinctions further.[2]

It was, therefore, necessary that a new policy should be formulated. This, Sir James insisted, should not be influenced by appeasement of impatient extremists but must be based on sound economic and social principles which would not only bear defence against factious opposition, but must also command the support of those Sudanese who were prepared to take logical and liberal points of view. After all '. . . it is the Sudanese, northern and southern, who will live their lives and direct their affairs in future generations in this country; and our efforts must, therefore, be concentrated on initiating a policy which is not only sound in itself, but which can be made acceptable to and eventually workable by patriotic Sudanese, northern and southern, alike'.[2] Sir James then stated that the Sudan Government should henceforth 'act upon the fact that the peoples of the Southern Sudan are distinctively African and Negroid, but that geography and economics combine . . . to render them inextricably bound for future development to the middle-eastern and Arabicised Northern Sudan'.[2]

[1] Dirdiri Muḥammad 'Uthmān, a District Judge who was a member of the sub-committee, records that Sir James Robertson described the report as 'an indictment of the Government and not a report' (*Mudhakkirati*, Khartoum, 1961, p. 40).

[2] Civil Secretary to the Legal and Financial Secretaries, Directors of Departments, and Governors of the Southern Provinces, 16 Dec. 1946 (CS/I.C.I., Archives, Khartoum).

The reactions of the British administrators working in the South were varied and interesting. The District Commissioner of Raja, for instance, felt that

the statement of policy is very welcome, as the old Southern Policy was one which no one, I think, could sincerely follow. One welcomes particularly the abandonment of the ridiculously artificial (and ineffective) barriers erected 16 years ago. It is a waste of time to query anyone called 'Amat' [i.e. Aḥmad] and 'Issen' [i.e. Hassan] and then ascertain and write down his tribal name, knowing full well that as soon as he went out of the door his friends would continue to know him not as Ngerebaya or Hgerekudu but by his Arabic name.[1]

The Governor of Juba wrote:

I do not regard the excision of the southern Sudan and its attachment to neighbours on the south as practical politics, not in the best interests of the people themselves, for they would be 'Cinderellas' even more than they are now. Whatever I may have felt in the past, recent developments in the Sudan and in East Africa have convinced me that neither attachment south nor isolationism are possible.[2]

He was, therefore, in full agreement with the proposed new policy.

Others, however, had only a qualified welcome for it. Thus, the Governor of Wau observed that:

Everybody is agreed upon the Civil Secretary's main contention that the South is bound up with the North and that the two have got to hang together as one country.

There is a unanimous feeling that the gap between pay, status and conditions of Northern and Southern staff is unjustified, that this gap splits them into two communities and gives the South a legitimate sense of grievance and that the principle must be accepted of equal pay for equal work.

All agree that restrictions on Northern traders should be withdrawn and that there should be no bar to Southerners going to work in the North if they wished.

All agree that religious discrimination, such as has existed though it may not have been admitted, must cease.

It is the subject of safeguards for the integrity of the South which most needs discussion for the formulation of a concerted attitude. My own

[1] District Commissioner, Raja, to District Commissioner, Western District, 12 Feb. 1947 (CS/I.C.I.). Fifteen years earlier he wrote to the Governor, Bahr al Ghazal: 'I suggest that it is not consistent that I should insist on them using their proper, tribal names and dropping their foreign (Arabic) ones when the Missionaries are permitted to baptise them with another foreign (Italian) one.' 17 Jan. 1932 (CS/I.C.I., Archives, Khartoum).

[2] 23 Dec. 1946 (CS/I.C.I., Archives, Khartoum).

opinion, tending to a measure of regional autonomy, or eventual federation of two rather different entities on an equal basis, and a plain statement that the British will hold the fort till the South doesn't need a garrison, have been stated separately.[1]

Two months later, fourteen British administrators working in the South were 'perturbed by the Minutes of the Administration Conference'. Though they were in agreement with the Civil Secretary's views and the main recommendation of the Conference, they signed a collective letter in which they protested that no Southerners were present at the Conference (a fact which, of course, was itself the result of the operation of Southern Policy) and that the peoples of the Southern provinces were only represented by two Governors. They, therefore, called for 'the institution of an Administration Conference for the Southern Sudan, to meet in the South'.[2]

In reply, the Civil Secretary reassured the signatories of the letter that the Government was fully aware of its responsibilities, that it had taken no decision about the Southern provinces, and that the recommendations of the Sudan Administration Conference had not yet been considered. 'As Chairman of that Conference the Civil Secretary [simply] allowed the Northern Sudanese to speak their minds and they did so.' Finally, Sir James indicated that he was 'willing to call a Conference such as suggested to meet in Juba'.[3]

The Juba Conference was held on 12 and 13 June 1947. Under the Chairmanship of the Civil Secretary, it was attended by the Governors of the Southern provinces, the Director of Establishments, seventeen Southern chiefs and mission-educated men, and six Northerners.

The terms of reference of the Conference were:

1. To consider the recommendations of Sudan Administration Conference about the Southern Sudan.
2. To discuss the advisability of the Southern Sudanese being represented in the proposed Assembly, and if it is decided to be advisable, to decide how such representation can best be obtained in the present circumstances; and whether the representation proposed by the Sudan Administration Conference is suitable.
3. To discuss whether safeguards can be introduced into the forthcoming legislation setting up the new assembly, to ensure that the Southern

[1] Governor, Wau, to Governor, Equatoria: 6 Jan. 1947 (CS/I.C.I., Archives, Khartoum). The idea of federation advocated by the Governor of Wau was later on picked up by some Southern Sudanese.

[2] Letter to Civil Secretary dated 10 Mar. 1947 (CS/I.C.I., Archives, Khartoum).

[3] Governor, Juba, to Deputy Governor, Wau, 30 Apr. 1947 (CS/I.C.I., Archives, Khartoum).

Sudan with its differences in race, tradition, language, customs and outlook is not hindered in its social and political advancement.

4. To discuss whether or not an Advisory Council for the Southern Sudan should be set up to deal with Southern affairs from which representatives might be appointed to sit on the Assembly as representatives of the Southern Sudan.
5. To consider the recommendations of the Sudan Administration Conference in paragraph 13 of their report which deal with matters not strictly relevant to the political development of the Sudan, which the Conference recommended as essential if the unification of the Sudanese people is to be achieved.[1]

After a lengthy discussion, during which various aspects of their terms of reference were discussed, the Juba Conference concluded that it was the wish of the Southern Sudanese to be united with the Northern Sudanese in a united Sudan; that the South should, therefore, be represented in the proposed Legislative Assembly; that the number of Southern representatives should be more than thirteen, as had been recommended by the Sudan Administration Conference; that they should be elected by Province Councils in the South and not by an Advisory Council for the Southern Sudan; that trade and communications should be improved between the two regions, and that steps should be taken towards the unification of the educational policy in the North and South.[2] Certain subjects, however, were left unresolved. Prominent amongst these was the question of whether it was necessary to introduce safeguards into the new constitution, and also whether Southern representatives should be full members from the start, or simply watch the proceedings at first until they had some experience of procedure. Over these (and a few other) matters there was some difference of opinion, but the nature of the Conference, as Sir James reminded his audience, was only exploratory and did not call for full agreement over every single issue. And, as was the case with the recommendations of the Sudan Administration Conference, it was pointed out: 'The decisions, if any, would be taken by the Central Government.'[2]

The matter was brought before the Governor-General's Council during its 559th Meeting, on 29 July 1947. It was then resolved that the main proposals of the Sudan Administration Conference be

[1] Civil Secretary's Memorandum on Juba Conference, 15 May 1947 (CS/I.C.I., Archives, Khartoum). For the recommendations of the Sudan Administration Conference mentioned in (5) see p. 166, n. 2 above.

[2] The Record of Discussions of the, Juba Conference (CS/I.C.I., Archives, Khartoum).

accepted in principle and that 'the proposal that the Legislative Assembly should be representative of the whole Sudan and that its scope should not be limited to the Northern Sudan be accepted, but that safeguards be introduced into the legislation setting up the new constitution which will ensure the healthy and steady development of the Southern people'.[1]

3. *The making of the new constitution*

From the point of view of the Egyptian Government (and that of the Sudanese nationalists, irrespective of religious and political differences) the creation of an all-Sudanese Assembly was not, as such, a subject for debate; it was a belated correction of a long-standing injustice, for which they had for many years criticized the British administration of the Sudan. Their criticisms of the new proposals were directed against what was, in their view, the failure of these proposals to give the Sudanese an adequate share in the government of their country—that they offered 'too little, too late'. The degree to which the Sudanese held this view and the conclusions they drew from it regarding participation in the Assembly varied, as usual, between the supporters of the Independence Front and the advocates of the Unity of the Nile Valley. Whereas the former were, in the last resort, prepared to accept the recommendations of the Administration Conference as representing one more step on the road to self-government and eventual independence, the Unionists were, like the Egyptian Government, strongly critical of the new proposals and rejected them as wholly inadequate.

At its 559th meeting of 29 July—i.e. a week before the Anglo-Egyptian dispute was brought before the Security Council—the Governor-General's Council decided that the proposals of the Administration Conference be submitted to the Governments of Egypt and Britain for their consideration. The British Government approved them as being 'well calculated to achieve the proclaimed purposes of the Co-Domini, namely, the progressive development of self-Government in the Sudan'.[2] The Egyptian Government, on the other hand, sent a Note in which the proposals were criticized in some

[1] Minutes of the 559th Meeting of the Governor-General's Council, held in the Palace, Khartoum, on 29 July 1947 (Archives, Khartoum).

[2] In *Proceedings of the Eighth Session of the Advisory Council*, 3–10 Mar. 1948, p. 20.

detail. Unless 'the defects pointed out in the note', said the President of the Council of Ministers, 'were removed and other amendments proposed in it were introduced, the Royal Egyptian Government could not approve of these recommendations'. While fully maintaining their position as defined before the Security Council, the Egyptian Government were sincerely desirous 'as emphasised on several occasions' of enabling the Sudanese to govern themselves, and did not wish to see the Sudanese miss any opportunity of increasing their share in the government of their country. But, though this was supposedly the objective of the Sudan Administration Conference, their recommendations implied the exact opposite. To begin with, the proposed system did not allow for 'the proper and full representation of the Sudanese'. In the South, representatives were 'frankly' appointed by Provincial Governors, while in the rural areas of the Northern Sudan, the definition of electors and constituencies was left to the discretion of Provincial Governors. Besides, ten of the proposed seventy members of the Assembly were to be directly appointed by the Governor-General. 'If we add that civil servants may be permitted to sit as members of the Legislative Assembly while retaining their posts, we may well inquire to what extent will the Legislative Assembly . . . be removed from the influence of the executive authorities even within the bounds of its limited jurisdiction?'

With regard to the powers of the Assembly, the memorandum continued, no one would have suggested that the Sudanese were, at that time, in a position to exercise full legislative rights. But if the purpose of the Assembly was to train them in self-government, then they should not, as the Administration Conference recommended, be given a purely consultative voice in law-making. The Assembly should, at least, be given the power to postpone the passage of an unacceptable piece of legislation until the next session, though it would not be too much to give them the right finally to reject such legislation. In particular, the Assembly should be given the authority 'as from now, to approve taxation in accordance with the well-known principle: "no taxation without representation"'.

While the powers of the Assembly should thus be increased, those of the Governor-General who, in accordance with the existing proposals, had 'absolute powers to approve or reject legislation', should be reduced. He should not either reject or approve a legislation passed by the Legislative Assembly and the Executive Council, except with the consent of the Egyptian and British Governments. The relationship between the Sudanese and British members of the Executive Council should, likewise, be altered so that the former should have a greater share of responsibility. In accordance with the existing proposals, the four *ex-officio* members, though a minority, held all the most important positions in the Government and, in addition, also had the final word in the choice of the Under-Secretaries, from amongst whom the six Sudanese members of the Executive Council were chosen. In order to correct this serious imbalance 'it is essential that the Sudanese should have a share of the key positions in the Executive Council and should also have all the other posts in the Sudan Government'. And, 'without prejudicing the right of the Sudanese', Egyptians should also be appointed to the Council, 'so that [they] may help the Sudanese in training in self-government'.[1]

In reply, the Governor-General informed the President of the Council of Ministers that the Sudan Government had accepted the Report of the Sudan Administration Conference in principle, but that in preparing the Ordinance they had 'already anticipated many of the points made in Your Excellency's Note'.[2] An *aide-mémoire* which was distributed to members of the Advisory Council made the same point, adding that the new Ordinances would go substantially further than the Report. 'The anxiety of the Royal Egyptian Government to give greater responsibility to the Sudanese than is visualised in the Report . . . is shared by the Sudan Government. . . . It is the wish of the Sudan Government to give the Sudanese now as much responsibility as they can undertake without imperilling good government.'[3]

However, the draft Ordinance did not, as was promised in the *aide-mémoire*, 'go substantially further' than the report of the Administration Conference; nor did it meet 'most of the modifications suggested' by the Egyptian Prime Minister, as the Governor-General had said it would. On the contrary, as the Explanatory Note states,

[1] *Proceedings of the Eighth Session of the Advisory Council*, pp. 20–5.

[2] Ibid., p. 26.

[3] Ibid., p. 27. *The Times* commented: 'These Egyptian proposals seem to represent an attempt to outbid Britain for the support of those Sudanese who are eager to obtain a share of immediate political power, but it is by no means certain that they are conceived in the best interests of the country as a whole. . . . Even so, the suggestions for giving increased power to the proposed legislative assembly deserve examination, provided that the members of the assembly are, in fact, representative of the country as a whole and not merely of the urban educated classes' (9 Jan. 1948).

'in most respects the Ordinance follows fairly closely the lines recommended by the Sudan Administration Conference'.[1]

The main differences between the two were, firstly, that, whereas the Conference had recommended that Under-Secretaries should be appointed to serve in Government Departments, the Ordinance provided that the Governor-General 'may', in addition, appoint Ministers to one or more of the several Departments of Government. As the Explanatory Note stated, however, it was 'not proposed to appoint Ministers at the outset, as it is intended that potential Ministers should first gain experience and prove themselves as Under-Secretaries'.[1] And whereas, in accordance with the Conference's report, the Assembly was to have chosen the Under-Secretaries, the Ordinance provided that, since these were intended to develop into Ministers, they should be appointed in the same way as Ministers, i.e. by the Government—thus leaving the Assembly with even less power than had been recommended by the Administration Conference. Defending this point in the Advisory Council, the Civil Secretary said that in no Cabinet Government anywhere in the world were Ministers chosen by the Assembly; they are chosen by the Prime Minister to speak on behalf of the Government. But the obvious difficulty with this argument, as Mirghani Ḥamza was quick to point out, was that the analogy of the Prime Minister in England, which was quoted by the Chairman, was no parallel to the situation in the Sudan, since the Prime Minister himself was appointed by a majority of the members of Parliament and, though he selected his own Ministers, he was responsible to Parliament for their action, so that, if he lost the confidence of Parliament, he and his team would be dismissed and replaced by another. The Legal Secretary's comment was that Lord Hailey, whose opinion had been sought on this very point, had insisted that Under-Secretaries must be Government appointments if the situation was to work and the Chairman repeated that this was one of the illogicalities inevitable at that stage on the road to self-government. Until full party Government with its corollary of Ministerial responsibility was established, he declared, this temporary arrangement would have to be accepted.[2]

The second modification introduced in the draft Ordinance was also more apparent than real. For, although Government Servants

[1] *Proceedings of the Eighth Session of the Advisory Council*, p. 54.
[2] Ibid., pp. 39 and 58–9.

were generally disqualified from appointment as members of the Executive Council, the Kaid (Commander-in-Chief of the Sudan Defence Force) and the three Secretaries were exempted from this ruling, and the Governor-General was given the power to declare, by order, that certain Government Servants should not be so disqualified. And although a Government Servant could not become a Minister, he could be appointed an Under-Secretary, a member of the Council or a nominated member of the Assembly. In this connection it is interesting to note that, although a Government servant could thus be *appointed* a member of the Assembly, he could not stand for *election* to the Assembly. This, Mirghani Ḥamza pointed out, might be taken to imply that the Government only wanted members of the Assembly who would speak as the Government wished. In reply, the Chairman said that the opinion of the Council at the previous session was that a Government servant should not stand for election.[1]

In the draft Ordinance, the number of members was raised from about seventy, as recommended by the Conference, to about ninety, of whom sixty-five were to be elected instead of sixty. Thus, although the number of elected members was greater, their proportion, compared with those who were to be appointed, was reduced. One reason for this, stated the Explanatory Note, was the provisional decision not to allow Government servants to stand for election. 'If there were no nominations apart from the Under-Secretaries, etc., the largest and most influential section of educated opinion would be barred from the Assembly except as holders of office.'[2] Needless to say 'educated opinion' especially in the Congress, was not impressed by this argument and continued to prefer free elections to official appointments as it did, in general, direct elections to indirect elections. To the dismay of this section of public opinion, however, the Ordinance provided for direct elections in only ten constituencies (of which half were in Omdurman and Khartoum) the remaining members being either directly appointed by the executive or chosen, by means of indirect elections, under the suspect supervision of Governors and District Commissioners.

The powers of the Assembly and the Executive Council were as circumscribed in the draft Ordinance as they had been in the report of the Administration Conference. Unlike the Advisory Council,

[1] *Proceedings of the Eighth Session of the Advisory Council*, p. 73.
[2] Ibid., p. 54.

the Assembly was entitled to hold debates and pass resolutions on any subject but, as in the case of the Advisory Council, 'all resolutions', stated the draft of the Legislative Assembly, 'shall have effect as recommendations to the Council'.[1] But neither the Assembly nor the Executive Council had the power to act, in any way, except with the approval of the Governor-General. In particular, the Assembly had no power to pass legislation affecting the constitution of the Sudan, its relations with foreign powers, or relations between the Sudan Government and the Governments of Britain and Egypt. Under the existing constitution of the Sudan, the Governor-General, in person, had been vested by the British and Egyptian Governments with very wide powers of which, under the terms of the 1899 Agreement, he could not divest himself. Both the report of the Administration Conference and the draft Ordinance were aimed at creating a Legislative Assembly and an Executive Council which exercised certain powers within the framework of the existing system. At the very best, therefore, they could provide for representative, but not responsible, government. Responsibility, in the last resort lay with the Governor-General, who alone had the constitutional right to make or unmake any law in the Sudan so long as the Anglo-Egyptian regime continued to exist.[2] This was as abundantly clear in the draft Ordinance as it had been in the Conference's report.

For this reason, and because it did not provide for 'the proper and full representation of the Sudanese' and failed to take cognizance of the other suggestions they had made, the Egyptian Government rejected the draft Ordinance. The Advisory Council on the other hand approved the draft in principle and, in the course of a lengthy discussion, indicated that, in their view, the Assembly should have some say in the appointment of some members of the Executive Council, that the Sudanese in the Council should not be in a minority,

[1] Ibid., p. 41.

[2] In this connection Shaikh Abu Shama 'Abd al-Maḥmoud not incorrectly pointed out that the principal obstacle in the path of progress towards full self-government was the existence of the Anglo-Egyptian regime, and that, unless the Governor-General and the governments of Egypt and Britain divested themselves of their rights as co-rulers, the country would move from one experiment to another without actually reaching the desired end. 'Since the Governor-General's powers must be relinquished ultimately,' he asked 'why not delegate them now?' In reply, the Chairman said that although Shaikh Abu Shama's views would be recorded in the proceedings, he could not, in his capacity as an official of the Sudan Government, make any answer to them (ibid., p. 63).

that there were already certain Sudanese fitted to be Ministers and that Ministers could be appointed at once in at least four Government Departments: namely, Education, Health, Agriculture, and Economics and Trade.

Having been approved by the British (but not by the Egyptian) Government, 'The Executive Council and Legislative Assembly Ordinance, 1948' was published, in its final form, on 19 June 1948. It endorsed two of the recommendations of the Advisory Council, but was otherwise substantially the same as the draft Ordinance. The two modifications were that Ministers, as well as Under-Secretaries, were to be appointed and that at least half the members of the Executive Council were to be Sudanese. But the Council's recommendation that the Assembly should have some say in the appointment of some members of the Executive Council was disregarded. Instead, the Ordinance provided that the Assembly was to elect one of its members to be Leader of the Assembly. The Leader would be appointed Minister by the Governor-General, and in consultation with him the Governor-General would appoint Ministers. But the Governor-General could dismiss Ministers or Under-Secretaries and appoint others in their place. He had the power to define special matters (defence, currency, and the status of religious and racial minorities) on which the Assembly could not legislate without the consent of the Executive Council, and the reserved matters on which the Assembly could not, under any circumstances, legislate (i.e. the Ordinance itself, foreign relations, Sudanese nationality, and relations between the Sudan Government and the Governments of Egypt and the United Kingdom). In addition, the Governor-General continued to have the last word in all the actions of the Assembly and the Council. He could dissolve the former, veto the decisions of the latter and, finally, he could amend or suspend the Ordinance.

As may be expected, the Graduates' Congress and the Unionists who continued to speak in its name were strongly critical of the Ordinance and organized demonstrations in all the principal towns of the Sudan in order to protest against the establishment of an Assembly which they, not incorrectly, conceived had some of the appearances but none of the substance of democratic institutions and which failed to give the Sudanese an effective share in the government of their country. Demonstrations involving clashes with the police were particularly violent on polling day—15 November, when ten people were killed and over a hundred injured.[1] A boycott of elections in the ten urban constituencies where polling was by direct election was also organized by the Congress and the Unionists, and as a result only 18 per cent of the registered electorate voted[1]—compared with an average of about 50 per cent in the sixty-five urban centres in which direct elections were held in 1953.[2] The Independence Front on the other hand 'fought' the elections and, naturally, won the majority of seats in the Assembly. This was formally opened on 15 December 1948, and the occasion was accompanied by more hostile demonstrations during which Ismā'īl al-Azhari, the leader of the Ashigga party, was arrested.

4. *Towards self-government: the conflict of parties and policies*

It is obvious that, compared with the Advisory Council, the Legislative Assembly and the Executive Council represented a considerable advance towards the closer association of the Sudanese with the government of their country. Apart from the budget, which was only once introduced in the Advisory Council (during its final session), the Assembly and the Executive Council discussed and actively participated in the formulation of a number of important laws covering such matters as the nationalization of the Jazīra Scheme, labour legislation, the introduction of the Arabic language in the administrative and educational systems of the Southern provinces and, most importantly, the amendment of the constitution with a view to giving the Sudanese self-government in preparation for self-determination.

Nevertheless, the Assembly and the Executive Council fell short of the expectations of the Sudanese. Less than fourteen months after they had been inaugurated, the Legal Secretary observed: 'there is no doubt that the present arrangements are far from that "democratic self-government" that all Sudanese political parties want (whatever else they differ in)'. He continued:

First of all, the Executive Council is not responsible to the Assembly; then there are the, on paper, limitless powers of the Governor-General to interfere in every and any decision and alter it to his liking. A third

[1] G. Kirk, *Survey of International Affairs: The Middle East, 1945–50* (London, 1954), p. 142.

[2] *Report of The Sudan Electoral Commission*, Sudan, no. 1 (1954), Cmd. 9058, p. 17.

major objection is the position of Secretaries in the Council. . . . Lesser objections are the presence of nominated members in the Assembly and insufficient representation of the intelligentsia, those who take the most interest in politics, and can take an active part in them; and the small number of direct elections.[1]

Four months earlier the Civil Secretary complained that some of the nominated members, though they 'do fill a gap', did not play a very conspicuous part in the Assembly's proceedings. Also 'the weight and solidity of the tribal country members [did] not make for rapid comprehension of complicated legislation'. Sir James, therefore, wondered whether it might not be a good idea to create a graduates' constituency and a few more constituencies covering the small towns, so that the existing state of imbalance between the educated and other members of the Assembly might be mended.[2] 'In the present Assembly', he elaborated afterwards, 'out of the sixty-five elected members there are only twelve who are sufficiently educated and intelligent to take a real share in committee work. Of these two are tribal leaders. . . . On the other hand, some of the so-called "educated" [nominated] members . . . have played little part in the Assembly or in committee.'[3] He went as far as declaring in public that some members of the Assembly did not adequately represent their constituencies.[4]

The points thus made by the Legal and Civil Secretaries were among the most important reasons why 'all Sudanese political parties (whatever else they differed in)'[5] were dissatisfied with the Assembly and the Executive Council. The Unionist parties and the Khatmiyya, as we have seen, had boycotted the new institutions and the Ashigga at any rate continued their relentless campaign against them until they were finally dissolved. The Independence Front and the Anṣār, though they, consistently with their programme, did not boycott the Assembly and the Council, were also dissatisfied. In addition to those points which they, in common with other groups, held against the Assembly and the Council, the Mahdists had special reasons for discontent. They had never completely recovered from

[1] Note on 'The Executive Council and Legislative Assembly Ordinance, 1948', dated 4 Feb. 1950 (file SCR/1.A.20, vol. i, Archives, Khartoum).

[2] Civil Secretary to all Governors, District Commissioners, and the Commissioner of Port Sudan, 19 Nov. 1949 (file SCO/1.A.20/9, Archives, Khartoum).

[3] The Civil Secretary to the Governor, Bahr al Ghazal, 17 Dec. 1949 (file SCO/1.A.20/9, Archives, Khartoum).

[4] *al-Ra'i al-'Aām Daily*, Khartoum, 7 Oct. 1949.

[5] The Legal Secretary's statement quoted above.

the shock of the Ṣidqi–Bevin Protocol and had since come to be increasingly suspicious of the British and Sudan Governments. They feared that the Sudan might, under Arab and American pressure, be 'sold out' to Egypt in a bargain over the Suez Canal—a point on which Sir Anthony Eden subsequently revealed that the Mahdists were right.[1] Their doubts and fears increased when it became known, towards the end of 1949, that Anglo-Egyptian negotiations were to be resumed. They (especially Sayyid 'Abd al-Raḥmān al-Mahdi)[2] therefore became increasingly anxious to achieve immediate self-government, as a first step towards independence. The decision of the United Nations Organization at about the same time, that the former Italian colonies of Libya and Somaliland were to become independent was a further stimulus to the independence movement in the Sudan.

In 1949 and 1950, however, the Sudan Government felt that 'any demand for self-government in the near future is . . . premature'[3]—and even as late as 20 February 1952 the Foreign Office informed the Civil Secretary: 'It is not yet His Majesty's Government's policy that the Sudan should be prepared for self-determination by 1953.'[4] Accordingly, the Civil Secretary directed that 'we must play for time'[5] while one of his colleagues stated that 'the job of the British in this country is to delay the day of self-government as long as possible without alienating those Sudanese whose co-operation we cannot afford to lose'.[6]

Both in order to achieve this end and to soften the opposition therefore, it was decided, six months after the inauguration of the Assembly, that the Ordinance should be amended. 'What is required',

[1] Sir Anthony Eden describes how the United States Government, especially after the abrogation of the Anglo-Egyptian Agreement and the treaty of 1936 in October 1951, continued to urge the British Government to recognize King Farouq as King of the Sudan—as part of a 'package deal'; see the memoirs of Sir Anthony Eden, *Full Circle* (London, 1960), pp. 230–8.

[2] It was frequently reported in 1949 and 1950 that Sayyid 'Abd al-Raḥmān al-Mahdi was 'the prime mover' or 'the main pressure' behind this movement; that not all the leaders of the Umma Party were agreed that the time had come for full self-government; but that he was pushing them along the road to immediate self-government.

[3] 'Note on Amendment to the Ordinance to Secure Khatmia Participation' by W. H. T. Luce, 2 Nov. 1949 (file no. SCO/1.A.20/9, Archives, Khartoum).

[4] Dispatch no. JE/1015/15, dated 20 Feb. 1952 (file no. SCO/1.A.20/9, Archives, Khartoum).

[5] Civil Secretary to the Governor-General, 9 Jan. 1950 (file no. SCO/1.A.20/8, Archives, Khartoum).

[6] 'Note on the Amendment to the Ordinance to Secure Khatmia Participation' quoted above.

wrote the clerk of the Assembly 'is something on the lines of a Royal Commission on which, while the Assembly members should be in the majority, reasonable Khatmia (now divorced from the Ashigga) should be strongly represented.'[1] It was considered that the participation of the Khatmiyya in the proposed Commission and the reformed Assembly would be possible, because they, unlike the Ashigga and other die-hard Unionists were known to desire only a weak form of association with Egypt (dominion status) and were, therefore, not opposed, in principle, to participating in the Assembly but wished to see certain specific modifications of the Ordinance and the electoral system carried out.[2] Their co-operation was considered 'on every account desirable',[3] but more especially because it was hoped that they would act as a check on the Anṣār within the Assembly. Since the Khatmiyya were opposed to the idea of an independent Sudan under a Mahdist monarchy (the main reason why they were Unionists), it was argued, they would resist the plans of the Anṣār for immediate self-government and an early termination of the Anglo-Egyptian regime.[3]

A long and arduous process of informal consultations then ensued and on 19 March 1950, *Ṣawat al-Sūdān*, the organ of the Khatmiyya, published an editorial headed 'The Amendments Demanded by Some

[1] M. F. A. Keen, 16 July 1949 (file no. SCO/1.A.20/9, vol. i, Archives, Khartoum).

[2] The views of the Ashigga and the Graduates' Congress on the subject were clearly summarized in an article in *al M'ūtamar*, the organ of the Congress on 25 Nov. 1949. The article, which was entitled 'The Amendment to the Legislative Assembly Ordinance Makes Conditions Worse', stated that the Anglo-Egyptian regime would not come to an end unless the people were resolved to boycott it. 'However, in the ever watchful eye of imperialism it is essential to shatter the people's solidarity. . . . In pursuance of this end imperialism established the Advisory Council, the Sudanisation Committee and other devices which were successfully resisted by the citizens. . . . Imperialism therefore abandoned these institutions and created a new body, the Legislative Assembly to which ministers and under-secretaries have been appointed, although in its essence it is not different from the Advisory Council. . . . But imperialism would continue to make changes and amendments in order to entice new supporters from amongst those who have hitherto been affected by patriotism and enlisted themselves as nationalists. Every change and amendment therefore makes things worse from the national point of view. After all imperialism can easily make changes, amendments or even grant so-called independence so long as its interests are safeguarded.' It was against this background that Ismā'īl al-Azhari made his famous statement about the Assembly—'Lun nudkhulahā wa-lao jā'at kāmilatan mubarr'atan min kulli 'Aib' (i.e. 'We shall not participate in it even if it were to be made perfect and free from all defects').

[3] Note on the 'Amendment to the Ordinance to Secure Khatmia participation' quoted above.

Prominent Khatmiyya Leaders and Independents'. The amendments which were described in the article as both minimal and integral included the following:

Direct Elections

1. All elections to be direct in towns and villages, and in tribes where possible. There will be no objection, when direct elections are difficult, in some few places, for the introduction of the double-stage system, provided that the elections should be free and unrestricted in both stages and by secret ballot, and provided that no pressure is brought to bear on any person, so that the election would fully express the views of the people.
2. The complete abolition of the residence proviso because, apart from being contrary to democratic rules, it prevents capable persons from standing for election outside their zones.
3. Official elements, such as Nāẓirs, Omdas and Sheikhs, should not stand for election unless they first relinquish their posts.

The Powers of the Assembly

1. The Assembly to be granted full legislative and financial powers; its decisions should be binding on the Executive Council.
2. Its Speaker and Leader to be elected.
3. The Leader to be equal to a prime minister and should have the right to select the ministers and under-secretaries.
4. The principle of ministerial responsibility should be applied and the cabinet should be responsible to the Assembly.
5. The Assembly to have the right of forcing the whole cabinet to resign through voting of non-confidence.

The Executive Council

1. A Minister to be selected for every big department.
2. Small departments with similar functions to be amalgamated forming one Ministry.
3. All ministers to be members of the Executive Council and should exercise full ministerial powers in their relevant ministries.[1]

The proposals concerning the powers of the Assembly of the Executive Council were not formally discussed in the Assembly at the time, but were largely reflected in subsequent revisions of the constitution. Instead it was decided, on the suggestion of Abdalla Bey Khalīl, the leader of the Assembly, that the Sudanese should be given a majority in the Executive Council and that the number of

[1] Official translation.

Ministers be revised from three to four—preferably including one Khatmi Minister. This, the Governor-General commented, would

enable them [the Sudanese] to claim that they are now, in fact, self-governing as far as internal government is concerned. I have no fear that the work of the government in the Executive Council will go on . . . much the same as before and in any case there is the Governor-General's very wide powers of veto. The thing is beautifully simple. It would avoid the necessity for further experiments in constitution building through such rather complicated proposals as those recently put up by the Legal Secretary[1] for which the time is certainly not yet ripe unless we are forced from outside.[2]

Accordingly, a British member of the Council resigned and a Sudanese was appointed in his place (thus giving the Sudanese a majority of seven to six in the Council) but the number of Ministers remained at three as all the Khatmiyya who were invited to become Ministers refused to accept the appointment.[3]

The proposals of the Khatmiyya regarding the elections on the other hand were incorporated in a 'Memorandum on Suggested Amendments to the Executive Council and Legislative Assembly Ordinance' which was presented to the Assembly on 17 April 1950 by the Civil Secretary. The Memorandum having been discussed in some considerable detail, the Civil Secretary moved, on 6 November 1950, 'that the Assembly requests His Excellency the Governor-

[1] Considering the shortcomings of the Assembly and the Council, and trying to anticipate the possible effects of the approaching Anglo-Egyptian negotiations and avoid the danger of lagging behind the demands of those who were inclined to co-operate with the Government, the Legal Secretary suggested, in February 1950, a 'new jump' which he hoped would 'cure all the defects of the present scheme' and yet be 'reasonably safe'. According to his plan, the Sudanese were to be given 'an all-elected Assembly with an all-Sudanese cabinet responsible to the Assembly, with Defence and Foreign Affairs only reserved from it, i.e. full home-rule. . . . There would be more weighting of the constituencies in favour of the intelligentsia. . . . [But] . . . the Governor-General to have foreign affairs and defence still vested in him and to have definite powers to intervene . . . for the fundamental matters of preserving law and order, stopping bankruptcy, and seeing fair play for foreign communities (including the British officials).' The constitution thus established would last for ten years after which an International Commission 'preferably not from U.N.O. and including an Indian on it [would] decide whether the country was ready yet for full self-government, and if so whether the people were in a position to choose for themselves what their future status was to be and if so to run the referendum' (P/SCR/I.A.1/2, Archives, Khartoum).

[2] Confidential Memorandum, 13 Feb. 1950 (SCR/I.A.11, Archives, Khartoum).

[3] Civil Secretary's Note on a conversation with Mirghani Ḥamza on 19 May 1950 (SCO/I.A.20/9, Archives, Khartoum).

General to appoint an electoral commission to review the present constituencies and methods of election under the Executive Council and Legislative Assembly Ordinance, 1948, and to make recommendations thereon'. An amendment was moved to add the words:

and in view of the irreparable harm which would accrue to the good repute of this Assembly as a result of any attempt at political bargaining recommends that the commission be instructed that no change should be made in any constituency save where it can be overwhelmingly shown that it will make for the better representation of the country in the Assembly, and that, in particular, no new constituency of less than 80,000 inhabitants be constituted and no existing homogeneous group be split up merely because its numbers are large.

To this amendment the Leader of the Assembly moved a sub-amendment to omit all the words after '. . . the better representation of the country in the Assembly'. The sub-amendment having been approved the amendment was (after a tedious and repetitive discussion) defeated and Sir James's motion carried.[1] The Assembly then recommended that the residence qualifications for candidates be repealed in the case of constituencies in which elections were to be carried out by the direct method; that the Ordinance be amended to provide for additional seats in the Assembly to represent the educated classes; that *ex-officio* membership of the electoral colleges be abolished; that the residence qualifications for voters be reduced to six months, and that property qualifications be repealed.[2]

It is clear that these amendments went a long way towards meeting the requirements of the Khatmiyya with regard to the reform of the electoral system. The Khatmiyya, however, had from the start condemned the 'Memorandum on Suggested Amendments' not so much because it did not fully meet their objections to the existing electoral system, but because their other suggestions, about the powers of the Assembly and the Executive Council were completely ignored. 'What is the use of three or four constituencies for the educated class amidst a hundred constituencies represented by well known people?' asked *Ṣawt al-Sūdān* in April. 'What good will be obtained by adopting the traditions of the British House of Commons without its regulations and powers? Where is the [much-discussed] full self-government and sovereignty of the people over the country?'[3]

[1] *Proceedings of the First Assembly*, Second Session, no. 9, 1–7 Nov. 1950 (Khartoum), p. 380.

[2] Ibid., no. 11, 15–21 Nov. 1950 (Khartoum), pp. 449–50.

[3] *Ṣawt al-Sūdān*, Khartoum, 20 Apr. 1950.

Khatmiyya leaders, as has been mentioned above, subsequently refused to participate in the (slightly) modified Executive Council and continued to be critical of it and of the Assembly. And when the electoral Commission was established they also boycotted it.

In the meantime, the Anṣār and the Independence Front had been intensifying their campaign for immediate self-government and the termination of the 'hateful' Anglo-Egyptian regime. They approached the Khatmiyya towards the end of 1949 and early in 1950 with a view to reaching an agreement over this issue. They proposed that a number of the existing Legislative Assembly members should resign in order to allow some Khatmiyya members to take their place and that the Ministers be increased from three to eight and be divided equally between the Umma and the Khatmiyya. This having been done, steps would be taken to amend the Executive Council and Legislative Assembly Ordinance. The Khatmiyya, however, refused this offer, insisting that there must first be an amendment to the Ordinance after which new elections should be held.[1] Had it been possible for them to agree at that juncture, the whole situation would have been transformed. However, with such a long history of rivalry and mutual suspicion behind them, they almost invariably disagreed, and, for the time being continued following different paths towards what was afterwards seen to be their common objective of self-government and independence.[2]

Thus having failed to reach agreement with the Khatmiyya, the Anṣār had to concentrate their efforts on the Assembly, which was, after all, the constitutional channel formally recognized to speak for the Sudanese. Since all the Ministers and most of the Under-

[1] Civil Secretary to all Governors and the Commissioner of Port Sudan, 4 Jan. 1950 (SCO/I.A.20/9, Archives, Khartoum).

[2] The Government's view on this question was clearly stated in the 'Note on the Amendment to the Ordinance to Secure Khatmia Participation' dated 2 Nov. 1949: '. . . the job of the British in this country is to delay the day of self-government as long as possible. . . . The obvious answer to any demand for self-government in the very near future is that it is premature to talk of self-government while the Sudanese are divided among themselves and a large number of them have no part in the constitutional bodies. The absence of the Khatmia from the Assembly is therefore a useful weapon in our hands with which to counter any demands at the moment for self-government. We might strike a bargain with the Umma on the lines of—"We will not press amendments to the Ordinance to bring the Khatmia into the Assembly before it runs its three years if you will not press us now for self-government". This may sound a bit Machiavellian but I think in these days we must use any weapon we have.'

Secretaries were members of the Umma Party, the Anṣār had the advantage of being able to speak, within the Assembly, not merely as another political group but also, to some extent, as the Government. Even then, however, they could not hope to persuade the thirteen members from the Southern provinces to vote for immediate self-government, as these were solidly opposed to self-government and independence until 'backward areas . . . which had been neglected in the last fifty years . . . reached the standard of the North in civilization'.[1] The campaign for self-government, therefore, had to be directed, in the main, towards the tribal Shaikhs and country members from the Northern provinces. Some of these, however, were Khatmiyya and could not be dealt with in isolation from their national leadership, while most, being tribal Shaikhs, owed their position to the native administration of the existing regime and not to the Mahdiyya, which had almost completely destroyed tribalism and undermined the position of the Shaikhs. Unless they were already committed to the Umma Party, therefore, it could not be taken for granted that they would support immediate self-government. In January 1950, moreover, the Civil Secretary pointed out to all province Governors the significance of the 'intensive campaign' which had just been launched, and asked them to make it perfectly clear to the country members in their provinces that, although Ministers and Under-Secretaries supported the proposal for self-government, 'the Government as a whole' did not.

It is most important to take the opportunity of the present prorogation of the Assembly to correct the possible misapprehension among the country members. Would you please therefore show this letter to the senior District Commissioners in your provinces and ask them to explain to the Legislative Assembly members in their districts that in this matter the Ministers and Under-Secretaries are speaking as members of the Umma Party and not for the Government as a whole. My view is that the bulk of the people whom the country members represent have no desire to precipitate steps towards self-government at the present time, and that the Khatmia who are not yet fully represented in the Legislative Assembly, are entitled as much as the Umma and Ansar to have a say in the matter.[2]

[1] Sayyid Benjamin Lwoki (Equatoria) in the debate on self-government in Dec. 1950 (*Proceedings of the First Assembly*, Second Session, no. 14, 6–16 Dec. 1950 (Khartoum), p. 610). Sayyid Benjamin's remarks are typical of those made by other members from the Southern Provinces.

[2] Civil Secretary to all Governors and the Commissioner Port Sudan (SCO/I.A.*0/9, Archives, Khartoum).

It is not surprising therefore that when the Assembly was reconvened in March and several suggestions were made to the effect that the Sudan had reached the stage at which self-government should be assumed, a majority of the members disagreed.[1]

By November, when the resolution asking the Governor-General to constitute an electoral commission was passed, the struggle was still going on and the Umma party were by no means certain that they could carry the Assembly on a vote of immediate self-government. By this time, however, patience was running short and self-government was the subject of everyday talk. Meanwhile Anglo-Egyptian negotiations had been resumed, and on 16 November Sudanese opinion was jolted by a speech from the throne in which the Egyptian Government declared their intention to abrogate the 1899 Agreement and the Treaty of 1936 in preparation for the unification of the Nile Valley under the Egyptian crown. The Civil Secretary was asked, in the Assembly, what the reaction of the Sudan Government would be in the case of the Egyptian Government carrying out their threat. He replied: 'That is a hypothetical question and we must wait and see.'[2] The Umma Party was not satisfied and decided to press on with its demand for immediate self-government. On 13 December Sayyid Muḥammad al-Hāj al-Amīn moved that an address be presented to the Governor-General in the following terms: 'We the members of the Legislative Assembly of the Sudan are of opinion that the Sudan has now reached the stage at which self-government could be granted, and request Your Excellency to approach the Comdominium Powers with a request that a joint declaration of the grant of self-government be made before the end of the Third Session of the First Assembly, so that the next election may be held on this basis.'[3] Consistently with the approved policy of playing for time and delaying the day of self-government as long as possible[4] the Civil Secretary, using a number of arguments—including the un-Burkian one that 'a great number of the members had come from far away and were not able to consult their Constituents on this matter'—suggested that the motion had better be postponed until the next session, when it could be dealt with in

[1] *Proceedings of the First Assembly*, Second Session, no. 1, 6–14 Mar. 1950, p. 12 n.

[2] Ibid., no. 11, 15–21 Nov. 1950, p. 453.

[3] Ibid., no. 14, 6–16 Dec. 1950, p. 593.

[4] Above, p. 181 and p. 186, n. 2.

April or May.[1] However, the debate was continued on the following day, when Sayyid Yūsif al-'Agab, one of the country members who had obviously been canvassed by District Commissioners in accordance with the Civil Secretary's instructions, moved an amendment to the address, as follows:

We the members of the Legislative Assembly of the Sudan are of opinion that the Sudan has made good progress towards the stage at which full self-government can be granted, and request Your Excellency to press on urgently with such measures which, while consistent with the maintenance of good government throughout the country, will ensure, not only that such self-government shall be full and complete, but also that, in working towards that end, all sections of the community and all parties may co-operate in developing the institutions of government so as to hasten the day when this goal is attained.[2]

After a long and spirited debate, which continued all day and night and ended at 12.30 a.m. on 15 December, the amendment was defeated by thirty-nine votes to thirty-eight and the motion was carried, also by thirty-nine votes to thirty-eight.[3]

However, 'it [was] not yet His Majesty's Government's policy that the Sudan should be prepared for self-determination',[4] and the Governor-General could not be expected to act on a resolution which was passed with a majority of only one vote. Instead he adopted another resolution which had been passed by the Assembly six days before, on 9 December. The text of this was:

We, the members of the Legislative Assembly of the Sudan do request Your Excellency to appoint a Commission, of whose members at least half should be Sudanese, to re-examine the Executive Council and Legislative Assembly Ordinance, 1948, and, in respect of any of its provisions other than those dealing with the election of members of the Assembly, to make such recommendations to Your Excellency for its amendment as they may consider will increase the value, and enhance the efficiency, of the Assembly and Council as a practical instrument of democratic

[1] *Proceedings of the First Assembly*, Second Session, no. 14, 6–16 Dec. 1950, pp. 594–5. In Jan. 1950 he thought that a motion asking for self-government should not be discussed in the Assembly, since 'it is clearly a "reserved" subject and can be refused'. The Civil Secretary to the Governor-General, 9 Jan. 1950 (SCO/I.A.20/8). In December, however, refusal to allow the motion to be discussed would have been disastrous from the Government's point of view.

[2] *Proceedings of the First Assembly*, Second Session, no. 14, 6–16 Dec. 1950, p. 608.

[3] Ibid., p. 614.

[4] Dispatch no. JE/1015/15, dated 20 Feb. 1952, in SCO/I.A.20/9, Archives, Khartoum. See also p. 181 and p. 186, n. 2 above.

government with a full measure of parliamentary control, within the framework of the existing constitutional agreements.[1]

5. *Towards self-government: the Constitution Commission and the abrogation of the Agreement*

The Constitution Amendment Commission, as it was subsequently known, was, from the start, a subject of much controversy and political bargaining. For the Umma Party, whose drive for immediate self-government had recently been frustrated, it was only a second best, which they joined with a heavy heart and many misgivings. The Ashigga boycotted it as another device for prolonging British rule in the Sudan and preventing the unification of the Nile Valley. And the Khatmiyya refused to participate unless two basic conditions were fulfilled. In the first place, they insisted that the electoral commission which had only recently been set up (but which they had boycotted) should be dissolved and its functions be entrusted to the Constitution Amendment Commission. Secondly, they wanted the limiting words 'within the framework of the existing constitutional agreements' dropped from the Commission's terms of reference as approved by the Legislative Assembly on 9 December 1950.[2] The membership of the Commission was also debated, but it was finally agreed that educated men, representing different interests and shades of political opinion, should be strongly represented. With regard to the terms of reference of the Commission, the difficulty was overcome by the Governor-General issuing the following somewhat evasive statement when he convened the Commission: 'In response to resolutions of the Legislative Assembly of the 6th November, 1950, and of 9th December, 1950, I Robert George Howe, C.B.E., K.C.M.G., do now hereby convene a joint commission to examine the matters referred to in these resolutions and to recommend to me the next steps to be taken in the constitutional advance to full self-government.'[3] Since this implied the dissolution of the electoral commission, however, the Governor-General added that, when the electoral rules were being considered by the Constitution Amendment Commission, four named members of the dissolved

[1] *Proceedings of the First Assembly*, Second Session, no. 14, 6–16 Dec. 1950, p. 570 n.

[2] Letter from the Civil Secretary to the Governor-General at Port Sudan, 18 Jan. 1951 (SCO/I.A.20/9, Archives, Khartoum).

[3] *Report on the Work of the Constitution Amendment Commission* up to the date of its dissolution, by the Chairman, Mr. Justice R. C. Stanley-Baker, p. 38.

commission should be present. In view of the delicacy of the situation and in order to avoid a split between the British and Sudanese members of the Commission, the Chairman, Mr. Justice R. C. Stanley-Baker, was informed that too rigid an adherence to the terms of reference of the Commission was not necessary.[1]

The Commission was formally convened on 29 March 1951. Apart from the Chairman, the Secretary, and an 'Adviser', all members were Sudanese—seventeen, including the four who were to attend when electoral rules were discussed. The first meeting of the Commission was held on 22 April. This was devoted to the preliminary matter of settling the order of business; it was decided that the constitution should be considered before the electoral rules.[2]

In the meantime, Anglo-Egyptian relations were going from bad to worse, the Sudan question being a major issue in the conflict. In December 1950, the President of the Egyptian Council of Ministers formally protested against the Governor-General's decision to allow the motion on self-government to be discussed in the Legislative Assembly without the consent of the Egyptian Government. He demanded the immediate cessation of the debate and asked the British Government to instruct the Governor-General to act according to his request. The Egyptian Foreign Minister, Muḥammad Ṣalāh al-Dīn, who was then in London for negotiations, explained that failure to abide by the wishes of the President of the Council of Ministers would have an undesirable effect on the progress of the negotiations. In reply Mr. Bevin said that refusal to allow the discussion of the motion in the Assembly would have given rise to undesirable misunderstandings in the Sudan, and to unjustifiable suspicions about the current negotiations. He agreed, however, that it was unfortunate that discussions of that sort should have taken place at that juncture. He had, therefore, asked the Governor-General to do all he could in order to prevent any action being taken in Khartoum which might cause controversy between the British and Egyptian Governments.[3] It is possible that this was one reason why, although he did not stop the debate half-way (the session was, in any case, due to end) the Governor-General did not act upon the

[1] Civil Secretary to the Financial and Legal Secretaries, 18 Jan. 1951, SCO/I.A.20/8, Archives, Khartoum; *Report on the Work of the Commission*, p. 3.

[2] Ibid., p. 4.

[3] The Arabic text of the negotiations in *al-Sūdān: min 13 Fabrayir 1931 ila 12 Fabrayir 1953* (The Presidency of the Council of Ministers, Cairo, 1953), pp. 255–6.

resolution of the 15th on self-government, but instructed the Commission to consider the motions of 6 November and 9 December. However that may be, the negotiations between the British and Egyptian Governments were bound to end, as usual, in deadlock. Encouraged by American support (which was given in the vain hope that Egypt would be persuaded to join the Western system of defence) the Egyptian Government insisted that the only basis on which they would accept a settlement of the Sudan question was that of the Unity of the Nile Valley under the Egyptian crown.[1] The British Government reiterated their position with regard to the right of the Sudanese to determine their own destiny, and negotiations were broken off in total disagreement. On 8 October the Egyptian Government unilaterally abrogated the Agreement of 1899 and the Treaty of 1936, and on the 16th and 17th Fārouq signed two Acts of Parliament in accordance with which a new constitution for the Sudan was to be written. Under the new constitution, he was to be called 'The King of Egypt and The Sudan' and the two countries were to be united under the Egyptian crown. But there was to be a Sudanese Cabinet in which Ministers would be appointed and dismissed by the King, and a House of Representatives which would, with the consent of the King, make laws and approve the budget. Foreign affairs, defence, the armed forces, and currency, however, were to be reserved for the King and he was to have the right to dissolve the House at his will.[2]

The proposed Egyptian constitution was met, in the Sudan, with a storm of disapproval, in which all political parties, except the Ashigga, joined. The Ashigga were thereby isolated and embarrassed while the Anṣār and the Khatmiyya were brought 'closer together than ever before'.[3] And when, on 25 October, the Legislative Assembly passed a motion deploring 'the Egyptian Government's attempt to impose Egyptian Sovereignty on the Sudan without consulting the Sudanese people, and [refusing] to recognise the constitution promulgated by the Egyptian Government for the Sudan',[4] no one seemed to disagree.

[1] The Arabic text of the negotiations in *al-Sūdān*, p. 269, and the memoirs of Sir Anthony Eden, *Full Circle*, pp. 225–30.

[2] *al-Sūdān*, pp. 285–8.

[3] J. S. R. Duncan, *The Sudan—A Record of Achievement* (Edinburgh and London, 1952), p. 248.

[4] *Proceedings of the First Assembly*, Third Session, no. 7. 25–31 Oct. 1951, p. 340.

The announcement of the Egyptian Government with regard to the Agreement of 1899 and the Treaty of 1936 was denounced by the British Government as a unilateral action, which was, therefore, not valid. For the Sudanese, however, the action of the Egyptian Government in this respect had undoubtedly destroyed the juridical foundations of the Anglo-Egyptian regime and thus opened the way for full freedom. On 15 November Mr. Eden told the House of Commons that

In view of the uncertainty caused . . . by the Egyptian Government's unilateral action . . . His Majesty's Government finds it necessary to reaffirm that they regard the Governor-General and the present Sudan Government as fully responsible for continuing the administration of the Sudan. His Majesty's Government are glad to note that the Sudan has for some time been and is now moving rapidly in the direction of self-government. In their view this progress can and should continue on the lines already laid down. His Majesty's Government will, therefore, give the Governor-General their full support for the steps he is taking to bring the Sudanese rapidly to the stage of self-government as a prelude to self-determination, and now await the recommendations of the Constitution Amendment Commission. His Majesty's Government are glad to know that a Constitution providing for full self-government may be completed and in operation by the end of 1952.[1]

A majority of the Sudanese members of the Commission disagreed. They argued that the abrogation of the Agreement and the Treaty had left the Anglo-Egyptian regime without any legal basis; that the Governor-General, therefore, represented neither Egypt nor Britain nor the two together but was only the *de facto* ruler of the Sudan; that, consequently, neither he nor the British Government were legally entitled to say how or when the Sudanese were to have self-government or exercise their right of self-determination; that an International Commission should replace the Governor-General and the necessary steps for the formal termination of the regime and the declaration of the independence of the Sudan be taken.[2] Accordingly

[1] The Civil Secretary, on behalf of the Governor-General, read Mr. Eden's statement to the Legislative Assembly on 19 Nov.

[2] Sayyid al-Dirdīri Mūḥammad 'Uthmān, who was one of the first members to advocate this view, relates that he was subsequently invited to talk the matter over with the Governor-General. During the discussion, he refused to be moved 'a hair's breadth' from this position. The Governor-General then asked him whether in his view the British Government should sign the agreement proposed by the Egyptian Government concerning immediate self-determination for the Sudanese. Dirdīri answered: 'Yes, you should sign it without any hesitation.' Sir Robert asked 'Why?', and Dirdīri replied: 'Because when the Sudan Question

'the members of the Commission as individuals and with one exception'[1] sent a telegram to the United Nations Organization asking for an International Commission to implement this proposal and 'to advise the Sudanese on the setting up of a Constituent Assembly to exercise self-determination on or before December, 1953'.[2] The telegram did not produce the desired effect but a sub-committee of the Commission was appointed, on 29 October, to review the recommendation which had already been agreed in the light of the altered circumstances and to report to the Commission within a week.[3] The report of the sub-committee stated that in the opinion of the majority of the sub-committee,

the Condominium has always been a source of difficulties and grave problems . . . due to the conflicting views of the co-domini. The position has further been complicated by the new attitude of the co-domini; Egypt, on the one hand, claims that the condominium rule has come to an end and the Sudan will be granted self-government under the Egyptian Crown, and Britain, on the other hand, maintains that the condominium rule is still in force. This state of affairs will certainly hamper the constitutional development of the country and they are, therefore, solemnly resolved that the only alternative is to provide in the draft constitution for an International Commission. They further hold the view that a fixed date for self-determination be mentioned in the draft constitution. They consider that the Condominium Rule virtually ceased to exist and a long-term control by the one remaining co-dominus will lay the country open to outside interference and will prejudice the interests of the Sudanese people and thereby endanger peace and order.[4]

They, therefore, proceeded to make suggestions about the transfer of power to the Sudanese with a view to self-determination in or before December 1953. But the Chairman of the Commission and the Sudan Government—taking the lead of the British Government—could not accept this or any other suggestion based on an acceptance of the unilateral abrogation of the Agreement and the Treaty by the

was discussed at Lake Success and Naqrāshi Pasha went on about Egypt's right of conquest and the Unity of the Nile Valley under the Egyptian crown, your representative, Sir Alexander Cadogan, stood up and said that the Sudanese alone had the right to freely determine their own future. He was then applauded by the delegates of the free world and the Russian representative, for the first time, rose from his seat to congratulate your representative. . . . What would your position be to-day if you refused to agree?' The Governor-General, Dirdīri continues, was silent and then shook hands and said farewell (*Mudhakkirāti*, pp. 43–4).

[1] Duncan, p. 249.

[2] Quoted in Duncan, p. 249.

[3] *Report on the Work of the Constitution Amendment Commission*, p. 5.

[4] Ibid., p. 66.

Egyptian Government, since this would have undermined Britain's position not only in the Sudan but also, and more importantly, in the Suez Canal. The Commission was, therefore, divided over the report of its sub-committee and, after a fortnight's discussion, they could still reach no agreement. On 21 November six members, supporting the views of the sub-committee, submitted their resignations on the sovereignty issue and a seventh resigned because 'he felt unable to continue work in a Commission otherwise exclusively composed of members of the Legislative assembly'.[1] On the following day, the Chairman informed the Governor-General that 'in these regrettable circumstances, the Commission is unable to continue in the form in which it was convened by Your Excellency'.[1] In reply the Chairman was told that His Excellency 'sees no other alternative than to dissolve the Commission'.[2] Formal dissolution was ordered on 26 November. Meanwhile, two points had become quite clear. The first was that, 'however much legal pundits might argue, the Treaty and the Agreement had in fact been torn up by Egypt and the Sudan was free'.[3] The second was the growth of still closer relations between the Anṣār and the Khatmiyya. By January 1952, they were agreed that the Sudanese people should exercise self-determination by means of a plebiscite held under the supervision of the United Nations. In this they were supported by the Ashigga and the majority of Sudanese parties. A 'United Sudanese Delegation', backed by the representative of Pakistan, Sir Muḥammad Zhafrulla Khān and by Fāris al-Khouri, the Syrian delegate,[4] canvassed the idea at the United Nations and a formal Note, based on the suggestions of the sub-committee of the Constitution Amendment Commission and expressing the desire of the Sudanese people for self-determination by means of a plebiscite, was distributed to the representatives of states at the United Nations. In the meantime, the Egyptian Government persisted in its campaign against the continued existence of the British administration in the Sudan after the abrogation of the Treaty and the Agreement and against the wishes of the Sudanese.

Under the circumstances it was natural that when he was asked, by Sir Zhafrulla Khān, whether Britain would evacuate the Sudan if the Sudanese opted for independence in the proposed plebiscite, Mr. Eden's reply was 'Why not?'[4] And whereas a year before, British officials in the Sudan felt that it was their duty to delay the

[1] Ibid., p. 41.
[2] Ibid., p. 42.
[3] Duncan, p. 249.
[4] Dirdīri, p. 53.

day of self-government as long as possible,[1] the Civil Secretary—prompted by a letter from a District Commissioner who continued to follow the old line—wrote to all Governors and District Commissioners informing them that their duty, under the altered circumstances, was 'to hasten along with our plans for self-government and to explain carefully to the people our reasons for so doing'. He continued:

It is often argued that we would be doing the majority of the Sudanese a greater service by prolonging the period of our control. Taking the long view I do not believe this is true. In so doing we should quickly lose the trust and confidence of the educated Sudanese. This group, though small in number, has, in fact, great actual, and even greater potential, power. . . . We want to do the best we can for the Sudan and unfortunately time is not on our side because of events outside our control. This is partly due to the national aspirations of many of the educated Sudanese, which have been stirred by recent events in neighbouring countries, and partly due to the actions of the other Co-dominus—Egypt, which claims the sovereignty of the Sudan and is endeavouring by every means to undermine the trust and confidence which the Sudanese have in the British officials of this country, and in the intentions of Her Majesty's Government. . . . Our primary duty as I see it is to keep, at all costs, the goodwill and trust of the Sudanese people as a whole, educated and non-educated, urban and rural. This will enable us to assist them as friends and allies after they have assumed control, and at a time when they will be in greatest need of assistance. . . . These are the views of His Excellency the Governor-General and of Her Majesty's Government.[2]

The British Government, however, were determined that progress towards self-government should proceed along the lines that had already been laid down and without reference to the juridical effects of the abrogation of the Agreement. In particular, they did not want the proposed new constitution to include 'specific directions about when and how the Governor-General should consult the sovereign authority'—whoever that may be. They also insisted that the Governor-General should

appear to 'represent' the sovereign authority in the fullest sense of the word, and to be himself the final arbiter in any dispute which may arise. We should therefore prefer to see all reference to the sovereign authority removed from the amendments to the Constitutions. . . . [Also] there are, of course, many reasons why we should be opposed to transferring

[1] Above, p. 181 and p. 186, n. 2.

[2] J. W. Robertson to 'All Governors, with copies to District Commissioners', 12 Feb. 1952 (CS/SCO/I.A.20/9, vol. i, Archives, Khartoum).

sovereignty to an international commission, not least of which is that the whole business of setting-up such a commission, drawing up its terms of reference, and deciding to whom it would be responsible, would involve an intolerable waste of time. Failing an international commission, it would be embarrassing either for Her Majesty's Government or presumably for the Sudan Government to be forced to specify who the sovereign authority is. To say that it is the Condominium Powers acting under the 1899 Agreement would now be unacceptable in the Sudan, and there are many reasons against our declaring that it is Her Majesty's Government alone. This is an additional, and in our view, a powerful, reason for omitting all reference to the sovereign authority from the new Constitution.[1]

6. *The Self-Government Statute: drafts, debates, and diplomacy*

The Constitution Amendment Commission was dissolved on 26 November 1951, without having completed its task and without having considered a formal report.[2] On the basis of the minutes of the meetings of the Commission up to the time of its dissolution, however, the Chairman prepared a report embodying certain recommendations on the principles of which the new constitution was to be based. The Stanley-Baker recommendations made no mention of the question of sovereignty over which the Commission broke up and, in general closely followed the lines which had been suggested two years before by the Legal Secretary in his proposed constitutional 'jump' which, he hoped, would satisfy the Sudanese and yet be 'reasonably safe'.[3] The Chairman's report recommended the establishment of a 'fully "self-governing" Constitution of the Parliamentary democratic type, embodying a "Cabinet" system of government'.[4] Key Ministries were to have 'Advisers' who would work within the framework of the policy-directives laid down by Ministers. In the event of a fundamental disagreement between a Minister and his Adviser, the issue would be referred to the Council of Ministers. 'If the Governor-General does not agree with the decision of the Council, he may refer the matter back to the Council with his views. If these are not accepted, the Governor-General should reserve the

[1] Roger Allen to J. Robertson (FO/J.E/1015/15, 20 Feb. 1952, SCO/I.A.20/9, Archives, Khartoum).

[2] *Report on the Work of the Constitution Commission*, p. 1. Duncan wrongly states that the Commission had, in fact, completed its report before it was dissolved, p. 250.

[3] Above, p. 184, n. 1.

[4] *Report on the Work of the Constitution Commission*, p. 7.

matter for the decision by the Sovereign Authority'[1]—presumably the British Government. There was to be a department of external affairs attached to the Governor-General's Office. Responsibility for Defence Policy was to remain with the Governor-General, but the Council was to discuss all major questions of policy. In order to reassure Southern representatives, many of whom were still under the influence of the discarded 'Southern Policy', there was to be a 'Minister for Southern Affairs who should himself be a Southerner selected by the Prime Minister in consultation with the Governor-General and with the Southern Members of Parliament'.[2] The Minister would be assisted by an 'Advisory Board for Southern Affairs, the members of which should be selected by the Minister in consultation with the Governors of the three Southern Provinces'.[3]

The report of the Chairman of the Constitution Amendment Commission was laid before the Legislative Assembly on 23 January 1952, and a protracted debate ensued which continued until the adjournment of the Assembly towards the end of February. In the course of the debate various aspects of the report were criticized but most of the criticism, as might have been expected, was directed against those parts of the report which recommended the creation of a special Minister for the Southern Provinces and a Board for Southern Affairs, whose members would be appointed by the Minister, in consultation with the Governors of the three Southern provinces—but without reference to the Prime Minister. This, it was pointed out, would weaken the position of the Prime Minister, not only because of the manner in which it was proposed the Board would be appointed, but because it would, in effect, create two cabinets in the country and constitute a relapse to 'Southern Policy' which all members were agreed was contrary to the wishes and interests of the Sudanese. The Southern provinces, moreover, were in no more backward a condition than other areas such as Darfur, the Beja area, or the Nuba Mountains, which were not granted Ministers for their own affairs. Had this been done, said a Southerner from Khartoum, 'the whole structure of the state might collapse'.[4] It was resolved,

[1] *Report on the Work of the Constitution Commission*, p. 18.

[2] Ibid., p. 14.

[3] Ibid., p. 21.

[4] Sayyid Zain al-'Aābdīn Bey 'Abd al-Tām, in the *Proceedings of the First Assembly*, Third Session, 9 Feb. 1952, p. 796. Sayyid Zain al-'Aābdīn said he was himself a Southerner and sympathized with the Honourable Members from the Southern provinces, but that if minority problems were created the whole structure of the state might collapse. For this reason, he opposed the recommendation.

therefore, that there should not be a special Minister for Southern Affairs, but that the Constitution should provide that at least one Minister must be from one of the Southern provinces.[1] To reassure the Southern Sudanese, as the Explanatory Note put it, the number was raised to 'not less than two' in the Draft of the Self-Government Statute which was laid before the Assembly on 2 April—and to three in the Transitional Constitution afterwards.

Following, mainly, the recommendations of the Assembly arising from its discussion of the report of the Chairman of the Constitution Amendment Commission, the Draft Statute provided that the Government should consist of an all-Sudanese Council of Ministers and an all-Sudanese Parliament of two Houses: a Senate and a Chamber of Deputies. The Chamber of Deputies was to consist of eighty-one members, of whom twenty-four would be elected by means of direct election in territorial constituencies and fifty-four by means of indirect elections. In addition, three members were to be returned by a Graduates' Constituency, in which persons who had completed fourth-year secondary school and passed final examinations would be qualified to vote. There were to be fifty Senators, of whom twenty would be appointed by the Governor-General and thirty elected by electoral colleges in the provinces. The Prime Minister would be elected by the Chamber of Deputies from among existing members and would thereupon be appointed by the Governor-General who would also appoint Ministers (not less than ten and not more than fifteen) on the advice of the Prime Minister. The Council of Ministers would be responsible to Parliament for all the executive and administrative functions of internal government. In accordance with the wishes of Sir Robert Howe, however, the Draft Self-Government Statute provided that the Governor-General should have a special responsibility for the public service and for the Southern provinces.[2] His Excellency would have the right to veto any bill which, in his opinion, adversely affected the contractual rights of the former or the 'special interests' of the latter. The Governor-General, moreover, would have an exclusive responsibility for external affairs during the transitional period. And, should he be satisfied that by reason of political deadlock, non-co-operation, or boycott the government of the Sudan could not be carried on under

[1] Ibid., p. 794.

[2] The Governor-General to the Civil Secretary, 2 Mar. 1952 (SCO/I.A.20/9, Archives, Khartoum).

the constitution, the Governor-General would have the right to proclaim a constitutional emergency and thereupon suspend the constitution and assume full powers. He would be entitled to do the same in case of imminent financial collapse or breakdown of law and order.

The powers of the Governor-General as stated in the Draft Statute were inevitably criticized both in and outside the Legislative Assembly and, of course, in Egypt. Other criticisms were directed against the fact that the proposed constitution did not mention the date for self-determination and was equally silent over the question of sovereignty over which the Constitution Amendment Commission had broken down.[1] These, however, were points over which the Sudan Government and the British Government were not, at that stage, prepared to make any concessions, and the Draft of the Self-Government Statute, as finally approved by the British Government on 21 October, merely reproduced the provisions of the original Draft on these matters. Instead of stating that the Governor-General shall have 'exclusive responsibility' for external affairs however, the approved Draft used the less obtuse expression that he 'shall remain responsible for external affairs', and, whereas the original Draft described him as 'the constitutional head of the Constitution', the approved version more lucidly stated that he shall be 'the Supreme Constitutional Authority' in the Sudan.

By abrogating the Agreement and the Treaty, Egypt had, in the meantime, forfeited her constitutional right to (and could not consistently) approve or amend the Draft Self-Government Statute which the Sudan Government sent to the Egyptian and British Governments in May. To have accepted the invitation to approve or suggest amendments to the Draft would have meant, by implication, that the Egyptian Government agreed that the abrogation had no validity and was, therefore null and void. Egypt, however, was not prepared to see her position in the Sudan, such as it was, undermined. The only way in which this could be avoided, in the altered circumstances, was to reach a political agreement with the Sudanese parties which opposed the policy of the Unity of the Nile Valley under the Egyptian crown. The Wafd government which abrogated the Treaty and the Agreement was dismissed by the King, and the new government of Najīb al-Hilāli invited the Mahdists to negotiate a settlement. If agreement could be reached with the Anṣār, the Independence Front,

[1] *Proceedings of the First Assembly, Third Session*, no. 18, 7 Apr. 1952, p. 57.

the Unionists, and the Egyptian Government would face the British Government as one front and the latter would, therefore, be obliged to make concessions over the powers of the Governor-General and the date of self-determination, and a final settlement of the question of sovereignty would thus be possible. Seeing this possibility and, like the Egyptian Government, hoping that it would finally be realized in a manner acceptable to them, the Mahdists accepted the invitation. On 27 May Sayyid 'Abd al-Raḥmān sent a 'personal' mission to start negotiations with Hilāli Pasha. The Egyptian Government offered to withdraw the constitution by means of which they had proposed, during the previous year, to declare the Sudan an Egyptian territory under the Egyptian crown and to accept, instead, any constitution on which the Sudanese agreed. The Egyptian Government would also accept the decision of the Sudanese over the date on which they chose to exercise self-determination by means of a plebiscite over the subject of union with Egypt or complete independence. In return, Hilāli Pasha asked the Mahdi's mission to accept temporarily, the nominal sovereignty of King Fārouq over the Sudan. This was, of course, both psychologically and constitutionally unacceptable to the champions of 'al-Istiqlāl al-Tām'—complete independence. From their point of view the first condition of any agreement was that no reference should be made to Egyptian sovereignty, nominal or otherwise, over the Sudan. Instead, they suggested that a tripartite (Anglo-Egyptian-Sudanese) commission should be formed to act, together with the Governor-General, as the supreme constitutional authority in the Sudan during the transitional period; that Egypt should approve or suggest amendments to the Draft Self-Government Statute; and that the plebiscite over the question of unity or independence be conducted under the supervision of a freely-elected Sudanese government.[1] Hilāli Pasha acquiesced in the last suggestion; acceptance of the second would have been humiliating and inconsistent for any Egyptian Government; and, as the spokesman of the Royal Egyptian Government, Hilāli Pasha could not give his consent to any agreement which did not concede the sovereignty of the Egyptian crown over the Sudan. Deadlock thus having been reached, Sayyid 'Abd al-Raḥmān's mission returned to the Sudan on 12 June 1952. On 23 July General Najīb (himself half Sudanese and a former student of the Gordon

[1] Tāha, pp. 91–2. Also the memoirs of Sayyid 'Abd al-Raḥmān al-Mahdi, *Jihadun fi-Sabīl al-Istiqlāl* (Khartoum, n.d.), pp. 93–5.

College) and his young service officers (many of whom, including Jamāl 'Abd al-Nāṣir, had served in the Sudan and knew the Sudanese well) staged the *coup d'état* which eliminated the monarchy and transformed Egypt. Their first diplomatic success was the signing of the agreement with the Mahdists which former Egyptian governments had failed to achieve—thereby paving the way not only to self-government but also to self-determination.

CHAPTER VII

The State of Local Government

THE purpose of this chapter is to give a general view of developments in the field of Local Government, as distinct from Native Administration, after 1937.

1. *Objections to Native Administration*

Native Administration, as we have seen,[1] was from the start repugnant to the educated core of the nationalist movement in the Sudan—for a number of reasons. As advocates of national unity, they wanted to strengthen the allegiance of the Sudanese to their country, not to their various tribes and localities. Native administration, however, was by definition based on the opposite premiss and aimed not only at protecting, but at reviving and strengthening tribal bonds. The fact that these had been almost completely destroyed by the Mahdiyya and by over twenty years of Direct Rule made the Government's policy of regenerating tribalism particularly abhorrent; and if British liberal opinion was shocked by 'the spectacle . . . of young administrators searching for lost tribes and vanished chiefs, and trying to resurrect a social system that had vanished for ever',[2] Sudanese nationalists could not but feel indignant at a policy which they conceived was not only holding up the progress of their country but was actually trying to turn the clock back. Nationalist disapproval was augmented by the fact that the resuscitated tribal institutions were used as a brake on the development of Sudanese nationalism and to reduce the role of the educated class in the administration. Behind a façade of Nāẓirs, Shaikhs, and Chiefs who were nothing but the tools[3] of the imperialists, it was pointed out, Governors and District Commissioners exercised wide powers over the people without any checks either from London (or Cairo)

[1] Chapters III and IV.

[2] Sir James Currie (above, p. 66).

[3] Dr. A. H. Marshall subsequently described native authorities as having been 'merely projections of the District Commissioners' (*Report on Local Government in the Sudan*, Khartoum, 1949, p. 7).

or from the enlightened class which they now arrogantly dismissed as 'the small, but vocal, minority', which was, allegedly, alienated from the people and not interested in their fates. 'Does education estrange a man from his people?' asked Maḥjoub; on the contrary it enables him to achieve a better understanding of them and of their needs and how to satisfy them. And why are the educated a minority? 'Because', he answered, 'the control of education is in the hands of those who want to maintain the *status quo*; had they attended to the first duty of all civilized governments, i.e. the adequate provision of education it would not have been possible to describe the educated as a minority.'[1] As budding advocates of parliamentary democracy, the young intelligentsia found the hereditary principle, in accordance with which tribal leaders were chosen, unacceptable. They wanted to see, not a tradition-bound society, based on a static, even archaic, economy, but a rational and dynamic society, in which merit and service, and not the accident of birth, counted. As against these ideals, the administration held up the traditional order of tribes and chiefs as models of practical wisdom, natural dignity, *amour propre*, and the happiness which romantics have always seen in the lives of backward peoples and which, accordingly, they have felt should be 'protected' from what were usually called the 'hazards' of civilization. To this the nationalists retorted that the 'state of nature' or of 'noble savagery', to which the protagonists of native administration wanted to confine the Sudanese, was indeed the negation of human dignity and prevented human fulfilment. The Southern provinces, it was often protested, had been kept—owing to the pernicious combination of Native Administration and Southern Policy—in a state of shameful backwardness—a human zoo to satiate the idle curiosity of the tourist and the vanity of the arrogant District Commissioner. For the same reason, the argument continued, vast areas of the Northern Sudan had been artificially maintained as feudal museums in which people and things were carefully insulated from the presumed worries and strain of modern life. 'Why did the imperialists spoil their own feudal paradise?' asked Maḥjoub; 'let them give education to the people, help them to get rid of disease and enjoy the wealth and products of their country in full—the people are more interested in the "misery" that goes with these things than in the imaginary happiness in which, it is alleged, they are now basking.'[2]

[1] Muḥammad Aḥmad Maḥjoub, *al-Ḥukouma al-Maḥalliyya Fi-l-Sūdān*, 'Local Government in the Sudan' (Cairo, 1945), pp. 72–3. [2] Ibid., p. 71.

By 1936 such views and feelings were commonplace among the politically conscious Sudanese, especially the educated class, and in due course, the Administration acquiesced. Sir Douglas Newbold wrote:

Gradually we found native administration tending to ossify or fossilize and become a privileged salaries hierarchy whose budget was largely a Civil List (e.g. Minor Indian States). No seed of progress: no scope for educated or ambitious citizens: acquired a feudal and reactionary tone: was hostile to or ignorant of towns: depended on hereditary system. So we began to rationalize our native administration on lines of modern local government, i.e. so as to rest more on popular consent and be acceptable to educated Arabs, and to be trained and equipped to deal with the new social and economic problems, e.g. sanitation, soil erosion, town planning.[1]

2. *The coming of Local Government*

The first step in the direction of developing Local Government as distinct from Native Administration was taken in 1937 with the promulgation of the three Local Government Ordinances[2] of that year. These applied to Municipalities, i.e. the larger towns with a high proportion of European inhabitants,[3] e.g. Khartoum and Port Sudan; Townships, or smaller towns with small or no European communities, e.g. Kasala and al-Ūbayyid; and Rural Areas—the rest of the country. But none of these Ordinances provided for the creation of full-blooded Local Government Authorities, independent

[1] Notes for a Lecture to the Arab Centre at Jerusalem, October 1944 (Henderson, pp. 531–2).

[2] In 1921 'The Khartoum Municipal Council' was established by order for the joint administration of Khartoum, Khartoum North, and Omdurman. The Council consisted of *ex-officio* members of the central government in the province and sixteen appointed members, half of whom were Sudanese. The Governor-General was empowered to dismiss any of the members, and the Council's powers were purely consultative and advisory. The Province Governor was the President of the Council; he had the power to appoint Committees and no subject could be discussed without his consent. All resolutions had to be expressed in English, but members could, with the permission of the President, address the Council in Arabic or any other language, e.g. Greek (*Laws of the Sudan*, 1941 edn., i. 291–3). A similar Council, one-third of whose members were Sudanese, was also established in Port Sudan, another town with a large foreign population. Needless to say, neither of these two Councils was an adequate local government authority.

[3] There have been no European settlers in the Sudan; those mentioned above were mostly either traders (mainly Greek) or members of the Political Service or their families.

from Governors and District Commissioners, and having the power to provide local services and make and execute laws of local applications. Instead, the Municipalities and Townships Ordinances enabled 'the Governor-General by warrant to authorise the Governor to delegate to any person or body of persons such powers as shall be specified in such warrant'.[1] In each case, the Civil Secretary, with the consent of the Governor-General in Council, could make 'standard regulations' within the limits of which Governors, except in cases of emergency, had the power to make 'local orders or regulations' for the purpose of providing, for example, for the orderly use and cleanliness of public streets and public squares, the impounding of stray animals, and the prevention of the pollution of river inlets and water courses.[2] In accordance with the Local Government (Rural Areas) Ordinance, on the other hand, the Governor-General was empowered 'to appoint by warrant any person either by name or by office and either singly or associated with a Council or any body of persons as the Local Authority'.[3] He could also authorize the Local Authority thus appointed to delegate all or any of its powers to any person or body of persons, and 'in particular may authorise the Local Authority of a nomadic tribe to delegate such powers to a person or body of persons in respect of a section or other part of the tribe in whatsoever such section or part is for the time being to be found'.[3] The main duties of the Authorities thus constituted were the maintenance of order in the prescribed areas, the execution of any 'lawful order' of the Governor, and the enforcement of ordinances which he was authorized to enforce.[4]

In so far as Municipalities and Townships were concerned, the result of the legislation of 1937 was, in the words of the Governor-General 'to coalesce in one body of local government law the heterogeneous sets of regulations made by governors under the old Public Health and Public Order Ordinances'.[5] In the countryside, the old system of Native Administration, with Shaikhs acting individually or in Council, was likewise continued under the Local Government (Rural Areas) Ordinance—the main difference being that Native Administration was now put on a territorial rather than a purely

[1] *Laws of the Sudan*, 1941 edn., i. 221 and 296.
[2] Ibid., pp. 222–3 and 297–8.
[3] Ibid., p. 365.
[4] Ibid., p. 366.
[5] *Annual Report* for 1938, Sudan, no. 1 (1939), Cmd. 6139, p. 9.

tribal basis.[1] This had the effect of encouraging the growth of tribal federations, which had already been taking place, and the settlement of problems affecting wide areas by a single body.

Although these changes could be described as a step in the right direction, local government—in the sense of local self-government, based on the election of representatives to sit on responsible bodies with corporate existence which make and execute laws for the provision of services—was still non-existent either in the towns, big or small, or in the countryside.

A further step was taken in 1942, the year in which the Graduates' Congress submitted their Memorandum. In his Note of 10 September, in which he asked the Governor-General's Council to investigate the expediency of forming an Advisory Council for the Northern Sudan, Newbold also suggested the extension of town councils with executive powers and financial independence and the creation of Province Councils.[2] These suggestions were approved and—except in the case of Province Councils—were implemented, not by the passage of new Ordinances, but by introducing a series of amendments (some had been introduced before 1942) to those of 1937. Under the new legislation, the first statutary Municipal Council was set up in Port Sudan in 1944 with eighteen members of whom twelve were elected.[3] But the first official elections ever held in the Sudan took place in al-Ūbayyid two years earlier, when the town had the further distinction of having the first fully executive Council with an independent budget and substantial responsibilities in the management and financing of local affairs.[3] In rural areas, the creation and consolidation of kindred local administrations in larger units continued, and the first Rural District Councils (or 'gisms'), embodying smaller units, were set up in 1944. One of these covered the rural area of Khartoum Province outside the three Municipalities (of Khartoum, Khartoum North, and Omdurman) which early in 1945 replaced the joint Khartoum Municipal Council of 1921; the other District Council covered the rural area around Gaḍārif.[3]

Unlike Municipalities, Townships, and Rural Areas, Provinces had not, previously, been used as Local Government Authorities, and a new ordinance was, therefore, needed. Accordingly, the Local

[1] *Annual Report* for 1937, Sudan, no. 1 (1938), Cmd. 5985, p. 10.

[2] Henderson, pp. 533–4.

[3] *Report on the Sudan for the Years 1942–1944*, Sudan, no. 2 (1950), Cmd. 8098, p. 12.

Government (Province Councils) Ordinance, 1943, was promulgated in August of that year.[1] The explanatory note of the Ordinance stated that

> just as, in 1910, owing to the increasing complexity of administration it was 'deemed expedient to associate a Council with the Governor-General in the discharge of his executive and legislative powers' so now, with the recent growth of Local Government, it is deemed expedient to associate Councils, composed of Local Authorities and enlightened citizens, with Governors of Provinces in the exercise of their Local Government powers.[2]

Section 5 of the Ordinance provided that not less than one-half of the members of any Province Council were to be appointed, either by nomination or after election, from amongst persons who were members of Local Government (Rural or Urban) Authorities in the Province in question, and that the remaining members were, in accordance with the provisions of the Order which created the Council, to be representative of 'the more important social and economic interests in the Province'. Apart from serving as electoral colleges from amongst whose members members of the Advisory Council were selected in the manner described above,[3] the functions of the Province Councils were to advise the Governors as to the carrying out of their powers and duties as the supervising and co-ordinating authorities under local government legislation, and to exercise any power or duty conferred upon the Governors and delegated by them to the Councils.[4] However, it soon became an open secret that not all Governors were enthusiastic about delegating any of their powers to Province Councils and the Governor-General reported that they 'could meet too rarely and were too remote from local affairs ever to develop into executive local government bodies'.[5] Province Councils, therefore, continued to exist mainly for the purpose of electing members of the Advisory Council and, subsequently, of the Legislative Assembly—with the advice of the Governors.

By 1947 all six Northern Provinces had such Councils, and during the following year a Province Council was established in each one of the three Southern provinces. The number of Municipalities rose, by 1947, to five, in one of which (Omdurman) a Sudanese chairman

[1] *Report on the Sudan for the years 1942–1944*, Sudan, no. 2 (1950), Cmd. 8098, p. 12.

[2] p. ii of the explanatory note to the Local Government (Province Councils) Ordinance, 1943 (Special supplement to the *Sudan Government Gazette*, no. 731).

[3] Above, pp. 137 ff.

[4] Section 6 of the Local Government (Province Councils) Ordinance, 1943.

[5] *Annual Report* for 1947, Sudan, no. 1 (1949), Cmd. 7835, p. 17.

had, for the first time, been elected and thus replaced the British District Commissioner. The latter, however, continued to act as an adviser. The number of warranted Town Councils rose from one in 1942 to five in 1947 and there were also four 'unwarranted' Councils in the smaller towns of Kousti, Shandi, al-Dāmar, and Wādi Ḥalfa and an 'unofficial' town council in Wau, Baḥr al-Ghazāl Province. The rest of the country continued to be covered with a net of overlapping councils of various types and dimensions.[1] Some of these, as Dr. Marshall observed in 1948, were

> really the native authorities operating under the umbrella of a warrant. The councils are composed of Nazirs, Omdas and Sheikhs. The executive is an Assistant District Commissioner or Mamur—usually part-time, most of the work being done by the tribal hierarchy, who regard the council meetings (held three or four times a year) largely as gatherings of tribal functionaries.... As the judiciary is largely manned by the same personnel there is thus a complete blend of judicial, legislative (or policy-making) and executive functions in the same persons.[2]

By contrast, the Urban Authorities, especially in the larger towns, were well on their way to attaining the status of fully fledged Local Authorities.[3] But in none of them had a separate Local Government service been created and the executive officers were, as a rule, seconded from the Central Government service and 'subject to transfer without consultation with the local authorities'.[3] Many Councils did not have offices of their own and used rooms in the 'Markaz', the seat of Central Government in the Districts. Besides, most Councils suffered 'financial straight jacketting'[4] at the hands of the District Commissioner (himself usually the Chairman), the Province Governor, and the Financial Secretary at Khartoum. The total expenditure of all Local Authorities during 1949 was about £880,000 (compared with about £14,000,000 for the Central Government) and, apart from reserve funds created by each Authority accumulating its own surpluses, there was no means of meeting capital expenditure except by gift from the Central Government.[5] Revenues—derived from rates, market dues, licences, etc.—were simply not sufficient to guarantee financial independence from the Central Government or make possible the provision of important local services. In order to break the vicious circle which was thereby created, the sub-committee of the

[1] *Annual Report* for 1947, Sudan, no. 1, Cmd. 7835, pp. 17–18.
[2] *Report on Local Government in the Sudan* (Khartoum, 1949), p. 10.
[3] Ibid., p. 9. [4] Ibid., p. 8. [5] Ibid., pp. 8–9.

Sudan Administration Conference on Local Government 'favoured the grant of [adequate] financial powers to the Municipal, Town and Rural Council',[1] but failed to make any suggestions beyond this general statement. It recommended the development of Local Government in the Sudan 'along democratic lines', and made a number of suggestions, mainly about the method of elections in Municipalities and Townships. Unlike the report of the sub-committee on Central Government, however, the report on Local Government did not, except indirectly, form the basis of subsequent legislation. It was not even discussed by the whole Conference which, following the setting-up of the Legislative Assembly, ceased to exist before it considered the work of the sub-committee. However the Local Government Advisory Board continued the work of the sub-committee of the Administration Conference and decided, among other things, that the English, not the managerial, system should be the basis of future development of Local Government in the Sudan,[2] and that an expert from England should be commissioned[3] 'to enquire into and report on the policy and practice of the Sudan Government in respect of Local Government and to make recommendations upon any matter arising from the enquiry'.[4] Dr. A. H. Marshall, the City Treasurer of Coventry, was invited. He arrived in the Sudan in November 1948, and stayed for six months, during which he conducted an inquiry in accordance with his terms of reference. His report, which was published in April of the following year, was, as indicated above, highly critical of the existing agglomeration of Local Authorities and of their position *vis-à-vis* the Central Government on the one hand and the agents of Native Administration on the other. Dr. Marshall, as may be expected, did not suggest that Central Government supervision over Local Government Authorities should be ended; he agreed that it should continue with a view to imposing certain minimum standards and to suspending recalcitrant or inert Authorities. He insisted, however, that Central Government Departments should not be allowed to continue the existing practice of dealing separately with Local Government Authorities and to that end recommended the creation of one Department whose concern it would be to co-ordinate general policy and supervise Local

[1] *Report of the Sudan Administration Conference*, report to the Conference by Sub-Committee 'B' concerning Local Government (Khartoum, 1946), p. 17.

[2] *Annual Report* for 1947, Sudan, no. 1 (1949), Cmd. 7835, p. 17.

[3] *Annual Report* for 1948, Sudan, no. 1 (1951), Cmd. 8181, p. 8.

[4] *Report on Local Government in the Sudan*, p. 3.

Authorities. He recorded his satisfaction with the Government's recent decision rejecting pyramidism (i.e. making the Central Government the apex of a pile of Authorities beginning with village Councils and passing upwards through local District and Province Councils, each being responsible to the layer above) in favour of setting up a network of autonomous Local Authorities side by side with the newly formed Legislative Assembly. Within this general framework, Dr. Marshall recommended the establishment of all purpose Local Government Authorities, which would be autonomous bodies enjoying corporate existence and answerable to the electorate both for the making of laws and for their execution. He emphasized the need for such Authorities having independent tax revenues sufficient to meet substantial parts of their expenditure and pointed out, as an 'inevitable concomitant of central supervision', the need for having a system of grants-in-aid for those services for which the state demanded a national minimum standard of performance. Dr. Marshall also insisted that 'unless local government can be given . . . a high priority in manpower, no further development should be undertaken' and that, although the basic structure of the new system must be the same throughout the country, there should also be sufficient flexibility to allow for the wide divergence of conditions in the Sudan.[1]

Dr. Marshall's report was discussed and its recommendations were, in principle, unanimously approved by the Legislative Assembly and the Executive Council in the autumn of 1949. As such, it formed the basis of the Local Government Ordinance, 1951, which 'marked the end of . . . years of direct experiment with local government as a development from the "native administration" of an earlier era'[2] and provided for the organization of Local Government Councils on a common basis throughout the Sudan, until after independence. The general direction and supervision of the new system was entrusted, in the first instance, to an Assistant Civil Secretary for Local Government within the Civil Secretary's Office. On 4 May 1954 a fully fledged Ministry of Local Government was established. Today this remains the pivot of Local Government in the Sudan.

[1] Ibid., pp. 12–15.

[2] *Report on the Sudan in 1950–1951*, Sudan, no. 1 (1956), Cmd. 9798, p. 1.

CHAPTER VIII

The Transfer of Power

1. *The Agreements of 1952 and 1953*

OUR predecessors had always assumed that Great Britain's insistence on protecting Sudan's 'right to self-determination' was merely an excuse for depriving Egypt of its right to a say in the determination of Sudan's future. And, indeed, so long as Egypt was ruled by a King whose realm, in theory, included the Sudan as well as Egypt, it was impossible for them to play what they could not but regard as a British game. It seemed to me, however, that having rid ourselves of a King who had been as unpopular in Sudan as he had been in Egypt, we could beat the British at their game simply by calling their bluff.

Thus wrote General Najīb in his autobiography,[1] and his statement accurately summarized the attitude of the new Egyptian Government towards the Sudan. The effect of this 'diplomatic coup', as it has rightly been called,[2] was to accelerate the process of bidding for Sudanese support in which Egypt and Britain had already been engaged, and thus to facilitate a speedy settlement of the Sudan question.

The first step was the resumption, on Egyptian initiative, of negotiations with the Mahdists and the Independence Front which had been broken off in June 1952—a few weeks before the *coup d'état*.[3] Since they were prepared to concede the right of the Sudanese to self-determination as a matter of principle and not merely for the purpose of political manœuvre,[4] it is not surprising that the 'Free Officers' were able to reach agreement with the Umma Party less than two months after they had assumed power. The object of the agree-

[1] Muḥammad Najīb, *Egypt's Destiny* (London, 1955), pp. 241–2.

[2] John Marlowe, *Anglo-Egyptian Relations 1800–1953* (London, 1954), p. 393.

[3] Above, pp. 200–2.

[4] It will be recalled that, when the recommendations of the Sudan Administration Conference were being discussed, the Egyptian Government declared that they were sincerely desirous 'as emphasised on several occasions' of enabling the Sudanese to govern themselves. And on 16 Nov. 1951 the Egyptian Minister of Foreign Affairs, speaking at the U.N.O., challenged the British Government to withdraw their forces and agents from the Sudan in preparation for a plebiscite to be held in an atmosphere free from outside intervention.

ment, which was signed on 12 October 1952, was to enable the Sudanese to exercise their right of self-determination, in complete freedom from outside intervention, either by declaring the independence of the Sudan from Egypt and Britain, or by accepting some form of association with Egypt. Self-determination would be preceded by a transitional period during which the Sudanese would have full self-government and the Anglo-Egyptian administration be liquidated. During the transitional period the Governor-General would exercise his discretionary powers in conjunction with a commission on which a British representative would sit with two Sudanese representatives appointed by an elected Sudanese parliament, an Egyptian, and an Indian or a Pakistani appointed by his own government. A similar commission would be responsible for conducting and supervising elections. A Sudanization committee would, within three years, complete the Sudanization of the administration, the police, and all other government posts that might affect the freedom of the Sudanese at the time of self-determination, and a public service commission would ensure the freedom of the civil service from political interference.[1] To make doubly sure that the right to self-determination would be exercised in a free and neutral atmosphere, and in order to reinforce their original Agreement, the Mahdists and the Egyptian Government of General Najīb concluded another 'gentleman's agreement'. The 'gentleman's agreement' added, among other things, that 'monies which Egypt would want to spend in order to help her brother the Sudan [during the transitional period] . . . should be given to the Sudanese Government for dispensation',[2] and that the Press of the two countries should refrain from publishing provocative materials harmful to the spirit of fraternal co-operation between Egypt and the Sudan.

On the basis of these Agreements a further document was signed, after arduous negotiations in which the late Major Ṣalāh Sālim played an important role, on 10 January 1953, by the leading political parties in the Sudan, including the Ashigga (now joined by seven other unionist groups in a single National Unionist Party),[3] the Socialist Republicans, and the Umma. 'Ittifāqiyat al-Aḥzāb', i.e. The Political Parties Agreement, as it came to be known, was, in effect, the Egypto-Sudanese answer to objections raised by the British Government in

[1] The text of the Agreement is in Ṭāha, pp. 104–7. [2] Ibid., pp. 108–10.

[3] The creation of the National Unionist Party was, in large measure, due to General Najīb and Major Ṣalāh Sālim.

the course of Anglo-Egyptian negotiations regarding the termination of their, nominally, joint regime in the Sudan. It endorsed the provisions of the two earlier Agreements between the Independence Front and the Egyptian Government in connection with the Sudanization of the administration, and added that, should qualified Sudanese not be available at the time of self-determination, three years later, all British and Egyptian personnel should be replaced by other neutral nationalities. It was agreed, secondly, that a Governor-General's Commission be established before the elections and simultaneously with the promulgation of the new constitution. The Commission would be constituted in accordance with the proposals submitted by the Egyptian Government during the negotiations and would, in the absence of the Governor-General, act—under the chairmanship of the Indian or Pakistani member—as the supreme constitutional authority in the country. Elections would be direct wherever possible, the practicality or otherwise of holding such elections being determined by the Electoral Commission, which would be constituted in accordance with the proposals submitted by the Egyptian Government. All British and Egyptian troops would be evacuated before self-determination. Responsibility for the maintenance of internal security would then belong to the Sudanese Armed Forces under the direction of the Sudanese Government. The Governor-General would thus cease to be the supreme military authority in the Sudan. With regard to the British proposal that the constitution should contain certain special safeguards for the three Southern provinces it was agreed that 'any resolution passed by the Commission which he regards as inconsistent with his responsibility to ensure fair and equitable treatment of all the inhabitants of the various provinces of the Sudan, should be brought by the Governor-General to the attention of the two Contracting Governments, each of which must give an answer within one month of the date of formal notice. The Commission's resolution shall stand unless the two Governments agree to the contrary.' Finally, the parties agreed, unanimously, to boycott elections held under any constitution which was not based on the agreed minutes of their convention.[1]

Faced with this situation the British Government, which had always professed the right of the Sudanese to self-government and

[1] *al-Sūdān* (The Presidency of the Council of Ministers, Cairo, 1953), pp. 297–9; Ṭāha, pp. 113–15; Dirdīri, pp. 65–71.

self-determination as opposed to the Unity of the Nile Valley under the now vanished Egyptian crown, had no alternative but to accept the unanimously agreed Egyptian-Sudanese views on the matter. The result was the Anglo-Egyptian Agreement Concerning Self-Government and Self-Determination for the Sudan.[1] This was signed on 12 February 1953—exactly four months after the Egyptian Government conceded the right of the Sudanese to self-determination to the Independence Front.

The preamble of the Agreement stated that the Governments of Egypt and the United Kingdom 'firmly believing in the right of the Sudanese people to self-determination and the effective exercise thereof at the proper time and with the necessary safeguards, have agreed as follows . . .'. Article 1 provided for the establishment of full self-government for the Sudanese during the transitional period preceding self-determination. In Article 9 it was stated that the transitional period 'shall not exceed three years'. The transitional period was described, in Article 2, as 'a preparation for the effective termination of the dual Administration [and shall therefore] be considered as a liquidation of that Administration'. During this period, the Article continued, the sovereignty of the Sudan shall be kept in reserve for the Sudanese until self-determination was achieved. In Article 5 the two Contracting Governments affirmed that it was 'a fundamental principle of their common policy to maintain the unity of the Sudan as a single territory'. Articles 3, 4, 7, and 8 provided for the establishment of a Governor-General's Commission, a Mixed Electoral Commission, and a Sudanization Committee, each of which was to act and be composed in the manner agreed in Ittifāqiyat al-Aḥzāb. Several amendments were then made in the Self-Government Statute, which had been approved by the British Government in October 1952, in order to bring it into line with the requirements of the changed situation. In its new form the Self-Government Statute was promulgated on 21 March 1953,[2] and thus became the constitutional charter of the country until 31 December 1955, when, with further amendments, it became the Transitional Constitution of the (independent) Sudan.

[1] See Appendix VII.

[2] The Self-Government Statute and the text of the Agreement were published together in a Special Legislative Supplement to the *Sudan Government Gazette*, no. 854.

2. *The first national elections*

In order to put the machinery envisaged in the Anglo-Egyptian Agreement of 1953 into operation it was necessary, first of all, to arrange for the election of the first Sudanese Parliament and Government. The holding and supervision of the elections, it had been agreed, would be entrusted to a Commission of six, of whom three were to be Sudanese, the remaining three being a Britisher, a citizen of the U.S.A., and an Indian who, by the terms of the Agreement, was to be the President of the Commission. By 25 March (four days after the promulgation of the Self-Government Statute) all the non-Sudanese members of the Electoral Commission had arrived in Khartoum, but a delay in the constitution of the Governor-General's Commission necessarily caused a similar delay in the appointment of the Commission's Sudanese members.[1] The Commission's terms of reference required it to arrange for elections to be held 'as soon as possible',[2] but on 5 May it declared that 'to its great regret' it was compelled to postpone elections until after the rainy season—a precedent which was understandably followed in all subsequent elections. In the meantime the Commission tackled the difficult task of revising the electoral rules and drawing up revised lists of direct and indirect constituencies—a subject which was fervently discussed throughout the country, for obvious reasons. One of the most controversial topics was whether or not tribal leaders should be allowed to stand for elections while maintaining their official position as government agents. The Commission finally decided against their exclusion, but following its terms of reference (that elections should be direct whenever possible) it decided that elections in sixty-eight constituencies should be direct and in twenty-four constituencies indirect—instead of thirty-five and fifty-seven respectively as originally provided in the Statute.[3] The number of members to be elected in the graduates' constituency was also raised from three to five. For the purpose of elections to the Senate the Commission endorsed the Statute's provisions that each one of the nine provinces should form a single constituency and that all thirty elected Senators (twenty were to be appointed by the Governor-

[1] *Report of the Sudan Electoral Commission*, 1953, Cmd. 9058, p. 4.

[2] Annex II to the Anglo-Egyptian Agreement.

[3] J. S. R. Duncan correctly states that 'under pressure from conservative opinion in the Provinces we had overdone the protection of the provincial voter' (*The Sudan's Path to Independence* (Edinburgh and London, 1957), p. 161).

General) should be chosen by means of indirect elections. Whereas the Statute had provided that only Sudanese members of Provincial and Local Government Councils were to act as electoral colleges, the Commission decided that the Senate would be more sound if the electorate was widened to include other categories. Accordingly graduates, certain teachers, holders of intermediate school-leaving certificates in the South, and candidates for election to the House of Representatives were included as qualified voters for the Senate.[1]

Previous elections having been systematically, and effectively, boycotted by the majority of the politically conscious sections of the population, the 1953 elections were the first ever contested by all registered political parties in the country. For this reason and because of the general condition of the country—vast, with a poor system of transport and a population largely nomadic and mostly illiterate—a variety of special arrangements had to be made in order to secure the effective participation of those qualified to vote. Instead of holding elections simultaneously throughout the country for instance, it was found more practicable to arrange for polling to take place over several weeks beginning on 2 November and ending on the 10 December. Within any given constituency, however, voting was generally restricted to one and the same day. Because of nomadism some polling stations had to be situated outside their constituencies, and the vast area of the country coupled with the inadequacy of trained staff capable of running elections obliged the Commission to charge some polling parties with the responsibility of supervising as many as five or six polling stations. Illiteracy and general backwardness made it imperative, in most areas, to adopt various alternatives to the usual method of voting by ticket. Tokens and colours were, therefore, widely used. But in five constituencies, two in the Nuba Mountains and three along the Ethiopian frontiers, the Electoral Commission felt that people were so 'unsophisticated' that the system of voting by acclamation had to be adopted. Some members of the Commission, however, opposed the use of this method (requiring voters to queue up behind the candidate of their choice) anywhere in the country.

During the elections several complaints were made about interference on the part of Egyptians, British members of the administration, and tribal leaders, and a small number of charges under the Corrupt Practices Ordinance were brought to the attention of the

[1] *Report of the Sudan Electoral Commission*, pp. 6–10.

Electoral Commission. But owing largely to the co-operation of the political parties, the mobilization of the radio and the Press for the cause of civility, and a general feeling that the world was watching and that therefore nothing but the best behaviour would suffice, the first national elections in the Sudan were conducted—entirely by Sudanese—with a remarkable degree of orderliness and propriety. Altogether about 50 per cent of the qualified voters participated in the elections, which, in the opinion of the Commission, was entirely satisfactory.[1] 'Whatever the nature and the extent of the influences that may have been exerted on them', the Commission concluded, '. . . the electorate had everywhere the opportunity of voting freely for the representatives of their choice, and . . . consequently the results of the elections substantially represent the will of the Sudanese people.'[2]

* * * * *

The results, according to a senior British member of the Sudan Political Service, dismayed many people in the Administration.[3] Their favourite Republican Socialist Party, composed mainly of tribal shaikhs and chiefs, which had been hailed by British officials as a major breakthrough in the familiar pattern of Sudanese politics,[4] suffered a crushing defeat in the elections, and the handful of R.S.P. members who were returned to Parliament afterwards decided to back the winning side. Out of 97 seats in the House of Representatives the National Unionist Party, under the leadership of Sayyid Ismā'īl al-Azhari, won 51; the Umma Party won 22; and the remaining 24 seats were divided between the R.S.P. (3), the Southern Party

[1] *Report of the Sudan Electoral Commission*, p. 17.

[2] Ibid., p. 18.

[3] Duncan, p. 164.

[4] Duncan, *The Sudan—A Record of Progress*, p. 265. On 18 Mar. 1947 the Egyptian Wafdist paper *al-Balāgh* published a Sudan Government secret document, no. SCR/36.M.8 of 9 Apr. 1945, in which the Civil Secretary expressed his satisfaction with the recently established Umma Party as an 'antidote' to the Congress and Unionist Movement. The Public Relations Officer of the Sudan Government confirmed the authenticity of the document, which was henceforth extensively used by the Unionists to present the Umma Party as an instrument of British policy. From 1950 onwards, however, the Umma Party, as we have seen, began pressing for the immediate termination of the Anglo-Egyptian regime. It was then generally felt that the Sudan Government, having failed to secure the participation of the Khatmiyya in the Legislative Assembly for the purpose of resisting the Umma policy, sponsored the R.S.P. as an 'antidote' against the Anṣār and their demand for immediate self-government and self-determination. The leader of the R.S.P. did not sign the Political Parties Agreement of 10 Jan. 1953—the Party being represented by two senior members.

(9), non-party members (11)—and there was one 'Anti-Imperialist', i.e. a member of the then clandestine Communist Party. Of the 30 electoral seats in the Senate the N.U.P. won 22, and of the 20 Senators appointed by the Governor-General 10 were members of the victorious party.

3. *Sudanization and self-determination*

The first Sudanese Parliament was convened on 1 January 1954, and on the 6th Sayyid Ismā'īl al-Azhari became the first Sudanese Prime Minister. Under his leadership the process of finally bringing the Anglo-Egyptian regime to an end and handing over to the Sudanese was accelerated.

Apart from Parliament and the Council of Ministers the most important feature of the new system was the Sudanization Committee. This was appointed on 20 February 1954. Like the Governor-General's Commission and the Electoral Commission, the Sudanization Committee had a mixed membership. One member was British, another Egyptian, and three were Sudanese. Unlike these two Commissions, however, the Committee had a Sudanese Chairman[1] and three non-voting members. But the Chairman was not permanent, the office being held by the three Sudanese members on a rotary basis of one month each—thus guarding against the possibility of vested interest growing around a key office of particular importance and sensitivity during the transitional period. The non-voting members of the Committee were the Chairman of the Public Service Commission (himself a Sudanese) and two members of his Commission, one Sudanese, the other British. The functions of the non-voting members were purely advisory, and the Chairman of the Sudanization Committee was authorized to use 'his discretion from time to time to determine how many and which of the non-voting members shall attend the meetings'[2] of the Committee.

The duties of the Committee were 'to complete [under the direction of the Council of Ministers] the Sudanisation of the Administration, the Police, the Sudan Defence Force, and any other government post that may affect the freedom of the Sudanese at the time of Self-Determination . . . within a period not exceeding three years'.[3]

[1] The Chairman of the Governor-General's Commission was a Pakistani, that of the Electoral Commission an Indian.

[2] Minutes of the Meetings of the Sudanisation Committee, Archives, Khartoum.

[3] Annex III to the Anglo-Egyptian Agreement of 12 Feb. 1953.

Beginning its formal meetings on 7 March it co-opted and interviewed a large number of civil servants, army officers, police, etc., and invited evidence by means of correspondence from a small number of persons, including the Speaker of the House of Representatives.

The proceedings of the Committee were in general characterized by the eagerness of the Sudanese members, supported by the Egyptian member, to complete the Sudanization of every branch of the Public Service as soon as possible, while the British member and some of the British officials who were interviewed urged—in the interest of efficiency and continuity—a slower pace of Sudanization, especially with regard to the Judiciary, the Army, certain technical posts, and in the Southern provinces in general. Some of them went as far as suggesting that British administrators should be retained as 'advisers' in certain Departments. As may be expected, however, the overriding political consideration explicitly stated in the Agreement and in the Committee's terms of reference was given priority over all other considerations. The main point, it was correctly and repeatedly pointed out, was to ensure the free and neutral atmosphere necessary for the proper exercise of self-determination. British and Egyptian employees of the Sudan Government, whether they were administrators, judges, or technical experts, were politically obsolete; their continued existence in the Sudan was likely to infringe the freedom and neutrality of the atmosphere in which self-determination would take place. Some lowering of technical standards was inevitable, at any rate in the short run, when the very fact of quick handing-over within the prescribed limit of three years was bound to have an adverse effect on efficiency. But this was likely to be a transient phase, after which adequate standards would be restored—if necessary with the help of technicians and advisers from neutral countries. Able and experienced Sudanese, however, were to be found in almost every field of the Public Service, partly as a result of the implementation of previous programmes of Sudanization, and arrangements could be made to train more. In the meantime, however, the first essential was to ensure the free and neutral atmosphere required by the Agreement. To facilitate this a Bill to provide for the payment of compensation and post-service benefits to expatriate officials consequent upon their retirement from the service of the Sudan Government was introduced into the House of Representatives on 8 July. At about the same time a campaign for the collection of 'Māl al-Fidā'' (literally, 'ransom money') was launched in order to popularize the policy of quick and wholesale Sudanization and raise additional funds for the payment of compensations. Generous compensations were paid for those whose contracts had to be prematurely terminated as a result of Sudanization or who, for other reasons, wished to resign before the end of the transitional period, on 12 February 1956. Under the circumstances the Sudanization Committee was able to finish its work several months before the deadline. This was formally declared on 2 August 1955.[1]

* * * * * *

In the meantime the future of the Sudan, whether it should become completely independent from both Egypt and Britain or be linked in some form of association with Egypt, was being vigorously discussed throughout the country. The victory of the N.U.P. in the elections and the subsequent appointment of Ismā'īl al-Azhari as Prime Minister in January 1954, seemed to suggest that the Sudanese would finally choose union with Egypt. For the majority of the Unionists, including the Khatmiyya, however, co-operation with Egypt during the lifetime of the Anglo-Egyptian regime was only a means of achieving the independence of the Sudan and not a preliminary step towards the political fusion of the two countries. This view of 'Unionism' as a means rather than an end had been gradually developed after the disappointments of 1924 (as we have seen in Chapter IV), and it was fostered throughout by the oscillation of Egyptian governments and advocates of the Unity of the Nile Valley between the notion that this was based on sovereignty, conquest, and the right of the Egyptians to rule the Sudan on the one hand, and the contradictory view that it was based on the fraternity and brotherhood of the Egyptians and the Sudanese on the other. Even in its heyday during the forties, therefore, the Unity of the Nile Valley, as far as the Sudanese were concerned, was essentially a means of resisting British rule in the Sudan rather than an expression of a desire to be governed by the junior partner in the dual administration —under the Egyptian crown. Unionism, furthermore, served the purpose of resisting and counteracting the rumoured plans of the Anṣār for the creation of a Mahdist monarchy in the Sudan. On 3 August 1953, however, Sayyid 'Abd al-Raḥmān al-Mahdi allayed

[1] *Weekly Digest of Proceedings in the House of Representatives*, no. 8, Third Session, Tuesday, 16 Aug. 1955, p. 397.

the fears of his political and sectarian opponents by publicly declaring that he was not interested in monarchy but favoured the establishment of a democratic republican regime in the Sudan.[1] Considering these factors, therefore, it is not surprising that, with the progressive liquidation of British rule in the Sudan, 'the Sudan for the Sudanese' began to gain the support of an ever widening circle of nationalists. The motto was no longer seen as an instrument either of the Mahdists as such or of British policy in the country, but as a genuine expression of Sudanese patriotism. On 1 March 1954, moreover, the Anṣār, already embittered by their unexpected defeat in the elections, clearly and violently demonstrated that they would not, under any circumstances, accept any form of association with Egypt and that the unity of the country would be jeopardized unless the Sudan became independent. The 1st of March had been chosen for the ceremonial opening of Parliament. A large number of foreign visitors, including General Najīb, had been invited for the occasion. Determined to let the world and the Egyptians in particular know that the Sudanese wanted only independence, Anṣār demonstrators clashed with the police and security forces to whom the arrangements of the day had been entrusted. Hundreds of people were injured and several were killed. The ceremony was cancelled and the guests, including General Najīb, left Khartoum the same day or shortly after. Even those who were genuinely convinced that the Unity of the Nile Valley was the best policy for Egypt and the Sudan began wondering whether the realization of this aim would be possible in the near future. It was obvious that a policy of complete independence would not only be expedient, but would also satisfy the nationalist aspirations of the Sudanese. A section of the N.U.P.—significantly led by three prominent Khatmiyya figures (Sayyids Mirghani Ḥamza, Khalafalla Khālid, and Aḥmad Jaly), all of whom were then Ministers and members of the Cabinet—withdrew their support from Prime Minister Ismā'īl al-Azhari because he would not immediately declare himself in favour of independence and, with the blessings of Sayyid 'Ali al-Mirghani duly given on 2 January 1955, launched a separate 'Republican Independence Party' of their own.[2] This was subsequently reinforced by an unprecedented personal and political reconciliation between Sayyid 'Ali al-Mirghani and Sayyid 'Abd al-Raḥmān al-Mahdi. In the dramatic statement which they jointly issued on the occasion—on 3 December—the two Sayyids announced that they

[1] The text of the statement in Ṭāha, p. 120. [2] *Ṣawt al-Sūdān*, 3 Jan. 1955.

were resolved to work together for 'the welfare, happiness, freedom and complete sovereignty' of the Sudan and appealed to their followers and all Sudanese people to follow suit.[1]

A number of subsidiary factors contributed to this process of growing support for independence. Amongst these was the humiliating dismissal by 'Abd al-Nāṣir of General Najīb from the leadership of the Egyptian Government. Najīb, who was half Sudanese and had played an important part in concluding the Agreements of 1952 and 1953, was held in high regard by the Sudanese. More important was 'Abd al-Nāṣir's suppression, first of the Muslim Brotherhood, with which the Sudanese generally sympathized,[2] and then of the Egyptian communists whose counterparts in the Sudan were thereby also alienated.[3] Numerous complaints had been made about Egyptian interference in the elections during 1953, and soon afterwards the Egyptian radio and Press—regardless of the Gentleman's Agreement of 1952—launched a violent and indiscreet campaign for the Unity of the Nile Valley. 'Egyptian interference', as it was resentfully dubbed by the nationalists irrespective of party allegiance,[4] increased, as more Sudanese declared their preference for independence—and the process gathered momentum with the growth of Egyptian pressure.[5]

[1] Ibid., 4 Dec. 1955 and the memoirs of Sayyid 'Abd al-Raḥmān al-Mahdi, p. 165. In this statement the two Sayyids also called for the formation of an all-party coalition government—a suggestion which had previously been made by the Umma Party and the recently formed R.I.P. but was strongly resisted by Azhari and his ruling N.U.P.

[2] The extent of the disapproval of 'Abd al-Nāṣir's handling of Najīb and the Muslim Brotherhood was indicated, among other things, by the extraordinary popularity of a poem which was written (in a magisterial and resonant Arabic style) by Ustādh Aḥmad Muḥammad Sālih, a prominent figure in Sudanese literary circles, who was subsequently appointed a member of the Supreme Commission which replaced the Governor-General as the constitutional head of the independent Sudan. The poem, entitled 'Ilā Najīb Fī 'Alya'hi' ('To Najīb In His Glory'), was first published in *al-Ra'y al-'Aām* (*Khartoum Daily*) of 26 Nov. 1954.

[3] In these days the Sudanese Communist Party was also critical of 'Abd al-Nāṣir for having concluded the Anglo-Egyptian Treaty of 1954. He was therefore seen by the S.C.P. not only as a fascist dictator but also as a paid agent of Anglo-American imperialism. It was against this background that the S.C.P. then joined with the Umma Party in calling for independence as against unity with Egypt.

[4] *al-Ra'y al-'Aām*, 27 July 1955.

[5] The abject failure of this policy induced President 'Abd al-Nāṣir to call it off and dismiss the man most closely identified with it, Major Ṣalāh Sālim, towards the end of 1955. By that time, however, the die had been cast and the country was firmly set on its path to independence.

On 16 March 1955 the Prime Minister, Sayyid Ismā'īl al-Azhari, himself declared that he was in favour of independence. 'Those who govern you today', he told an enthusiastic audience, 'will not surrender you either to the Egyptians or to the British.'[1] The Umma Party and the Anṣār announced their approval of the new policy of the N.U.P. and promised to support Azhari 'both inside and outside of Parliament'.[2]

By the beginning of August when the Sudanization Committee completed its work, therefore, the country was united[3] in its desire for independence. All that remained was for this to be formally endorsed.

The procedure of self-determination as laid down in the Anglo-Egyptian Agreement of February 1953 was long and complicated. The agreement stipulated that, at the end of the transitional period, the Sudanese Parliament would pass a resolution expressing their desire that arrangements for self-determination be put in motion. The Governor-General would notify the British and Egyptian Governments of the resolution. The Sudanese Government would then draw up a draft law for the election of a Constituent Assembly. When this had been approved by Parliament the Governor-General would, with the agreement of the Commission, give his consent to the law. Detailed preparations for the process of self-determination, including safeguards ensuring the impartiality of the elections of the Constituent Assembly, would then be made, subject to international supervision. The Constituent Assembly would then decide the future of the Sudan by 'choosing to link the Sudan with Egypt in any form' or by 'choosing complete independence'.[4]

To have gone through this procedure at a time when the Sudanese were clearly united in their wish for independence would have been superfluous. Given the attitude of the Egyptian Government at the time moreover, it could easily lead to undesirable complications. On

[1] *Ṣawt al-Sūdān*, 16 Mar. 1955.

[2] Note submitted by the Independence Front to the Prime Minister (Ṭāha, p. 146).

[3] Sayyid Muḥammad Nour al-Dīn, the deputy president of the N.U.P., together with a small and short-lived group of supporters, broke away from the party because of its change of policy *vis-à-vis* Egypt and, for a while, continued to advocate the old policy of union with Egypt. Other splinter groups briefly experimented with such unintelligible (some would almost certainly say nonsensical) notions as Istiqlāl Ittiḥādi—i.e. unionistic independence—and Ittiḥād Istiqlāli—literally, independential union—before finally joining the ranks of those who stood for independence pure and simple.

[4] Article 12.

16 August Parliament unanimously passed a resolution expressing the desire of the members that arrangements for self-determination be put in motion forthwith.[1] Two days later, a mutiny of troops broke out in one of the Southern provinces. This had been encouraged by the Egyptian Government as a means of bringing pressure to bear on Parliament in order to induce it to change its attitude with regard to the question of unity versus independence.[2] The Egyptian Government then urged the Governor-General to declare a constitutional emergency and send a formal request for Anglo-Egyptian troops to be sent to the South in order to restore peace. The British Government, having nothing to gain by such a move and consistent with its policy of keeping 'at all costs the goodwill and trust of the Sudanese people',[3] refused to accept the suggestion. The disorders in the South were finally ended without outside help—but only after over three hundred Northerners, including women and children, had been massacred. The mutiny and the continued hostility of the Egyptian Government confirmed the Sudanese Government and Parliament in their belief that the end of the Anglo-Egyptian regime should be brought about as soon as possible and without recourse to the procedures visualized by the signatories of the Agreement.

On 29 August Parliament unanimously resolved that direct plebiscite was the best method to ascertain the true wish of the Sudanese as regards self-determination.[4] It soon became apparent, however, that the holding of the plebiscite was itself likely to be a long process and that in the unsettled conditions of the Southern provinces it might even prove impossible. On the 19 December therefore another resolution was unanimously approved. The resolution read as follows: 'We, the Members of the House of Representatives in Parliament assembled, declare in the name of the Sudanese people that the

[1] *Weekly Digest of Proceedings in the House of Representatives*, no. 8, Third Session, Tuesday, 16 Aug. 1955, p. 144.

[2] Having devoted many years of their lives to the implementation of the old Southern Policy, many British administrators found it extremely difficult to accept the new policy of unity between the North and the South. Thus the Governor of Wau, who in 1947 accused the Civil Secretary of 'sacrificing his conscience', continued, even after the commencement of the transitional period, to insist that the Northern and Southern provinces of the Sudan should be treated differently and that what applied to the former could not operate in the latter (Richard Owen to the Civil Secretary, 23 Feb. 1952, B.G.P./S.C.R./I.C.I., Archives, Khartoum).

[3] Above, p. 196.

[4] *Weekly Digest of Proceedings in the House of Representatives*, no. 9, Third Session, 22–9 Aug. 1955, p. 454.

Sudan is to become a fully independent sovereign state.'[1] The Arabic version of the resolution read: '. . . the Sudan *has become* a fully independent sovereign state'. It was a *fait accompli* which neither Egypt nor Britain could prudently refuse to accept.

On the same day the House of Representatives also unanimously resolved that a committee of five Sudanese be elected by Parliament to exercise the powers of the Head of State under a temporary constitution.[2] The Transitional Constitution of the Sudan was approved, on 31 December, in a joint session of the members of the House and the Senate.[3] It was a modified form of the Self-Government Statute on which the existing system was based. Article 2 declared the Sudan 'a Sovereign Democratic Republic'. Article 10 provided for the election, by Parliament, of a Supreme Commission which, as Head of the State, was, except in certain specified cases, to discharge its functions on the advice of the Council of Ministers. Article 67 asserted, for the first time, the sovereignty of the Sudanese Parliament in international affairs. It provided that 'No treaty, agreement or convention with any other country or countries or any decision made in any international convention, association or other body, shall have effect in the Sudan unless ratified and affirmed by Parliament by law.' A number of continuation clauses were also introduced to keep the existing institutions in motion until new legislation was enacted. The Transitional Constitution having been approved by Parliament on the 31 December, independence was formally celebrated on the following day, 1 January 1956.

* * * * * *

The Transitional Constitution, as indicated by its title, was a temporary arrangement which was hurriedly contrived at the eleventh hour[4] in order to facilitate the country's orderly passage to indepen-

[1] *Weekly Digest of Proceedings in the House of Representatives*, no. 13, Third Session, 19–24 Dec. 1955 p. 586.

[2] Ibid., p. 589.

[3] *Weekly Digest of Proceedings in the House of Representatives*, no. 14, Third Session, 26 Dec. 1955 to 1 Jan. 1956, p. 668.

[4] In the course of a talk to the Political Science Staff Seminar of the University of Khartoum on 22 Jan. 1967 Sayyid Aḥmad Mutwalli al-'Atabani, who, as Attorney-General, was chiefly responsible for the drafting of the Transitional Constitution, told the story of how five amendments proposed, on the last day, by the Umma Party, became the subject of hard bargaining that went on until the small hours of 31 Dec. Agreement having been finally reached the amendments were hurriedly typed, duplicated, and pasted on copies of the original draft of the Constitution, which were handed out to M.P.s just before the com-

dence. It was the intention of its makers to replace it, at an early date, with a permanent constitution which would adequately reflect the character, the needs, and the aspirations of the Sudan and the Sudanese. As it happened, however, the country—more than a decade after the achievement of independence—is still engaged in the pursuit of that illusive object. In the meantime the Sudan has passed through three constitutionally distinct phases: the first, during which it was governed under the Transitional Constitution as originally promulgated, lasted until 17 November 1958; the second, commencing on that date, was the military regime of General Ibrahim 'Abboud and his military junta; and, finally, the period since October 1964 when the military were—dramatically and almost miraculously—overthrown and civilian government was restored under a modified version of the Transitional Constitution of 1956. Throughout these three phases Sudanese politics and society have been dominated by three main issues: that arising from the country's dependence on one cash crop—cotton; the question of the Southern Sudan—by far the knottiest problem inherited from the British colonial administration; and the continued search for a permanent constitution. The interactions between these and other related factors—principally the battle of nation-building at home and the country's involvement in various, often conflicting, policies abroad—will be analysed in a later study of government and politics in the independent Sudan.

mencement of the joint Parliamentary session in which the Transitional Constitution was finally adopted.

APPENDICES

I. Cromer's Original Draft of the Anglo-Egyptian Agreement of 1899 229
II. The Anglo-Egyptian Agreement of 1899 233
III. Supplemental Agreement for the Administration of the Sudan, 1899 235
IV. Kitchener's first 'Memorandum to Mudirs' 237
V. The Governor-General's Council Ordinance, 1910 241
VI. Civil Secretary's Memorandum on Southern Policy, 1930 244
VII. Anglo-Egyptian Treaty, 1936: Article 11, Annex, and Note (3) 250
VIII. Civil Secretary's Memorandum on Revision of Southern Policy, 1946 253
IX. Anglo-Egyptian Agreement concerning Self-Government and Self-Determination for the Sudan, 1953 257

APPENDIX I

Cromer's Original Draft of the Anglo-Egyptian Agreement of 1899

WHEREAS certain provinces in the Soudan which were in rebellion against the authority of H.M. The Khedieve have now been reconquered by the joint military and financial efforts of H.B.M.'s Govt. and the Govt. of H.H. The Khedieve.

And whereas it has become necessary to decide upon a system for the administration of and for the making of laws for the said reconquered provinces under which due allowance may be made for the backward and unsettled conditions of large portions thereof and for the varying requirements of different localities.

And whereas it is desired to give effect to the claims which have accrued to H.B.M.'s Govt. by right of conquest to share in the present settlement and future working and development of the said system of administration and legislation.

And whereas it is conceived that for many purposes the districts of Wady Halfa and Suakin may be most effectively administered in conjunction with the reconquered provinces to which they are respectively adjacent.

Now it is hereby agreed and declared by and between the undersigned duly authorized for that purpose as follows:

ARTICLE 1

Unless it be otherwise authorized the word 'Soudan' in this agreement means all the territories south of the 22nd parallel of latitude which:

(i) have never been evacuated by Egyptian troops since the year 1882, or

(ii) which, having before the late rebellion in the Soudan been administered by the Government of H.H. The Khedieve, were temporarily lost to Egypt and have been reconquered by H.B.M.'s Government and the Egyptian Government acting in concert, or

(iii) which may hereafter be reconquered by the two Governments acting in concert.

ARTICLE 2

The British and Egyptian flags shall be used together, both on land and water, throughout the Soudan except in the town of Suakin in which locality the Egyptian flag alone shall be used.

ARTICLE 3

The supreme military and civil command in the Soudan shall be vested in one officer termed the 'Governor-General of the Soudan'. He shall be appointed by Khedievial decree on the recommendation of H.B.M.'s Government and shall be removed only by Khedievial decree with the consent of H.B.M.'s Government.

ARTICLE 4

Laws, as also orders and regulations with the full force of law for the Government of the Soudan and for regulating the holding disposal and devolution of property of every kind herein situate may from time to time be made, altered or abrogated by proclamation of the Governor-General. Such laws, orders and regulations may apply to the whole or any named part of the Soudan and may either explicitly or by necessary implication alter or abrogate any existing law or regulation.

Proclamations of the Governor-General shall be issued only with the prior consent of H.H. The Khedieve, acting under the advice of his Council of Ministers, and of H.B.M.'s Government, through H.B.M.'s Agent and Consul General in Cairo.

Nevertheless the parties whose consent is so required may from time to time exempt from the obligation to receive such prior consent proclamations of the Governor-General in respect of any such clauses of administrative or executive matters as may be specified in any instrument conferring such exemption. Proclamations issued without prior consent by virtue of exemption shall be forthwith notified to H.B.M.'s Agent and Consul General in Cairo and to the President of the Council of Ministers of H.H. The Khedieve within a period of   from date of issue and shall be subject to such power of revision or rescission as may be reserved by the instrument creating the exemption.

ARTICLE 5

No Egyptian law decree ministerial arrete or other enactment hereafter to be made or promulgated shall apply to the Soudan or any named part thereof save in so far as the same shall be applied by proclamation of the Governor-General in manner hereinbefore provided.

ARTICLE 6

The whole of the Soudan revenue shall be at the disposal of the Egyptian Government. The Egyptian Government shall be solely responsible for all the civil and ordinary military expenditure in the Soudan but H.B.M.'s Government undertakes to bear the whole cost of any British troops that may be stationed in the Soudan, other than special expeditionary forces.

In the event of any extraordinary circumstances occurring which may necessitate the despatch of a special British expedition to the Soudan the question of the division of cost shall form the subject of a special arrangement between the two Governments.

ARTICLE 7

In the definition by proclamation of the conditions under which Europeans of whatever nationality shall be at liberty to trade with or reside in the Soudan, or to hold property within its limits, no special privileges shall be accorded to the subjects of any one or more Power.

ARTICLE 8

Import duties on entering the Soudan shall not be payable on goods coming from Egyptian territory. Such duties may, however, be levied on goods coming from elsewhere than Egyptian territory, but in the case of goods entering the Soudan at Suakin or any other port on the Red Sea littoral they shall not exceed the corresponding duties for the time being levied on goods entering Lower Egypt from abroad. Export duties may be levied on goods leaving the Soudan whether for Egyptian territory or elsewhere.

ARTICLE 9

The jurisdiction of the Mixed Tribunals shall not extend nor be recognized for any purpose whatsoever in any part of the Soudan except in the town of Suakin.

ARTICLE 10

Until and save so far as it shall be otherwise determined by proclamation, the Soudan, with the exception of the town of Suakin, shall be and remain under martial law.

ARTICLE 11

No consuls, vice consuls or consular agents shall be accredited in respect of nor allowed to reside in the Soudan without the previous consent of H.B.M.'s Government.

ARTICLE 12

The importation of slaves into the Soudan, as also their exportation, is absolutely prohibited. Provisions shall be made by proclamation for the enforcement of this regulation.

ARTICLE 13

It is agreed between the two Governments that special attention shall be paid to the enforcement of the Brussels' Act of July 2nd, 1890, in respect of the import, sale and manufacture of firearms and their munitions and distilled or spirituous liquors.

APPENDIX II

The Anglo-Egyptian Agreement of 1899

AGREEMENT between Her Britannic Majesty's Government and the Government of His Highness the Khedive of Egypt, relative to the future administration of the Sudan.

WHEREAS certain provinces in the Sudan which were in rebellion against the authority of His Highness have now been reconquered by the joint military and financial efforts of Her Britannic Majesty's Government and the Government of His Highness the Khedive; and WHEREAS it has become necessary to decide upon a system for the administration of and for the making of laws for the said reconquered provinces, under which due allowance may be made for the backward and unsettled condition of large portions thereof, and for the varying requirements of different localities; and WHEREAS it is desired to give effect to the claims which have accrued to Her Britannic Majesty's Government, by right of conquest, to share in the present settlement and future working and development of the said system of administration and legislation; and WHEREAS it is conceived that for many purposes Wadi Halfa and Suakin may be most effectively administered in conjunction with the reconquered provinces to which they are respectively adjacent:

NOW IT IS HEREBY AGREED AND DECLARED by and between the undersigned, duly authorized for that purpose as follows:

ARTICLE I

The word 'Sudan' in this agreement means all the territories south of the 22nd parallel of latitude, which:

1. Have never been evacuated by Egyptian troops since the year 1882; or
2. Which, having before the late rebellion been administered by the Government of His Highness the Khedive, were temporarily lost to Egypt, and have been reconquered by Her Majesty's Government and the Egyptian Government, acting in concert; or
3. Which may be hereafter reconquered by the two Governments acting in concert.

ARTICLE II

The British and Egyptian flags shall be used together, both on land and water, throughout the Sudan, except in the town of Suakin, in which locality the Egyptian flag alone shall be used.

ARTICLE III

The supreme military and civil command of the Sudan shall be vested in one officer, termed the 'Governor-General of the Sudan'. He shall be appointed by Khedivial Decree on the recommendation of Her Britannic Majesty's Government and shall be removed only by Khedivial Decree, with the consent of Her Britannic Majesty's Government.

ARTICLE IV

Laws, as also orders and regulations with the full force of law, for the good government of the Sudan, and for regulating the holding, disposal, and devolution of property of every kind therein situate, may from time to time be made, altered, or abrogated by Proclamation of the Governor-General. Such laws, orders, and regulations may apply to the whole or any named part of the Sudan, and may, either explicitly or by necessary implication, alter or abrogate any existing law or regulation.

All such Proclamations shall be forthwith notified to Her Britannic Majesty's Agent and Consul-General in Cairo, and to the President of the Council of Ministers of His Highness the Khedive.

ARTICLE V

No Egyptian law, decree, ministerial arrete, or other enactment hereafter to be made or promulgated shall apply to the Sudan or any part thereof, save in so far as the same shall be applied by Proclamation of the Governor-General in manner hereinbefore provided.

ARTICLE VI

In the definition by Proclamation of the conditions under which Europeans, of whatever nationality, shall be at liberty to trade with or reside in the Sudan, or to hold property within its limits, no special privileges shall be accorded to the subjects of any one or more Power.

ARTICLE VII

Import duties on entering the Sudan shall not be payable on goods coming from Egyptian territory. Such duties may however be levied on goods coming from elsewhere than Egyptian territory, but in the case of goods entering the Sudan at Suakin or any other port on the Red Sea littoral, they shall not exceed the corresponding duties for the time being leviable on goods entering Egypt from abroad. Duties may be levied on goods leaving the Sudan, at such rates as may from time to time be prescribed by Proclamation.

ARTICLE VIII

The jurisdiction of the Mixed Tribunals shall not extend, nor be recognized for any purpose whatsoever, in any part of the Sudan, except in the town of Suakin.

ARTICLE IX

Until, and save so far as it shall be otherwise determined by Proclamation, the Sudan, with the exception of the town of Suakin, shall be and remain under martial law.

ARTICLE X

No Consuls, Vice-Consuls, or Consular Agents shall be accredited in respect of nor allowed to reside in the Sudan, without the previous consent of Her Britannic Majesty's Government.

ARTICLE XI

The importation of slaves into the Sudan, as also their exportation, is absolutely prohibited. Provision shall be made by Proclamation for the enforcement of this Regulation.

ARTICLE XII

It is agreed between the two Governments that special attention shall be paid to the enforcement of the Brussels Act of the 2nd July 1890 in respect of the import, sale, and manufacture of firearms and their munitions, and distilled or spirituous liquors.

Done in Cairo, the 19th January 1899.

Signed: { BOUTROS GHALI
CROMER

APPENDIX III

Supplemental Agreement for the Administration of the Sudan, 1899

AGREEMENT made between the British and Egyptian Governments Supplemental to the Agreement made between the two Governments on 19th January 1899 for the future administration of the Sudan.

WHEREAS under our Agreement made the 19th day of January 1899, relative to the future administration of the Sudan, it is provided by Article VIII, that the jurisdiction of the Mixed Tribunals shall not extend nor be recognized for any purpose whatsoever in any part of the Sudan except in the town of Suakin:

And WHEREAS no Mixed Tribunal has ever been established at Suakin and it has been found to be inexpedient to establish any such tribunal in that locality by reason notably of the expense which the adoption of this measure would occasion:

And WHEREAS grievous injustice is caused to the inhabitants of Suakin by the absence of any local jurisdiction for the settlement of their disputes and it is expedient that the town of Suakin should be placed upon the same footing as the rest of the Sudan:

And WHEREAS we have decided to modify our said Agreement accordingly in manner hereinafter appearing:

Now, it is hereby agreed and declared by and between the undersigned duly authorized for that purpose, as follows:

ARTICLE I

Those provisions of our Agreement of the 19th day of January 1899 by which the town of Suakin was excepted from the general regime established by the said agreement for the future administration of the Sudan, are hereby abrogated.

Done at Cairo, the 10th of July 1899.

Signed: { BOUTROS GHALI
CROMER

APPENDIX IV

Kitchener's first 'Memorandum to Mudirs'

THE absolute uprootal by the Dervishes of the old system of Government has afforded an opportunity for initiating a new Administration more in harmony with the requirements of the Soudan.

2. The necessary Laws and Regulations will be carefully considered and issued as required, but it is not mainly to the framing and publishing of laws that we must look for the improvement and the good government of the country.

3. The task before us all, and especially the Mudirs and Inspectors, is to acquire the confidence of the people, to develop their resources, and to raise them to a higher level. This can only be effected by the District Officers being thoroughly in touch with the better class of native, through whom we may hope gradually to influence the whole population. Mudirs and Inspectors should learn to know personally all the principal men of their district, and show them, by friendly dealings and the interest taken in their individual concerns, that our object is to increase their prosperity. Once it is thoroughly realized that our officers have at heart, not only the progress of the country generally, but also the prosperity of each individual with whom they come into contact, their exhortations to industry and improvement will gain redoubled force. Such exhortations, when issued in the shape of Proclamations or Circulars, effect little; it is to the individual action of British officers, working independently, but with a common purpose, on the individual natives whose confidence they have gained that we must look for the moral and industrial regeneration of the Soudan.

4. The people should be taught that the truth is always expected, and will be equally well received whether pleasant or the reverse. By listening to outspoken opinions, when respectfully expressed, and checking liars and flatterers, we may hope in time to effect some improvement in this respect in the country.

5. In the administration of justice in your province you should be very careful to see that legal forms, as laid down, are strictly adhered to, so that the appointed Courts may be thoroughly respected; and you should endeavour, by the careful inquiry given by your Courts to the cases brought before them, to inspire the people with absolute confidence that real justice is being meted out to them. It is very important that the Government should do nothing which could be interpreted as a sign of weakness, and

all insubordination must be promptly and severely suppressed. At the same time, a paternal spirit of correction for offences should be your aim in your relation with the people, and clemency should be shown in dealing with first offences, especially when such may be the result of ignorance, or are openly acknowledged. In the latter case, they should be more than half pardoned in order to induce truthfulness.

6. Be careful to see that religious feelings are not in any way interfered with, and that the Mohamedan religion is respected.

7. Mosques in the principal towns will be rebuilt, but private mosques, takias, zawiyas, sheikhs' tombs, etc., cannot be allowed to be re-established, as they generally formed centres of unorthodox fanaticism. Any request for permission on such subjects must be referred to the Central authority.

8. Slavery is not recognized in the Soudan, but as long as service is willingly rendered by servants to masters it is unnecessary to interfere in the conditions existing between them. Where, however, any individual is subjected to cruel treatment, and his or her liberty interfered with, the accused can be tried on such charges, which are offences against the law, and in serious cases of cruelty the severest sentences should be imposed.

Inspectors

You should divide your province into two approximately equal districts, and hold each Inspector responsible for the exact execution of all Orders and Regulations in the district allotted to them.

Duties of Inspectors

The Inspector is the Mudir's Staff Officer in charge of the district to which he is appointed by the Mudir. He will be responsible for the execution and enforcement in his district of all Orders and Regulations that are issued for the administration of the province, and for the smartness and discipline of the police.

He will be careful to strictly carry out the law as laid down, and make the Court over which he presides respected, and to see that the Mamurs in his district give proper punishments according to their powers.

It will be one of his most important duties to supervise the operations of the police and to see that they thoroughly investigate all criminal cases, and are employed in such a manner as to insure the maintenance of public security.

He will not be a channel of communication between Mamurs and the Mudirieh, that is, Mamurs will forward direct to the Mudirieh all Reports and Returns called for. He will, therefore, have no office staff, but will make himself acquainted with the work of the Mamurs of his district either in the central office or while inspecting the Mamuriehs.

He will be most careful to see that there is no oppression nor illegal taxation in his district.

He will report to the Mudir any official who fails to set a good example in the district by leading a moral and respectable life, or who shows negligence or incapacity in the performance of his duties.

Mamurs

Instructions for Mamurs are as under. In addition to the duties specified it should be noted that they are responsible for the proper measurement of the land in their Mamuriehs and its correct registration.

Instructions to Mamurs

The new position you are about to take up is an important and responsible one.

You should always bear in mind that you are the recognized agent in your district of a just and merciful Government, and as such you should do all in your power to gain the confidence and respect of the inhabitants, who should, in their turn, be made to look to and respect the Government of which you are the Representative.

In order to acquire and hold this position, you should bear in mind the following points, which are essential to the good government of your district.

You should recollect that this country has just been relieved from most oppressive and tyrannical rulers, who have plundered and enslaved the population, and engendered in them feelings of moral and physical fear, which it may take long to eradicate; your object should, therefore, be to make the government of your district as great a contrast as possible to that of the Dervishes. Every effort should be made to induce the inhabitants to feel that an era of justice and kindly treatment has come, with, at the same time, a vigorous repression of crime, and a determination to put down with a strong hand any attempt of evil-doers to carry on the practices which, it is hoped, have disappeared with the flight of the Dervishes.

No doubt the local people will offer bribes, in order to try and secure the goodwill of their new rulers; these offers must be resolutely and absolutely refused, and the people made to understand that they can acquire no benefits by such means, but are more likely to be severely punished. In all their dealings with the Government they should be convinced of its unity of purpose and justice; nothing, therefore, should be taken from them without payment, in accordance with the fixed tariff, and every inducement should be given to them to bring their saleable articles and products to fixed market places, where it is most important the regulation price should be adhered to. You should also endeavour, by all means in your power, to encourage the inhabitants to increase the amount of cultivation in the district. It is especially necessary that the women should be in no way molested, and that the Mamur of the district should be not only an example of fairness and justice, but also of morality, by doing all in his power to improve the moral tone of the inhabitants in his charge, and by instilling into their minds that it is to him they should turn for a redress of grievances, being fully convinced that he will act as is best for their interest and advantage consistently with justice.

Every effort should be made to repress crime, and Mamurs have the power of sending offenders to prison for one day; but when, in their opinion, offences are committed which deserve more severe punishment, they should refer the case to the nearest Commandant, who will either deal with it in accordance with the military powers delegated to him, or will refer it to higher authority. Should it be discovered that you or any of your employees have been the recipients of bakshish of any kind from the local people, you will be liable to be tried by court-martial, and dismissed from the service.

In any case of difficulty or doubt, you should at once refer to the nearest Military Commandant, under whose general direction and guidance you will act.

APPENDIX V

The Governor-General's Council Ordinance, 1910, for Creating a Council to Assist the Governor-General

WHEREAS by virtue of the Agreement dated the 19th January, 1899, between the Government of Her late Britannic Majesty and the Government of His Highness the Khedive the Governor-General is invested with the supreme military and civil command in the Sudan, with the powers in the said Agreement mentioned.

And whereas with the approval of the two Governments aforesaid it is deemed expedient to associate a Council with the Governor-General in the discharge of his executive and legislative powers:

Now It Is Hereby Enacted As Follows:

1. This Ordinance may be cited as the Governor-General's Council Ordinance 1910.

2. A Council to be known as the Governor-General's Council shall be created, composed of the Inspector General, the Financial Secretary, the Legal Secretary, and the Civil Secretary, as ex-officio members, together with not less than two or more than four additional members to be appointed by the Governor-General.

Every additional member shall be appointed for a period of three years and shall be eligible for re-appointment.

During the absence of an ex-officio member of the Council on leave or in the event of his incapacity through illness he shall be replaced on the Council by any officer who, either by special appointment or by virtue of his office is competent to act for him generally.

During the absence or incapacity through illness of an additional member, any other person may be appointed by the Governor-General to act temporarily as a member of the Council.

3. Meetings of the Council shall be presided over by the Governor-General. If the Governor-General shall not be present, then, subject to the provisions of section 13, the senior member of the Council who is present shall preside.

4. The Governor-General's Council shall in respect of all such things as under this or any other Ordinance are required to be done by the Governor-General in Council, exercise the powers conferred upon it by the Ordinance

in respect of all other matters which may be submitted to it shall act as Advisory Council to the Governor-General.

5. All Ordinances, Laws and Regulations to be made by proclamation of the Governor-General by virtue of the provisions of Article IV of the Agreement of the 19th January 1899 shall be made by the Governor-General in Council. Provided that this section shall not apply to any Regulations to be issued by the Governor-General in exercise of any power reserved to him independently of the Council by any Ordinance for the time being in force.

6. The annual budget shall be passed and all supplementary credits whether out of reserve or out of current revenue shall be granted by the Governor-General in Council.

7. All such things shall be done by the Governor-General in Council as shall be required so to be done by the provisions of any Ordinance for the time being in force or by the rules to be made in that behalf by the Governor-General in Council.

8. Subject to the provisions of sections 9 and 10 all things which require to be done by the Governor-General in Council shall be decided by the vote of the majority of the members present. In case of equality the Governor-General or the presiding member shall have a second or casting vote.

A record shall be kept of the decisions of the Council and of the votes of the individual members with respect thereto and any member dissenting from the decision of the majority may require a minute of the reasons for his dissent to be entered on the record.

9. The Governor-General whether present at a meeting of the Council or not may for reasons to be recorded in the record of the proceedings of the Council, overrule the decisions of the majority of the Council, and thereupon the decision of the Governor-General shall be deemed for all purposes to be the decision of the Council.

10. The Governor-General whether present at a meeting of the Council or not, may suspend the operation of any decision of the Council pending the reference thereof to the authorities mentioned in paragraph 2 of Article IV of the Agreement of the 19th January, 1899.

11. Rules not in conflict with the provision of this Ordinance may be made by the Governor-General in Council for regulating the proceedings of the Council, as to the places at which the Council may meet, and as to the appointment and duties of officials of the Council.

12. During the absence of the Governor-General on leave or in the event of his incapacity through illness to perform his duties, as also during every

vacancy in the office of Governor-General all the power of the Governor-General shall vest in the Governor-General's Council, unless the Governor-General shall have appointed an Acting Governor-General to act for him generally.

13. Whenever the Governor-General, while continuing to act as Governor-General shall be away from his Council, he may appoint an officer to preside over the Council in his place and to exercise all or any of the powers herein before conferred upon the Governor-General with respect thereto.

14. Whenever the Governor-General shall be away from his Council the Governor-General, if thereto authorized by a decision of the Council may exercise personally all or any of the powers of the Governor-General in Council.

15. Nothing in this Ordinance contained shall be interpreted as conferring upon the Governor-General in Council any power which if vested in the Governor-General in person would be in conflict with the provisions of the Agreement of the 19th January, 1899, or of any Agreement heretofore made between the Egyptian and Sudan Governments.

APPENDIX VI

Civil Secretary's Memorandum on Southern Policy, 1930

CS/I.C.I.

CIVIL SECRETARY'S OFFICE
Khartoum, 25th January, 1930

The Governor, Upper Nile Province, Malaka 1.
,, ,, Mongalla Province, Mongalla.
,, ,, Bahr el Ghazal Province, Way.

His Excellency the Governor-General directs that the main features of the approved policy of the Government for the administration of the Southern Provinces should be restated in simple terms.

In the strictly confidential memorandum which accompanies this letter an attempt has been made to do this, though it will of course be seen that innumerable points of detail arising are not dealt with *seriatim*.

2. Your attention is directed to Part II of the memorandum, and I should be obliged if you would forward, as soon as possible, your comments on the criteria suggested and any suggestions you may wish to make for additions to the list.

3. The carrying out of the policy as described may lead from time to time to various financial implications or commitments though it is hoped that these will not be great. It will be convenient that any such foreseen should be notified to the relevant authority without delay for consideration.

4. Application of the policy will obviously vary in detail and in intensity according to locality. It is essential however, that the ultimate aim should be made clear to all who are responsible for the execution of the policy, and the memorandum should therefore be circulated to and studied by all your District Commissioners. Sufficient copies for this purpose are sent herewith. Copies are also being sent to such Heads of Departments in Khartoum as are concerned.

CIVIL SECRETARY

Copies to: Director of Agriculture & Forests
,, ,, Works
,, Sudan Medical Service

Copies to: Director of Education
,, Veterinary Department
,, of Surveys
,, ,, Posts & Telegraphs
General Manager, S.G.R. & S.
Financial Secretary
Legal Secretary

For information and with special reference to paragraph 3 above. A separate letter on this point addressed to Heads of Departments follows from Secretary for Education, Health, etc.

CS/I.C.I.

STRICTLY CONFIDENTIAL

MEMORANDUM

PART I

The policy of the Government in the Southern Sudan is to build up a series of self contained racial or tribal units with structure and organisation based, to whatever extent the requirements of equity and good government permit, upon indigenous customs, traditional usage and beliefs.

The measures already taken or to be taken to promote the above policy are re-stated below.

A. PROVISION OF NON-ARABIC-SPEAKING STAFF (ADMINISTRATIVE, CLERICAL AND TECHNICAL)

(a) Administrative Staff

The gradual elimination of the Mamur, whether Arab or black. This has already begun, and it is intended that the process of reduction shall continue as opportunity offers.

(b) Clerical

It has been the recognised policy for some years that locally recruited staff should take the place of clerks and accountants drawn from the North and that the language of Government offices should be English.

In the Bahr El Ghazal Province the change to English has already been made and a large number of local boys are employed.

The process has to be gradual. It is recognised that local boys are not fit at present to fill the higher posts in Government offices, and the supply of educated English-speaking boys depends on the speed with which the two missionary Intermediate schools in Mongalla Province and the Intermediate and Stack Schools at Wau can produce them. The missions must retain a certain number of these boys as teachers for their Elementary Schools (which are an integral part of the educational system) but since the employment of local boys in Government offices is a vital feature of the general policy every encouragement should be given to those in charge of mission schools to co-operate in that policy by sending boys into Government Service. Province officials must aim at maintaining a steady supply of boys for the Elementary Vernacular schools which feed the Intermediate schools.

(*c*) *Technical*

Generally speaking, the considerations mentioned above apply also to the supply of boys for the technical departments—Agriculture, Medical, Public Works, etc.; but in certain cases it may not be essential that boys going to these departments should complete the Intermediate school course.

B. CONTROL OF IMMIGRANT TRADERS FROM THE NORTH

It is the aim of the Government to encourage, as far as is possible, Greek and Syrian traders rather than the Gellaba type. Permits to the latter should be decreased unobtrusively but progressively, and only the best type of Gellaba, whose interests are purely commercial and pursued in a legitimate manner should be admitted. The limitation of Gellaba trade to towns or established routes is essential.

C. FUNDAMENTAL NECESSITY FOR BRITISH STAFF TO FAMILIARISE THEMSELVES WITH THE BELIEFS AND CUSTOMS AND THE LANGUAGES OF THE TRIBES THEY ADMINISTER

(*a*) *Beliefs and Customs*

The policy of Government requires that officials in the South, especially administrative officials, should be fully informed as to the social structure, beliefs, customs and mental processes of pagan tribes. Study on these lines is of vital importance to the solution of administrative problems and, it is with this fact in view that a highly qualified expert has been detailed to work in the South.

(*b*) *Language*

The Rejaf Language Conference recommended the adoption of certain 'group languages' for use in schools. It is clearly impossible to develop all the languages and dialects of the Southern Sudan and the development of a limited number of them may tend to cause the smaller languages one by one to disappear, and be supplanted by 'group languages'.

It is of course, true that the adoption of this system carries with it the implication of the gradual adoption of a new, or partly new, language by the population of the areas in which the 'smaller languages' are used at present. Such a result is, indeed, inevitable in the course of time, for 'smaller languages' must always tend to disappear.

It is also recognised that in such places as Wau itself, Arabic is so commonly used that the local languages have been almost completely excluded. Special concessions may be necessary in these places.

The Rejaf Conference did not regard these factors as seriously affecting the policy of 'group languages', and it was held to be a matter of first importance that books for the study of the 'group languages' should be available for missionaries and officials and that a specialist should be appointed to study the question. A linguistic expert, Dr. Tucker, has therefore been appointed for a period of two years, and his chief function will be to advise as to the production of suitable books. The Secretary for Education and Health has already circulated a memorandum on his duties.

The production of grammars and vocabularies will facilitate the study of the local vernaculars. But this will take time and meanwhile it is the duty of our officers to further the policy of the Government without delay. *It cannot be stressed too strongly that to speak the natural language of the people whom he controls is the first duty of the administrator*. Arabic is not that language, and indeed to the bulk of the population of the South it is a new, or partly new, tongue. Officials should avoid the error of thinking that by speaking Arabic they are in some way conforming to the principle that the administrator should converse with his people in their own language.

D. THE USE OF ENGLISH WHERE COMMUNICATION IN THE LOCAL VERNACULAR IS IMPOSSIBLE

The time has not yet come for the adoption of a general *lingua franca* for the Southern Sudan, and it is impossible to foretell what, if ever that time comes, the language would be.

At the same time there are, without doubt, occasions when the use of a local vernacular is impossible, as, for instance in the case of heterogeneous groupings such as the Sudan Defence Force or the Police.

The recent introduction of English words of command in the Equatorial Corps of the Sudan Defence and their use in the Police Forces in the Provinces concerned is a step in the right direction, but more is required. Every effort should be made to make English the means of communication among the men themselves to the complete exclusion of Arabic. This will entail in the various units the opening of classes in which the men would receive instruction in English, and a concentrated effort on the part of those in authority to ensure that English is used by the men when local vernaculars cannot be. It is believed that in a comparatively short time men of these forces could learn as much English as they now know of Arabic.

It is hoped that those in charge of mission schools will assist in providing instructors for the classes referred to above.

Similarly, an official unable to speak the local vernacular should try to use English when speaking to Government employees and servants, and even, if in any way possible, to chiefs and natives. In any case, the use of an interpreter is preferable to the use of Arabic, until the local language can be used.

The initial difficulties are not minimised. Inability to converse freely at first will no doubt result in some loss of efficiency, and the dislike of almost every Englishman to using his own language in conversing with natives is fully recognised; but difficulties and dislikes must be subordinated to the main policy.

Apart from the fact that the restriction of Arabic is an essential feature of the general scheme it must not be forgotten that Arabic, being neither the language of the governing nor the governed, will progressively deteriorate. The type of Arabic at present spoken provides signal proof of this. It cannot be used as a means of communication on anything but the most simple matters, and only if it were first unlearned and then relearned in a less crude form and adopted as the language of instruction in the schools could it fulfil the growing requirements of the future. The local vernaculars and English, on the other hand, will in every case be the language of one of the two parties conversing and one party will therefore always be improving the other.[1]

In short, whereas at present Arabic is considered by many natives of the South as the official and, as it were, the fashionable language, the object of all should be to counteract this idea by every practical means.

PART II

PROGRESS OF POLICY

His Excellency the High Commissioner in approving this policy has suggested the need for criteria by which progress may be measured.

With this end in view it is intended to tabulate various important features of the policy and to set down the progress made at stated intervals.

It is suggested that the matters to be included in the table should be the following:

[1] Incidentally it may be argued that if a District Commissioner serving in the South is transferred to the North, a knowledge of Nilotic Arabic is more of a hindrance than a help to him in learning the Arabic of the Northern Sudan.

(*a*) The number of non-Mohammedans in relation to the total Government staff under headings of administrative, clerical, and technical, with a report on the use of English by Government employees of non-British origin.
(*b*) The number of British officials who have qualified in the local language.
(*c*) Number of immigrant traders of various nationalities from the North.
(*d*) Number of Mission schools, elementary, intermediate and technical respectively.
(*e*) Number of Government schools.
(*f*) The amount spent on education including:
Subsidies to mission schools.
Cost of Government schools.
Cost of supervisory educational staff.
(*g*) Introduction of English words of command in military or police forces, with a report as to the extent to which Arabic is disappearing as the language in use among the men of these forces.
(*h*) Notes on the progress of the use of English instead of Arabic where communication in the vernacular is impossible.
(*i*) Progress made in the production of text-books in the group languages for use in the schools, and grammars and vocabularies for use of missionaries and officials.

It is proposed to give information in the Annual Report under these heads for the years 1924, 1927, and 1930 and for each subsequent year.

APPENDIX VII

Anglo-Egyptian Treaty, 1936

Article 11, Annex, and Note (3)

ARTICLE 11

1. While reserving liberty to conclude new conventions in future, modifying the agreements of the 19th January and the 10th July, 1899, the High Contracting Parties agree that the administration of the Sudan shall continue to be that resulting from the said agreements. The Governor-General shall continue to exercise on the joint behalf of the High Contracting Parties the powers conferred upon him by the said agreements.

The High Contracting Parties agree that the primary aim of their administration in the Sudan must be the welfare of the Sudanese.

Nothing in this article prejudices the question of sovereignty over the Sudan.

2. Appointments and promotions of officials in the Sudan will in consequence remain vested in the Governor-General, who, in making new appointments to posts for which qualified Sudanese are not available, will select suitable candidates of British and Egyptian nationality.

3. In addition to Sudanese troops, both British and Egyptian troops shall be placed at the disposal of the Governor-General for the defence of the Sudan.

4. Egyptian immigration into the Sudan shall be unrestricted except for reasons of public order and health.

5. There shall be no discrimination in the Sudan between British subjects and Egyptian nationals in matters of commerce, immigration or the possession of property.

6. The High Contracting Parties are agreed on the provisions set out in the Annex to this Article as regards the method by which international conventions are to be made applicable to the Sudan.

Annex to Article 11

1. Unless and until the High Contracting Parties agree to the contrary in application of paragraph 1 of this Article, the general principle for the

future shall be that international conventions shall only become applicable to the Sudan by the joint action of the Governments of the United Kingdom and of Egypt, and that such joint action shall similarly also be required if it is desired to terminate the participation of the Sudan in an international convention which already applies to this territory.

2. Conventions to which it will be desired that the Sudan should be a party will generally be conventions of a technical or humanitarian character. Such conventions almost invariably contain a provision for subsequent accession, and in such cases this method of making the convention applicable to the Sudan will be adopted. Accession will be effected by a joint instrument, signed on behalf of Egypt and the United Kingdom respectively by two persons duly authorised for the purpose. The method of depositing the instruments of accession will be the subject of agreement in each case between the two Governments. In the event of its being desired to apply to the Sudan a convention which does not contain an accession clause, the method by which this should be effected will be the subject of consultation and agreement between the two Governments.

3. If the Sudan is already a party to a convention, and it is desired to terminate the participation of the Sudan therein, the necessary notice of termination will be given jointly by the United Kingdom and by Egypt.

4. It is understood that the participation of the Sudan in a convention and the termination of such participation can only be effected by joint action specifically taken in respect of the Sudan, and does not follow merely from the fact that the United Kingdom and Egypt are both parties to a convention or have both denounced a convention.

5. At international conferences where such conventions are negotiated, the Egyptian and the United Kingdom delegates would naturally keep in touch with a view to any action which they may agree to be desirable in the interests of the Sudan.

Note 3

Sir Miles Lampson to Moustapha El-Nahas Pacha

The Residency, Ramleh.
August, 12, 1936.

Sir,

In the course of discussions on questions of detail, arising out of paragraph 2 of Article [11] the suggestion for the secondment of an Egyptian economic expert for service at Khartoum, and the Governor-General's wish to appoint an Egyptian officer to his personal staff as military secretary, were noted and considered acceptable in principle. It was also considered desirable and acceptable that the Inspector-General of the Egyptian Irrigation Service in the Sudan should be invited to attend the Governor-General's Council when matter relating to his departmental interests were before the Council.

I avail, etc.

MILES W. LAMPSON

High Commissioner

APPENDIX VIII

Civil Secretary's Memorandum on Revision of Southern Policy, 1946

CS/SCR/I.C.I.

CIVIL SECRETARY'S OFFICE
KHARTOUM.

Subject: Southern Sudan policy

SECRET

16 December 1946

Financial Secretary	(2)
Legal Secretary	(2)
Kaid	(3)
Director of Agriculture & Forests	(3)
Director of Economics & Trade	(2)
Director of Education	(3)
Director of Medical Service	(3)
General Manager, Sudan Railways	(2)
Director Veterinary Service	(2)
Governor, Equatoria Province	(12)
Governor, Upper Nile Province	(10)

Will you please refer to Khartoum Secret Despatch No. 89 of 4th August 1945, of which copies were sent to you (or to your predecessors in Office) personally under this number.

2. You will see that in paragraph 2 of the despatch there are contemplated three possible political futures for the Southern Sudan. The crucial sentence is:

> 'It is only by economic and educational development that these people can be equipped to stand up for themselves in the future, whether their lot be eventually cast with the Northern Sudan or with East Africa (or partly with each).'

3. Since the despatch was written, and since the decisions on policy which it records were taken not only have further decisions on policy for the South been taken (of which a list is attached) but great changes have taken place in the political outlook for the country as a whole. Whatever may be the final effect, inside the Sudan, of the present treaty negotiations, it is certain that the advance of the Northern Sudan to self-government, involving the progressive reduction of British executive authority, and

public canvassing of the Southern Sudan question, will be accelerated. It is therefore essential that policy for the Southern Sudan should be crystallised as soon as possible and that it should be crystallised in a form which can be publicly explained and supported and which should therefore be based on sound and constructive social and economic principles. These principles must not only bear defence against factious opposition, but must also command the support of Northern Sudanese who are prepared to take logical and liberal points of view: while the relief of doubts now in the minds of British political and departmental staff who have the interests of the South at heart is also pressing and important.

4. You will see from the foregoing paragraph that I do not suggest that the future of the two million inhabitants of the South should be influenced by appeasement of the as yet immature and ill-informed politicians of the Northern Sudan. But it is the Sudanese, northern and southern who will live their lives and direct their affairs in future generations in this country; and our efforts must therefore now be concentrated on initiating a policy which is not only sound in itself, but which can be made acceptable to, and eventually workable by patriotic and reasonable Sudanese, northern and southern alike.

5. Apart from the recent rapid political development in the North the following conclusions have further emerged since His Excellency's 1945 despatch and enclosures were written:

(*a*) with reference to Appendix I to the despatch, Section 7 last sentence of penultimate paragraph, East Africa's plans regarding better communications with the Southern Sudan have been found to be nebulous, and contingent on the Lake Albert Dam. Whatever the possibilities, we have no reason to hesitate between development of trade between the South and E. Africa and development of trade between the Southern and the Northern Sudan. Our chance of succeeding depends I think upon confining ourselves to the one aim of developing trade in the South, and between the North and the South.

(*b*) In Education, I believe that while the South may hope to have secondary schools, it cannot hope to support post-secondary education, and I believe that Southerners should get this at the Gordon Memorial College—Arabic is not essential there, but should I think be taught to Southerners as a subject from intermediate school level upwards.

(*c*) The distinctions in rates of pay and other conditions of government service, the artificial rules about employment of Southerners in the north, attempts at economic separation, and all similar distinctions are becoming more and more anomalous as the growing demand for Northerners to be employed in Southern Development Schemes, the rapidly growing communication and travel between North and

South, and the very application of the policy of pushing forward in the South, break down the previous isolation of the Southern Provinces and strain these distinctions further.

6. The preceding paragraphs are an attempt to indicate briefly the reasons which have led me to think that an important decision on Southern policy must now be taken. The biennial report to His Britannic Majesty's Government is due early next year. Subject to your comments on this letter, I propose to advise His Excellency that in His Excellency's next report he asks His Britannic Majesty's Government to approve that two of the alternatives mentioned in paragraph 2 above be ruled out as practical politics at the present time. It may in the future be proved that it would be to the advantage of certain of the most southerly tribes, e.g. of Opari or Kajo Kaji, to join up with their relatives in Uganda. It may be that the feeling which now exists among a few of the wisest Northern Sudanese, that they should not, when self-governing, be asked to shoulder the financial and communal burden which they believe the South will always prove to be, may become an important political policy among them. But we should now work on the assumption that the Sudan, as at present constituted, with possibly minor boundary adjustments, will remain one: and we should therefore restate our Southern policy and do so publicly, as follows:

> 'The policy of the Sudan Government regarding the Southern Sudan is to act upon the facts that the peoples of the Southern Sudan are distinctively African and Negroid, but that geography and economics combine (so far as can be foreseen at the present time) to render them inextricably bound for future development to the middle-eastern and arabicised Northern Sudan: and therefore to ensure that they shall, by educational and economic development, be equipped to stand up for themselves in the future as socially and economically the equals of their partners of the Northern Sudan in the Sudan of the future.'

7. Certain changes of detail, in each sphere of Government activity in the South, would I think have to follow the approval and publication of a policy so defined. You will wish to suggest briefly the major points.

8. Will you please consider this matter carefully, consult the senior members of your staffs upon it (particularly of course those who have experience of the South), and let me have your views as briefly as possible. Those of any individual member of your staff which you wish to forward separately with your comments will also be welcome.

The views of Senior Sudanese in whose judgment and discretion you have confidence may also be asked for.

9. Finally I ask you to read again the late Sir Douglas Newbold's note to Council No. CS/SCR/I.C.14 of 3.4.44, reproduced as Appendix 'B' (1) to

the despatch, and to bear in mind that *urgency* is the essence of the problem. We no longer have time to aim at the ideal: we must aim at doing what is the best for the Southern peoples in the present circumstances.

(Sgd.) J. W. ROBERTSON,
Civil Secretary

Copies to: Governors: Blue Nile
Darfur
Kassala
Khartoum—2 copies each
Kordofan
Northern
Sudan Agent, Cairo (2)
Sudan Agent, London (2)

APPENDIX IX

Agreement between the Egyptian Government and the Government of the United Kingdom of Great Britain and Northern Ireland concerning Self-Government and Self-Determination for the Sudan (1953)

THE Egyptian Government and the Government of the United Kingdom of Great Britain and Northern Ireland (hereinafter called the 'United Kingdom Government'), firmly believing in the right of the Sudanese people to Self-Determination and the effective exercise thereof at the proper time and with the necessary safeguards, have agreed as follows:

Article 1

In order to enable the Sudanese people to exercise Self-Determination in a free and neutral atmosphere, a transitional period providing full Self-Government for the Sudanese shall begin on the day specified in Article 9 below.

Article 2

The transitional period, being a preparation for the effective termination of the dual Administration, shall be considered as a liquidation of that Administration. During the transitional period the sovereignty of the Sudan shall be kept in reserve for the Sudanese until Self-Determination is achieved.

Article 3

The Governor-General shall, during the transitional period, be the supreme Constitutional Authority within the Sudan. He shall exercise his powers as set out in the Self-Government Statute with the aid of a five-member Commission, to be called the Governor-General's Commission, whose powers are laid down in the terms of reference in Annex I to the present Agreement.

Article 4

This Commission shall consist of two Sudanese proposed by the two Contracting Governments in agreement, one Egyptian citizen, one citizen of the United Kingdom and one Pakistani citizen, each to be proposed by his respective Government. The appointment of the two Sudanese members shall be subject to the subsequent approval of the Sudanese Parliament when it is elected, and the Parliament shall be entitled to nominate candidates in case of disapproval. The Commission hereby set up will be formally appointed by Egyptian Government decree.

Article 5

The two Contracting Governments agree that, it being a fundamental principle of their common policy to maintain the unity of the Sudan as a single territory, the special powers which are vested in the Governor-General by Article 100 of the Self-Government Statute shall not be exercised in any manner which is in conflict with that policy.

Article 6

The Governor-General shall remain directly responsible to the two Contracting Governments as regards:

(*a*) external affairs;
(*b*) any change requested by the Sudanese Parliament under Article 101 (1) of the Statute for Self-Government as regards any part of that Statute;
(*c*) any resolution passed by the Commission which he regards as inconsistent with his responsibilities. In this case he will inform the two Contracting Governments, each of which must give an answer within one month of the date of formal notice. The Commission's resolution shall stand unless the two Governments agree to the contrary.

Article 7

There shall be constituted a Mixed Electoral Commission of seven members. These shall be three Sudanese appointed by the Governor-General with the approval of his Commission, one Egyptian citizen, one citizen of the United Kingdom, one citizen of the United States of America, and one Indian citizen. The non-Sudanese members shall be nominated by their respective Governments. The Indian member shall be Chairman of the Commission. The Commission shall be appointed by the Governor-General on the instructions of the two Contracting Governments. The terms of reference of this Commission are contained in Annex II to this Agreement.

Article 8

To provide the free and neutral atmosphere requisite for Self-Determination there shall be established a Sudanisation Committee consisting of:

(*a*) An Egyptian citizen and a citizen of the United Kingdom to be nominated by their respective Governments and subsequently appointed by the Governor-General, together with three Sudanese members to be selected from a list of five names submitted to him by the Prime Minister of the Sudan. The selection and appointment of these Sudanese members shall have the prior approval of the Governor-General's Commission;

(*b*) one or more members of the Sudan Public Service Commission who will act in a purely advisory capacity without the right to vote.

The functions and terms of reference of this Committee are contained in Annex III to this Agreement.

Article 9

The transitional period shall begin on the day designated as 'the appointed day' in Article 2 of the Self-Government Statute. Subject to the completion of Sudanisation as outlined in Annex III to this Agreement, the two Contracting Governments undertake to bring the transitional period to an end as soon as possible. In any case this period shall not exceed three years. It shall be brought to an end in the following manner. The Sudanese Parliament shall pass a resolution expressing their desire that arrangements for Self-Determination shall be put in motion and the Governor-General shall notify the two Contracting Governments of this resolution.

Article 10

When the two Contracting Governments have been formally notified of this resolution the Sudanese Government, then existing, shall draw up a draft law for the election of the Constituent Assembly which it shall submit to Parliament for approval. The Governor-General shall give his consent to the law with the agreement of his Commission. Detailed preparations for the process of Self-Determination, including safeguards assuring the impartiality of the elections and any other arrangements designed to secure a free and neutral atmosphere shall be subject to international supervision. The two Contracting Governments will accept the recommendations of any international body which may be set up to this end.

Article 11

Egyptian and British Military Forces shall withdraw from the Sudan immediately upon the Sudanese Parliament adopting a resolution expressing its desire that arrangements for Self-Determination be put in motion. The two Contracting Governments undertake to complete the withdrawal of their forces from the Sudan within a period not exceeding three months.

Article 12

The Constituent Assembly shall have two duties to discharge. The first will be to decide the future of the Sudan as one integral whole. The second will be to draw up a constitution for the Sudan compatible with the decision which shall have been taken in this respect, as well as an electoral law for a permanent Sudanese Parliament. The future of the Sudan shall be decided either:

(*a*) by the Constituent Assembly choosing to link the Sudan with Egypt in any form,
or

(*b*) by the Constituent Assembly choosing complete independence.

Article 13

The two Contracting Governments undertake to respect the decision of the Constituent Assembly concerning the future status of the Sudan and each Government will take all the measures which may be necessary to give effect to its decision.

Article 14

The two Contracting Governments agree that the draft Self-Government Statute shall be amended in accordance with Annex IV to this Agreement.

Article 15

This Agreement and its Attachments shall come into force upon signature.

SELECT BIBLIOGRAPHY

(A) A NOTE ON PRIMARY SOURCES

THIS study, as indicated in the acknowledgements and the main body of the text, is mainly based on unpublished documents—mostly secret and confidential—many of which have been written since the Second World War. Among the most useful, however, have been some of the older documents in the Public Record Office, London—particularly files Class FO/78, containing official correspondences between the British Agent and Consul-General in Cairo and the Foreign Office, and Class FO/633 which consists of the Cromer correspondence. By examining these papers it was possible to throw some fresh light, not only on the character and problems of the administration newly established in the Sudan at the beginning of this century, but even on the Anglo-Egyptian Agreement of 1899, about which so much has already been written.

The Wingate Papers kept—in numbered boxes—at the School of Oriental Studies, Durham University, are by far the most important source of information on the political and administrative development of the Sudan until the outbreak of the First World War—but also, include important documents on later phases of Sudanese history. The letters, memoranda, and other papers contained in the following boxes are particularly useful: 204, 238, 271, 272, 275, 276, 282, and 403.

The Milner Papers at the Library of New College, Oxford, are, of course, indispensable to a study of the Egyptian Revolution of 1919, and its repercussions on the administration of the Sudan, particularly in relation to Egypt, and on the development of Indirect Rule and Southern Policy. Particularly useful to this study were the files entitled 'Memoranda on the Sudan' and Appendices E and F.

As may be expected, however, the Central Archives at Khartoum are the richest source of information on these and other themes in the modern history of the Sudan. Devolution and Native Administration are best studied by reference to files Class I.F.I. Policy statements and correspondence relating to 'Southern Policy' are contained in files Class CS/I.C.I. Valuable information on 'Political Agitation' and the development of Sudanese nationalism until about the outbreak of the Second World War can be gathered from the Reports of the Intelligence Department and the 'Personality Sheets' of the C.I.D. Subsequent developments of these themes and of the constitutional problems and development of the Sudan until 1951 have been studied with the aid of files and documents at the Ministry of Interior—particularly Class SCR/I.A.20 and Class SCO/I.A.20 As the filing systems of the Central Archives and the Ministry of which the Archives Office is part are closely connected, however, I have not thought it necessary to distinguish between the two; both are designated 'Archives, Khartoum' in the text. Minutes of the Governor-General's Council are also kept at the Archives.

(B) PUBLISHED OFFICIAL SOURCES

1. *Annual Reports* of the Governor-General on the Administration, Finances, and Conditions: of Egypt and the Sudan (from 1898 to 1920), and of the Sudan (from 1921 to 1951/2). Ref. Nos.: C. 9231; Cd. 95, 441, 1012, 1529, 2409, 2817, 3394, 4580, 5633, 6149, 6682, 7358; Cmd. 957, 1487, 1837, 1950, 2544, 2742, 2991, 3284, 3403, 3697, 3935, 4159, 4387, 4668, 5019, 5281, 5575, 5895, 6139, 8097, 8098, 7316, 7581, 7835, 8181, 8434, 9798, and 9841.
2. *al-Sūdān min 13 Fabrayir 1841 ilā 12 Fabrayir 1953* (the Egyptian Government's 'Green Book') (Presidency of the Council of Ministers, Cairo, 1953).
3. *The Laws of the Sudan*: the 1941 and 1955 editions.
4. *Firmans granted by the Sultans to the Viceroys of Egypt 1841–73 with Correspondence Related Thereto* (1879): C. 2395.
5. *Correspondence relating to Claims of the Egyptian Government and Counter Claims of the British Government arising from the Operations in the Sudan* (1887): C. 5162.
6. *Correspondence with the French Government respecting the Valley of the Upper Nile* (1898): C. 9054.
7. *Further correspondence respecting the Valley of the Upper Nile* (1898): C. 9055.
8. *Despatch from H.M. Agent and Consul-General at Cairo Enclosing a Report on the Sudan by Sir William Garstin* (1899): C. 9332.
9. *Report of the Special Mission to Egypt* (1920): Cmd. 1131.
10. *Treaty of alliance Between H.M. Government in United Kingdom and the Egyptian Government 1936*: Cd. 5360, 1937.
11. *Draft Sudan Protocol (1946): Papers regarding the Negotiations for a Revision of the Anglo-Egyptian Treaty of 1936*: Cmd. 7179, 1947.
12. *Verbatim Records of the Discussions of the 175th, 176th, 179th, 182nd, 189th, 193rd, 198th, 200th, and 201st Meetings of the Security Council concerning the Anglo-Egyptian Dispute*, 1947.
13. *Proceedings of the Advisory Council for the Northern Sudan*, 1944–8.
14. *The First and Second Reports of the Sudan Administration Conference*, 1946.
15. *Report of the Committee on the Sudanisation of the Civil Service*, 1948.
16. *Report on Local Government in the Sudan*: by Dr. A. H. Marshall, 1949.

17. *Minutes and Weekly Digests of the Proceedings of the Legislative Assembly*, 1948–52.

18. *Report on the Work of the Constitution Amendment Commission*: by the Chairman, Mr. Justice R. C. Stanley-Baker.

19. *Draft of the Self-Government Statute as approved by Her Majesty's Government on 21.10.52.*

20. *Documents concerning Constitutional Development in the Sudan and the Agreement Between Britain and Egypt concerning Self-Government and Self-Determination for the Sudan, 1953*. Cmd. 8767.

21. *The Self-Government Statute, 1953.*

22. *Report of the Sudan Electoral Commission*, 1953. Cmd. 9058.

23. *Weekly Digest of Proceedings in the Senate and House of Representatives*, 1954–5.

24. *The Transitional Constitution of the Sudan, 1956.*

25. *Twenty-one Facts about the Sudanese, the First Population Census of the Sudan*, 1955–6.

(C) BOOKS

'ABBĀS, MEKKI: *The Sudan question*. London, 1952.

'ABD AL-ḤALĪM, M. and MAḤJOUB, M. A.: *Mawt Dunya*. Cairo, 1946.

'ABD AL-RAḤMĀN AL-MAHDI: *Jihād fi-Sabīl al-Istiqlāl*. Khartoum, n.d.

ARIAN ('IRYAN), ABDALLA EL: *Condominium and related situation in international law*. Cairo, 1952.

ARKELL, A. J.: *A history of the Sudan from the earliest times to 1821*. London, 1955.

'ATIYAH, E.: *An Arab tells his story*. London, 1946.

'AWAD, MUḤAMMAD: *Al-Sūdān al-Shamāly*. Cairo, 1950.

BADDOUR, A. F.: *Sudanese Egyptian relations*. The Hague, 1960.

COLLINS, R. O.: *The Southern Sudan, 1883–1878*. Yale University Press, 1962.

CROMER, EARL: *Modern Egypt*. London, 1911 (one vol.) edition.

DUNCAN, J. S. R.: *The Sudan—a record of achievement*. Edinburgh and London, 1952.

—— *The Sudan's path to independence*. Edinburgh and London, 1952.

EDEN, SIR A. E.: *Full circle*. London, 1960.

FABUMNI, L. A.: *The Sudan in Anglo-Egyptian relations*. London, 1960.

GAITSKILL, A.: *Gezira—a story of development in the Sudan*. London, 1959.

GRAY, R.: *A history of the Southern Sudan.*

HAMILTON, J. A. DE C. (ed.): *The Anglo-Egyptian Sudan from within*. London, 1935.

HENDERSON, K. D. D. (ed.): *The making of the modern Sudan*. London, 1952.

HILL, R.: *Egypt in the Sudan, 1820–1881*. London, 1959.

HOLT, P. M.: *A modern history of the Sudan*. 1961.

KHAIR, AḤMAD: *Kifāḥ Jīl*. Cairo, 1948.

—— *Maʿasi al-Injiliz Fil-Sudan*. Cairo, 1946.

KIRK, G.: *A survey of international affairs in the Middle East—1945–50*. London, 1954.

MACMICHAEL, SIR H.: *The Anglo-Egyptian Sudan*. London, 1934.

—— *The Sudan*. London, 1954.

MAḤJOUB, M. A.: *Al-Ḥaraka Al-Fikriyya Fil-Sudan*. Khartoum, 1941.

—— and 'ABD AL-HALIM, M.: *Mawt Dunya*. Cairo, 1946.

MARLOWE, J.: *Anglo-Egyptian Relations, 1800–1953*. London, 1954.

MARTIN, P. F.: *The Sudan in evolution*. London, 1921.

NAJĪLA, H.: *Malāmiḥ, Min al-Mujtama'a al-Sūdāni*. Khartoum, 1959.

NEGUIB (NAJĪB), GENERAL M.: *Egypt's destiny*. London, 1955.

'OMAR, A.-M.: *The Sudan question based on British documents*. Cairo, 1952.

'UTHMĀN, DARDIRI M.: *Mudhakkirati*. Khartoum, 1961.

RAFI'Ī, 'ABD AL-RAḤMĀN AL: *Miṣr Wal-Sūdān*. London, 1952.

SHUKRI, M. FUʿĀD: *Miṣr Wal-Siyāda 'Ala al-Sūdān*. Cairo, 1947.

ṬAHA, 'ABD AL-RAḤMĀN 'ALI: *Al-Sūdān lil-Sūdāniyyin*. Khartoum, 1955.

TOTHILL, J. D. (ed.): *Agriculture in the Sudan*. London, 1948.

TRIMINGHAM, J. S.: *The Christian approach to Islam in the Sudan*. London, 1948.

WINGATE, SIR R.: *Wingate of the Sudan*. London, 1955.

A Note on Anglo-Egyptian Writings on the Constitutional and Political Development of the Sudan: 1899–1956

As may be expected, Anglo-Egyptian writings on this subject reflected the Anglo-Egyptian dispute over the Sudan. Egyptian writings, whether of official spokesmen or private citizens concerned with the presentation of the Egyptian nationalist point of view, aimed at two main objectives: criticism of the British position and administration in the Sudan and the promotion of the Unity of the Nile Valley—under the Egyptian crown. And on the whole they were more successful in achieving the first than the second.

The chief weakness of the Unity of the Nile Valley as presented in these writings was that its advocates invariably spoke with two voices—emphasizing, on the one hand, the fraternal and cultural links that bound Egypt and the Sudan, while insisting, on the other, that the Unity of the Nile Valley was based on Egypt's juridical right as a conquering power to be master of the Sudan and rule the Sudanese. The French, then the British, and subsequently the Sudanese advocates of Independence found no difficulty in picking holes in the Egyptian case from a juridical angle, while unnecessary exaggerations in presenting the Egyptians and the Sudanese, from the Equator to the Delta, as one and the same people, ethnically as well as culturally (as Dr. Muhammad Salah al-Din, for instance, insisted) constituted an open invitation to British commentators and spokesmen to make fun of the Egyptian point of view.[1] Unnecessary and unwarranted exaggerations about the nature and extent of historical contacts between Egypt and the Sudan from the earliest times to the present day had a similarly weakening effect on Egypt's position and her advocacy of the Unity of the Nile Valley. As a result even legitimate Egyptian interests in the Sudan suffered—not only as a consequence of Egypt's weakened moral standing in the country but also by arousing the suspicion and hostility of large sections of the Sudanese. Among the Mahdists in particular this had the effect of creating a psychological barrier which has survived independence, the Suez war, and even the popularity of Pan-Africanism and Pan-Arabism. More damaging still from Egypt's point of view was the fact that successive Egyptian governments and spokesmen were almost unbelievably uninformed—sometimes even positively

[1] *Great Britain and Egypt, 1914–1951* (Royal Institute of International Relations, London, 1952), p. 139. For a typical presentation of the Egyptian point of view see A. F. Baddour, *Sudanese Egyptian Relations* (The Hague, 1960).

misinformed—about the nature of Sudanese politics in general and, in particular, about the motives which prompted certain sectors of Sudanese opinion to stand for unity with Egypt as against independence; and also about the nature and the limits of Sudanese, as distinct from Egyptian, Unionism. Hence the confusion, anger, and deep sense of hurt pride which overcame the Egyptians when Sayyid Ismā'īl al-Azhari, of all people, chose to lead the country to independence instead of unity with Egypt in 1955.

British writings about Sudanese politics and administration during the period under consideration, like their Egyptian counterpart, were aimed at serving the interests of the writers and their country.[1] On the whole, however, they were characterized by greater subtlety and dexterity and reflected a greater knowledge of Sudanese politics and society. It followed therefore that British writings were much more successful in achieving their ends. Main amongst these was the justification of Britain's control over the Sudan—first as an agent of Egyptian governments, after 1919 as a partner of Egypt in the Sudan. This, as we have seen, had always been a difficult task, but became infinitely more so after the outbreak of the Egyptian Revolution and the conferring of formal independence on Egypt in 1922. It was a measure of the success of British diplomacy and propoganda, however, that the resultant and radical change in the terms justifying Britain's presence in the Sudan was hardly noticed or discussed and that the notion of the Anglo-Egyptian regime in the Sudan having been a 'condominium' was almost unanimously accepted—albeit mainly by default—outside the circles of Egyptian jurists and politicians.

Much more difficult was the justification of the British administration *vis-à-vis* the Sudanese. Here the familiar arguments of good government, protection of the inhabitants, and the training of the Sudanese to run their own affairs were repeatedly used. The weaknesses, fallacies, and inconsistencies of these arguments became increasingly obvious as the Sudanese became better able to speak for themselves. The idea that the British had come all the way from Europe in order to build railways and start such projects as the Jazīra Scheme for the benefit of the Sudanese was one of the first to be attacked, while claims that the regime had been established for the purpose of training the Sudanese in the art of self-government were difficult to accept in view of the slow pace of Sudanization and constitutional development—and were obviously impossible to reconcile with the Government's attitude towards education (for example) after 1924, and the introduction of Native Administration, involving as it did the deliberate rehabilitation of tribalism in the Northern Sudan.

[1] See R. Hill's *Slatin Pasha* (London, 1965) for an interesting account of how Wingate and the British officer corps of the Egyptian army used information collected by the intelligence department in preparing a series of books and articles which, including Slatin's *Fire and Sword in the Sudan*, deliberately sought to paint the Mahdiyya 'in the blackest possible colours' as a weapon of war propaganda.

But the main failure of British administration in the Sudan was probably its 'Southern Policy'. And the chief weakness of British writings in this connection was not that they were aimed at justifying the policy in question—by any standard a difficult task indeed—but that with a few distinguished exceptions[1] they were aimed at covering up the facts of Southern Policy and pretending that it had never existed. Thus Sir Harold MacMichael, one of the chief architects of this policy, approvingly cites an official statement which spoke of Southern Policy as a 'protective barrier which it had been necessary in the past to build up against exploitation by Northern merchants and others', and writes of the 'suspicion' which it aroused among Northerners that the government was working for a separation between the two regions of the country.[2] Dr. Richard Gray writes on the problem of the Southern Sudan in a similar vein and refers to the claim that the 'protective' British policy in the South was carried to 'absurd lengths (biblical names and British shorts [instead of] Arab names and dress . . ., etc.)' in a way which implies that this claim was merely a Northern exaggeration and not a correct estimate of the situation. In the same manner he writes of the Closed Districts Order as if it were not created by the British but by Sudanese governments.[3]

In an equally misleading statement, published in *The Times* of 24 July 1962, Mr. J. A. Gillan (who, as Governor of Kordofan, was for many years concerned with the application of the principles of Native Administration and Southern Policy to the Nuba Mountains) argued that British administration in the Southern Sudan was based on tolerance towards Muslims and non-interference with the practice and propagation of the Islamic faith by the Arabs—citing, as evidence, the existence under British rule of 'respectable Arab communities . . . in every Southern town'.

But the boldest and most daring attempt to deny that Southern Policy ever existed was made by one who spent many years of his life executing it in person—not as a minor official but as the Governor of Equatoria during the heyday of Southern Policy. Mr. Martin Parr's statement on the subject was made in a letter which was published in the *Guardian* on 1 June 1964. The startling inaccuracy of Mr. Parr's statement was shown in a reply, by the present writer, which was published in the *Guardian* on 4 June 1964. This ran as follows:

'Mr. Parr (June 1) unfairly dismisses Mr. Wright's statement (May 28) that what is now happening in the three Southern provinces of the Sudan "is part of a sad procession of events set in train during British administration"

[1] The outstanding example of this is P. M. Holt, *A Modern History of the Sudan* (London, 1961)—i.e. five years after the independence of the Sudan.

[2] *The Sudan* (London, 1954), pp. 116–17.

[3] See the introduction to *The Problem of the Southern Sudan* (London, 1963). This is a heavily edited pamphlet which is published under the names of Joseph Oduhu and William Deng.

as misleading and incorrect. In support of his contention Mr. Parr says that the Southern provinces were never administered separately, that Arab dress and religion (by which I presume is meant Islam) were never forbidden there, and that "Northerners were always admitted to do jobs" in the Southern provinces.

'Each one of these statements is wrong. The Southern provinces were administered separately at least from 1922, when the Passports and Permits Ordinance was promulgated and subsequently used to transform these provinces into a series of "Closed Districts" until 1947 when, in the words of the Civil Secretary, "the distinctions in rates of pay and other conditions of Government Service, the artificial rules about employment of Southerners in the North, attempts at economic separation and all similar distinctions" were found untenable in the face of nationalist pressure and because of the "growing demand for Northerners to be employed in Southern development schemes". Until that time Arab clothes were not only forbidden in the South but, as one D.C. said in 1941, bonfires were made of them and "religious discrimination . . . though it may not have been admitted", as the Governor of Wau subsequently wrote, was in fact extensively and officially practised.

'This policy of separation and discrimination had been restated in 1930, when the then Civil Secretary informed senior British staff that "it is the aim of the Government to encourage as far as possible (Christian) Greek and Syrian traders rather than the Gallaba (i.e. Muslem-Arabs from the Northern Sudan) type. Permits to the latter should be decreased unobtrusively but progressively. The limitation of the Gallaba trade to towns or established routes is essential." And whereas Islam, Arabic language and Arab dress were until then "fashionable" in the South, they were to be counteracted "by every practical means".

'As an ex-Governor during the heyday of "Southern Policy" Mr. Parr surely knows all this and a lot more besides. He would also know that the purpose of this policy—officially stated as early as 1919—was the "assimilation" of the Southern provinces to the government of other East African "possessions". By 1946, when the folly of this policy was realized, it was too late, as Mr. Wright correctly said (May 27), and when the country became independent in 1956 the Southern provinces were far from integrated. The harm done by the fanatical and arbitrary policy of the Condominium regime in the Southern Sudan far outweighs that of memories of the slave trade. In spite of attempts to kindle—and exaggerate—these dark memories, slave trade in the Sudan is as dead as its even more grotesque counterpart in the West.'[1]

No reply was published.

[1] See p. 7, n. 4.

INDEX

abandonment of the Sudan, *see* Sudan.
'Abbas II, 25.
'Abbas Maḥmoud al-'Aqqād, 115.
'Abboud, *see* Ibrahim, 'Abboud.
'Abd al-Ḥalīm Muḥammad, Dr., 123 n., 124 n., 125 n.
'Abd al-Ḥamīd, 95.
'Abd al-Laṭīf Bey al-Baghdādi, 64.
'Abd al-Qādir Wad Ḥabboub, 90, 93.
'Abd al-Raḥmān al-Mahdi, Sayyid, 91, 94, 95, 96, 97, 99, 101, 118, 119, 120, 124, 131, 132, 138, 151 n., 157, 159, 181, 201, 221, 222, 223 n.
'Abdalla Bey Khalīl, 108, 148, 149, 153, 183.
'Abdal-Karīm Muḥammad, 148.
'Abdullah Bakr, 150.
Abul-Qāsim Aḥmad Hāshim, 99, 101.
Abyssinia, Invasion of, 84.
Advisory Board for Southern Affairs, 198.
Advisory Council for the Northern Sudan, 124, 128, 135, 136, 137, 140, 142, 143, 144, 145, 147 *passim*, 153, 157, 158, 159, 160, 163, 165, 166, 167, 174, 175, 179, 207.
Africa: Central, 2, 4, 7, 13, 36, 74; East, 4, 36, 71, 74, 84, 168, 169; North, 6; West, 1, 3.
Aḥmad Bey Abu-Sin, 16 n.
Aḥmad Jaly, 222.
Aḥmad Khair, 116 n., 125 n., 126 n., 145.
Aḥmad Muḥammad Ṣālih, 223 n.
Aḥmad 'Uthman al-Qādī, 148.
Aḥrār Party, 159.
Alexandria, 4.
'Ali 'Abd al-Laṭīf, 104, 105, 106, 108.
'Ali Badri, Dr., 148, 149, 152.
'Ali Bey al-Jārim, 122.
'Ali Dinār, 44, 95.
'Ali Yūsif, 90 n.
Allenby, Lord, 103, 107.
al-Nujūmi, *see* Amīr Abd al-Rahman.
American intervention, 181, 192.
Amir 'Abd al-Raḥmān al-Nujūmi, 23.
Anglo-American Imperialism, 223 n.
Anglo-Egyptian Agreement Concerning self-Government and self-determination, 215, 216, 224.
Anglo-Egyptian Agreement for the Administration of the Sudan, 1899 (Condominium Agreement), 32–8, 39 n., 47, 51–4, 56 n., 57, 62, 63, 85, 92, 101, 106, 124, 128, 132, 153, 155, 188, 197.
Anglo-Egyptian dispute, 172.
Anglo-Egyptian negotiations, 84, 105, 154, 181, 184 n., 188, 214.
Anglo-Egyptian regime, 2, 14, 44, 51 n., 63, 71, 81, 117, 134, 177, 182, 186, 191, 193, 218 n., 221, 225.
Anglo-Egyptian Treaty of Alliance, 1936, 84, 120, 122, 153, 154, 188, 192, 193, 195, 200.
Anglo-Egyptian troops, 225.
al-Anṣār', 89, 90, 94, 96, 97, 108, 115, 120, 130, 132, 157, 180, 182, 186, 187, 192, 195, 200, 218 n., 221, 222, 224, *see also* Umma Party and Independence Front.
al-'Aqqād, *see* 'Abbas Maḥmoud.
Arab revolt of 1916, 58, 94.
Arab clothing, 78, 79.
Arabic language, 42, 43, 62, 77, 78, 83, 102, 113, 166 n., 179, 205 n.
Arabization, 6, 7.
'Arafāt Muḥammad 'Abdalla, 113, 124 n.
Argīn, 23.
Arkell, J., 3 n.
Ashigga Party, 111, 131 n., 133, 140, 146, 154, 159, 179, 180, 182, 190, 192, 213.
Aswan, 14, 21, 41; Dam, 23.
Ataturk, 113.
Atbara, River, 4.
'Atiyah, Edward, 110, 116 n.
Atlantic Charter, 127, 153.
Atlantic Sea, 1, 7.
Attlee, Clement, 157.
Austrian Government, 72.
al-Azhari, *see* Ismā'il al-Azhari.

Babu Nimir, 149.
al-Baghdadi, *see* Abd al-Latif Bey.
Baḥr al-'Arab, 4.
Baḥr al-Ghazāl, 5, 15, 27, 70, 76, 77, 209.
Baḥr al-Jabal, River, 74.
Baker, Sir Samuel, 15, 17.
al-Balāgh, 218 n.
Barbar, 16 n., 17, 49 n., 50, 109.
Baring, Sir Evelyn, *see* Cromer.
Baro, River, 74.
Beja tribes, 50.
Belgian Government, 24, 28, *see also* Leopold.
Bevin, Ernest, 154, 155, 157, 181, 191.
'Bilād al-Sūdān', 1.
Boer War, 43, 92.
boundaries, *see* Sudan.
Brussels Act of 2 July 1890, The, 37.
British Administration, 109, 115.
British Empire, 59, 60, 71, 116, 122.
British Government, 19, 21, 22, 24, 26, 29, 30, 32–3, 38, 47, 63, 130, 140, 185, 193, 200.
British Imperial Idea, 100, 102.

Cabinet Government, 163.
Cadogen, Sir Alexander, 155, 156, 194 n.
Cairo, 17, 19, 20, 34, 51, 53, 57.
Cantwell Smith, Professor Wilfred, 89.
Capitulations, 29, 30.
Cecil, 32 n.
Central African Republic, 3, *see also* Africa.
Central Government, 171, 209, 210, 211.
Chief's Courts Ordinance, 70.
Chad, Republic of, 3.
Chamber of Commerce, 145.
Chamber of Deputies, 199.
Christian Missionary Societies, 71, 72, 73, 77, 81, 82, 123 n., *see also* Southern Policy and Missionaries.
Christianity, 6, 79, 81.
Circumcision (female), 151, 152.
Civil Secretary, 180, 211.
Civil Service, 45, 161, 173, 213; Indian, 45.
'Closed Districts', 128, 167, *see also* Southern Policy.
Communist Party, 133, 134 n., 219, 223 n.
Condominium Agreement, *see* Anglo-Egyptian Agreement, 1899.
Congo, 3, 72, 83.
Congress of Vienna, 37 n.
Constantinople, 14.
Constituent Assembly, 224.
Constitution Amendment Commission, 190, 191, 193, 195, 197, 198, 199, 200.
Constitutional Charter, 30.
Constitution, constitutional development, 14, 163, 164, 172 *passim*, 184, 196, 197, 199, 200, 201, 214, 225, 226, 227.
Copts, 73, 103.
Corrupt Practices Ordinance, 217.
Cotton, export of, 3; production of, 64, 227, *see also* al-Jazira.
Council of Ministers, 197, 219, 226.
Cripps, Sir Stafford, 127, 128, 135; Memorandum, 127.
Cromer, Lord (Sir Evelyn Baring), 19, 20, 21, 23, 24, 26, 29–32, 33 n., 34–8, 39, 41, 44, 45, 51–6, 58, 63, 71, 72, 91, 92, 100, 145.
Currie, Sir James, 65.
Curzon, Lord, 61 n., 99 n.

al-Dāmar, 209.
Darfur, 2, 5, 7, 15, 17, 44, 49, 95, 97, 137, 198; Baggara of, 78.
Defterdar, the, 14.
De La Warr Commission on Education, 122.
Depression, The, 84.
Dirdiri Muḥammad 'Uthmān, 102, 168 n., 193 n.
Direct Rule, 51, 203.
District Commissioners, 203, 204.
Dongola, 16 n., 17, 24, 49 n., 50, 74; Campaign, 25, 26.
Dual Control over Egypt's revenues, 18.
Dual Mandate in British Tropical Africa, The, 51.
Duncan, J. S. R., 216 n.

East African Federation, 8.
East India Company, 31.
Eden, Anthony, 181, 193, 195.
Education, 5, 41, 59, 65, 81, 82, 83, 91, 94, 109, 110, 111, 112, 113, 117, 118, 119, 122, 126, 128, 130, 135, 138, 141,

161, 166 n., 176, 178, 179, 180, 185, 190, 196, 203, 204, 205.
Edward 'Atiyah, *see* 'Atiyah.
Egypt, Egyptians, 3, 6, 13, 16, 24, 25, 32, 36, 37, 38, 51–2, 58, 60, 74, 75, 92, 98, 105, 115, 121, 130, 146, 154, 157, 188, 200, 201, 212, 213; independence of, 19, 21, 22, 63, 64, 83, 84.
Egyptian army, 40, 60, 65 n., 90, 92, 93, 107; immigration, 84; Irrigation Service, 84; Mutiny of 1900, 92, 93; nationalists, 13, 25, 26, 54, 58, 61, 62, 65, 90, 92, 93, 94, 100; Revolution, 38, 51, 58–9, 60, 64, 65, 71, 73, 97, 100; Sovereignty over the Sudan, 192, 221; subventions, 94; Treasury, 54, 55, 56, 71; Wafd Party, 106, 114, 120, 200, 218 n.
Electoral Commission, 215, 216, 217, 218, 219.
Equatoria, 167.
European intervention, 25.
Evans, Pritchard, 80.
Executive Council, 48, 147, 162, 163, 164, 173, 174, 176, 177, 178, 179, 183.
Executive Council and Legislative Assembly Ordinance, 184–5, 186.
Exiles to the Sudan, 17.

Faḥal, Ibrahim, 149.
al-Fajr, 115, 116, 124.
Faraḥ, *see* Khalīl.
Fāris al-Khouri, 195.
Farouq, King, 121, 181 n., 192, 200, 201, 212; Institute, 122.
Fascism, 84, 116.
al-Fāshir, 3, 106.
Fashoda, 62, 96 n.
al-Fil, *see* Shaikh Ahmad.
Fīlists, 119.
Foster, Arnold, 56 n.
French Government, 24, 25, 27, 28, 31, 62, 116.
Fu'ād I, 19.
Fūnj, Islamic Kingdom of, 6; period, 16.

Gandhi, 125 n.
Garibaldi, 15.
Gash Delta, 64, 94.
George V, 99.
Gessi, Romolo, 15.
Ghana (Gold Coast), 1.
'Give Us Education', 117.
Gordon, General Charles, 15, 17, 23, 31 n., 40 n., 41.
Gordon College, 94, 102, 109, 110, 117, 118, 119, 122, 125, 151, 154, 201–2.
Gorst, Sir Eldon, 46, 57, 90, 93.
Governor-General's Commission, 215, 216, 219.
Governor-General's Council, 57, 58, 136, 138, 139, 140, 160, 164, 171, 172.
Graduates' Constituency, 199.
Graduates' General Congress, 125, 126, 127, 129, 130, 131, 132, 136, 145, 159, 167, 178, 207.
Granville, Lord, 19, 20, 21, 22, 31 n.
Gray, Richard, 7 n.
Grenfell, General, 23.

Ḥadārat al-Sūdān, 101, 102, 103, 104, 105, 116.
Hailey, Lord, 165, 175.
Hākimdār, 16.
Ḥalfa, 2, 6, 50, 74, 106.
Ḥalfayat al-Mulouk, 3.
Ḥamid al-Sayyid, 149.
Hardinge, Lord, 59.
Ḥasan Najīla, 109 n., 110 n.
Ḥasan Ṣāliḥ, 105.
Ḥasan Ṣharīf, 105.
Ḥasan 'Ali Shikailawi, 149.
Henderson, K. D. D., 126 n.
Hicks, General, 19.
High Church Party, 72.
Higher Schools Advisory Committee, 141.
Ḥijāz, Ottoman Wali of, 16.
al-Hilāli, *see* Najīb.
House of Representatives, 192, 217, 218, 220, 225, 226.
Howe, Sir Robert George, 190, 193 n., 199.
Ḥusain, King, 98.

Ibrahim, 'Abboud, General, 8, 227.
Imperial Service Corps, 93.
Imperialism, 182 n., *see also* British Empire, Ottoman-Egyptian administration, Sudan and Africa.
Independence, 8, 9, 13, 115, 130, 134, 157, 158, 182, 187, 193, 213, 223, 224, 225, 226, 227.

Independence Front, 154, 156, 163, 172, 179, 180, 183, 186, 201, 212, 214, 215, 221, 222, 223, *see also* Umma Party and al-Anṣār.
India, 109, 117, 135, 205; routes to, 14.
Indian Congress, 125, 132.
Indirect Rule, 65–70.
Inspector of Southern Education, 82.
Institute of African Languages and Cultures, 80.
Islam, 5, 6, 13, 14, 18, 26, 60, 62, 83, 89, 91, 95, 104, 113, 123 n.
Ismā'īl al-Azhari, 99, 101, 102, 111, 125, 132, 179, 182 n., 218, 219, 221, 222, 223 n., 224.
Ismā'īl Pasha, 15, 17, 18, 19, 96.
'al-Istiqlāl al-Tām', 201.
Ittifāqiyat al-Aḥzāb, 213, 215, 218 n.

Jackson, Colonel, 91.
Jaly, *see* Ahmad Jaly.
Jamāl 'Abd al-Nāṣir, 202, 223.
al-Jārim, *see* 'Ali al-Jārim.
al-'Jazīra', 3, 70, 90, 94, 103 n., 107; Advisory Board, 141; Scheme, 64, 153, 179, *see also* Cotton.
Jazīra Aba, 96.
Juba, 169.
Juba Conference, 165, 170.

Kasala Province, 49 n., 50, 137.
Kenya, 3, 74.
Khalafalla Khālid, 222.
Khaldoun, Ibn, 1 n.
Khalīfa, 23, 24, 25, 27, 28, 39, 43, 89 n., 93, 97.
Khalīfa 'Abdullahi, 106.
Khalīl Faraḥ, 111.
Khartoum, 1, 4, 5, 20, 29, 37, 39, 41, 47, 49 n., 50, 51, 55, 64, 72, 74, 79, 103, 106, 107, 108, 137, 138, 154, 176; capital of the Sudan, 16; fall of, 23, 27; Military Hospital, 108; Municipal Council, 205 n.
al-Khatmiyya, 91, 130, 131, 132, 133 n., 134 n., 180, 182, 183, 184, 185, 186, 187, 190, 192, 195, 218 n., 221, 222, *see also* Unionists and National Unionist Party.
Khedive, 15, 20, 22, 26, 27, 31, 33, 34, 54, 65 n., 92; rights of, 32, *see also* Viceroy of Egypt.
Kitchener, Lord, 26, 27, 39, 41 n., 43, 52, 53, 92, 93, 96 n.; School of Medicine, 64, 122.
Kordofan, 7, 15, 20, 49, 137.

Lake Success, 155, 194 n.
Language Conference of Rajjāf, 82.
Lansdowne, Lord, 41 n., 42, 44, 72.
Lawrence, T. E., 113.
League of Sudanese Union, 104, 105, 108, 112.
Legislative Assembly, 142, 147, 160, 161, 162, 163, 164, 166, 171, 172, 173, 176, 177, 178, 179, 180, 181, 182, 183, 186, 187, 188, 189, 190, 191, 192, 199, 210, 211, 218 n.
Leopold, King, 49, 72, *see also* Belgian Government.
Libya, 3, 84, 127, 181.
al-Liwā', 92.
Local Government, 135, 161, 203, 205 *passim*; Advisory Board, 210; Ordinances, 122, 135–7, 211.
lukikos, 79, 80.

MacMichael, Sir Harold, 75, 77.
al-Mahdi, 18, 19, 20, 23, 28, 91, 96 n., 97.
Mahdist Period, 2, 20, 23, 66; risings, 18, 32, 62, 93, 155.
Mahdists, 24, 26, 43, 54, 89, 90, 91, 92, 96, 133, 180, 181, 182, 200, 202, 212, 213, 221.
Mahdiyya, 2, 39, 89, 131, 187, 203.
Maḥjoub, *see* Muḥammad Aḥmad.
Maghrib, 6, 58.
Makki 'Abbās, 148, 150, 165.
Makki Shibaika', 125.
Malakal, 4, 106.
'Māl al-Fidā'', 220.
Māmūrs, 16, 49, 50, 64, 68, 73.
Mangalla Province, 79.
Marchand, Captain, 27.
Marshall, Dr. A. H., 209, 210, 211.
martial law, 37, 41.
Mayall, R. C., 136, 161 n.
McIlwraith, Sir Malcolm, 33 n.
Milner, Lord, 60; Report of 1920, 59, 61, 62 n., 67, 74.
Milner Mission, 66, 67.
Mirghani Ḥamza, 149, 152, 165, 166, 175, 176, 184 n., 223.
Missionaries, 143, 167, *see also* Christian Missionary Societies.

'Moḥammedan Law', *see* Sharī'a law.
Mu'āwiya Muḥammad Nour, 115.
al-Mu'ayyid, 90.
Mudīr, 16.
Mudīriyyas, 49.
Muḥammad Aḥmad 'Abdalla, 18.
Muḥammad Aḥmad Maḥjoub, 113, 114, 115, 123 n., 125 n., 204.
Muḥammad al-Haj al-Amīn, 188.
Muḥammad al-Khalīfa Sharīf, 101, 104.
Muḥammad al-Mahdi al-Khalifa Abdullahi, 106.
Muḥammad Najīb, General, 212 n., 213, 223.
Muḥammad Nour al-Dīn, 224 n.
Muḥammad 'Ali Pasha, 2, 7, 14, 15, 17, 39, 96.
Muḥammad 'Ali Shawqi, 147, 150.
Muḥammad Bey Rāsikh, 16 n.
Muḥammad Ṣalāh al-Din, 191.
Muḥammad Zhafrulla Khān, Sir, 195.
Municipalities, 205, 207, 208, 210.
Municipalities and Townships Ordinances, 206.
Muṣawwa', 16.
Muslims, 5, 14, 16, 40, 55, 72, 75, 79, 102, 111, 133, 152.
Muslim-Arabic culture, 81, 89, 95, 113, 114, 223.
Muslim Brotherhood, 133, 134 n., 219, 223 n.
Mustafa Kāmil, 92.
Mustafa Abu al-'Ila, 148.

Nabi 'Īsa, 43, 90.
al-Naḥḥas Pasha, 121.
'Nahas College', 122.
al-Nahda, 116.
Najīb al-Hilāli, 200, 201, 212, 213, 222, 223.
Najīb, General, *see* Muḥammad Najīb.
Najīla, *see* Hasan Najīla.
Nāṣir, *see* Jamāl 'Abd al-Nāṣir.
Napoleon III, 14.
Naqrāshi Pasha, 155, 156, 194 n.
Nationalism, 58, 60, 61, 102, 109, 110, 111, 112, 113, 114, 115, 116, 118, 123, 130, 131 n., 132, 135, 140 *passim*, 156, 168, 172, 203, 204, 222, 223.
National Unionist Party, 213, 218, 221, 222, 223 n., 224, *see also* Unionist.
Native Administration, 49, 51, 67, 68, 70, 71, 79, 80, 81, 83, 117, 118, 122, 135, 145, 187, 203, 204, 205, 206, 210, 211.
Nazism, 84, 116.
Newbold, Sir Douglas, 128, 135, 136, 137, 140, 141, 142, 143, 144, 145, 146, 147, 161 n., 163, 205.
Nile, 3, 4, 13, 24, 57, 62, 74; Valley, 58, 98, 99, 124.
al-Nīl, 122.
Nilo-Hamites, 5.
Nilotics, 5.
Nour al-Din, *see* Muḥammad Nour-al-Dīn.
Nuba Mountains, 14, 49, 143, 198.
Nuba tribes, 5.
Nūbār Pasha, 22, 145.
Nubia, 6, 15.
Nubians, 5.
Nuḥ Abdullah, 149.

October Revolution, *see* Revolution of October 1964.
Omdurman, 27, 39, 42, 64, 89, 92, 96 n., 112, 127, 176; Battle of, 29 n., 93 n., Broadcasting Station, 127, 145; Graduates' Club, 94, 113, 124.
Onama, F. K., 8 n.
Ottoman-Egyptian administration, 2, 17, 36; army, 16.

'pacification', 43, 44, 46, 79, 93.
parliamentary system, 160, 164, 204.
Passports and Permits Ordinance, 75, 76.
Peace Conference, 59.
permanent constitution, 8.
Permits to Trade Order, 166.
Phipps, Major P. R., 46 n.
Political Parties Agreement, *see* Ittifāqiyat al-Aḥzāb.
Powers of Nomad Sheikhs Ordinance of 1922, The, 66, 68 n., 69, 70, 79, 80.
Press, 113, 147, 149, 150 n., 151, 218, 223; freedom of, 57.
Province Councils, 171, 207, 208, 211, 217.
Public Service Commission, 219.

al-Qā'id al-'Aām (El Kaid el Am), 48.
Qawmiyyīn Party, 159 n.
Qur'ān, 5, 103.

Raja, 169.
Rajjāf, 2, *see also* Language Conference of.
Ras Hofun, 16.
Rātib, 91.
Ra'ūf Pasha, 18.
Reconquest of Sudan, *see* Sudan.
Red Sea, 1, 2, 3, 6, 7, 50, 74.
Republican Socialist Party, 218.
Revolt of 1924, 102–7, 108, 112, 117, 119.
Revolution of October 1964, 8, 133, 227.
Rifa'at Bey, 108.
Robertson, Sir James, 159, 163, 168, 170, 171, 180, 185.
Roman Catholicism, 72.
Rosebery, Lord, 22 n.
Russian Government, 25.

Sa'ad Zaghlūl, 107, 114.
Sahara, 1, 3, 5.
Sa'īd, 14.
Ṣalaḥ al-Din, *see* Muḥammad Ṣalaḥ al-Din.
Ṣalāḥ Sālim, 213, 223 n.
Ṣāliḥ 'Abd al Qādir, 105, 107.
Salisbury, 24, 30 n., 31 n., 36, 42, 52, 53, 57, 92.
Sanousi of Libya, 44, 95.
Sawākin, 2, 16, 37.
Ṣawt al-Sūdān, 182, 185.
Sayyid Aḥmad Mutwalli al-'Atabāni, 226 n.
Sayyid 'Ali al-Mirghani, 91, 94, 98, 99, 101, 119, 131, 138, 151 n., 152, 222.
Sayyid Mirghani al-Sayyid al-Makki, 99.
Security Council, 155, 156, 172, 173.
Self-Government Statute, 199, 200, 201, 215, 226.
Shaikān, 20.
Shaikh Aḥmad al-Sayyid al-Fīl, 119.
Shaikh al-'Ulama, 125.
Sharī'a law, 40, 103.
Sharīf Pasha, 20, 21, 22.
Sharīf Yūsif al-Hindi, 94, 99, 101, 124.
Shawqi, *see* Muhammad 'Ali.
Shawqists, 119.
Shibaika, *see* Makki.
Shukriyya tribe, 16 n.
al-Ṣiddiq al-Mahdi, 159.
Ṣidqi Pasha, 154, 155, 157 n., 181.
Sinnar, 3, 15.
Sirdār, The, 53, 60, 65.
Slatin, Rudolf von, 40 n., 48, 90, 97.
Slaves, slave trade, 3, 7, 8, 14, 17, 37.
Sobāt, River, 4, 74.
Socialist Republican Party, 133, 213.
'Southern Policy', 6, 8, 70 *passim*, 109, 133, 156, 198, 204; abandonment of, 166 *passim*, *see also* Christian Missionary Societies and Closed Districts.
'Sovereign Democratic Republic', 226.
Special Mission of 1919, 60; Report of, 61, 62, 63.
Stack, Sir Lee, 59, 60 n., 65, 97, 103, 107; Memorial School at Wau, 83.
Stanley-Baker, R. C., 191, 197, *see also* Constitution Amendment Commission.
Stewart, Colonel, 20.
Sublime Porte, 14, *see also* Turkish Government and suzerainty.
Sudan Administration Conference, 158 *passim*, 165, 170, 171, 172, 173–7, 210, 212 n.
Sudan Defence Force, 49, 65, 93, 127, 176.
Sudan Denizen Ordinance, 151, 219.
Sudan: abandonment of, 20–23, 28; affairs of, 17, 18; derivation of name, 1; European intervention in, 17, 18, 33, 35; reconquest of, 23, 24, 31, 33 n., 36, 51 n., 55, 62.
Sudan Political Service, 45, 218.
Sudan Protocol, 155, 156.
'Sudanization', 65, 67, 158, 167, 168, 214, 219 *passim*; Committee, 182 n., 213, 215, 219, 221, 224.
Suez Canal, 15, 181, 195.
Sulayman Wad al-Zubair, 15.
Sultanates, 14, 16, 18, 21, 25, 26, 37.
'Supplementary Agreement', 36.
'Supreme Constitutional Authority', 200.
Surūr Muḥammad Ramli, 149.
'Sword of Victory', 99.

Talodi, 106, 107.
Tana, Lake, 4.
Ṭariqās, 7, 91, 94, 100, 119, 130, 157,

see also Anṣār Khatmiyya and Sharīf Yūsif al-Hindi.
Taxes, 17, 39, 40, 60, 173, 211.
al-Ṭayyib Hāshim, 99, 101.
al-Tijāni Yūsif Bashīr, 113.
Toshki, 23, 89.
'Toussoun Orphanage', 122.
Trade-unionism, 183.
Traders, 75.
Transitional Constitution, 199, 215, 226, 227.
Tribunals: Consular, 30 n.; mixed, 36.
Turkish Government, 31, 58, *see also* Sublime Porte.
Turkish suzerainty, 27.
Turko-Egyptian regime, 33, 96; Peace Treaty, 61.

'Ubaid 'Abd al-Nour, 111.
'Ubaid Ḥāj al-Amīn, 105.
al-Ubayyid, 20, 207.
Uganda, 3, 37, 74, 82, 83, 156, *see also* Onama.
'Umar Ṭūson, Prince, 121.
Umma Party, 131 n., 132, 133, 134 n., 144, 146, 153, 154, 157, 159 n., 181 n., 187, 188, 190, 212, 213, 218, 223 n., 224, 226 n., *see also* Independence Front and al-Anṣār.
Unionists, 132, 140, 141, 144, 145, 146, 157, 159, 172, 179, 180, 182, 201, 218 n., *see also* National Unionist Party and al-Khatmiyya.
United Nations Organization, 181, 184 n., 195, 212 n.
Unity of the Nile Valley, 102, 105, 116, 130, 132, 172, 188, 190, 192, 194 n., 200, 215, 221, 222, *see also* Unionists and Egyptian Sovereignty over the Sudan.
Universities, 44, 94, 111.
Upper Nile Province, 79, 80.
'Urābi Pasha, 18.
'Urābi Revolt, 20.
Urban Authorities, 209.

Viceroy of Egypt, 14, 15, *see also* Khedive.
Victoria, Queen, 89 n., 91 n.

Wad Ḥabboub, *see* 'Abd al-Qādir.
Wad Madani, 112, 125.
Wādi Ḥalfa, 21, 209.
Wafd Party, *see* Egyptian Wafd.
Wau, 77, 106, 107, 209; Governor of, 169.
Westermann, Professor, 80, 83.
White Flag League, 105, 106, 107, 112, 113.
Wilson, President, 58, 94.
Wingate, General Sir Reginald, 32 n., 42, 45, 46, 47, 58, 59, 60 n., 90, 91, 93, 95, 99, 100.
World War I, 44, 49, 94 *passim*.

Young Turks, 44.
Yūsif al-'Ajab, 189.

Zain al-'Aabdīn Bey, 'Abd al-Tām, 198 n.
Zaghlul, *see* Saad.
al-Zubair Ḥamad al-Malik, 150.
al-Zubair Pasha wad Raḥama, 15.

PRINTED IN GREAT BRITAIN
AT THE UNIVERSITY PRESS, OXFORD
BY VIVIAN RIDLER
PRINTER TO THE UNIVERSITY